Gestalt Therapy on the \

The Gestalt Therapy Page is the l. comprehensive web resource for information, resources, and publications relating to the theory and practice of Gestalt therapy.

Visitors can subscribe to News and Notes, a free email calendar of conferences, training programs, and other events of interest to the worldwide Gestalt therapy community.

The Gestalt Therapy Page includes an on-line store that offers the most comprehensive collection of books and recordings available – many available nowhere else!

Visit today: www.gestalt.org

The Gestalt Journal Press was founded in 1975 and is currently the leading publisher and distributor of books, journals, and educational recordings relating to the theory and practice of Gestalt therapy. Our list of titles includes new editions of all the classic works by Frederick Perls, Laura Perls, Paul Goodman, Ralph Hefferline, and Jan Christiaan Smuts. Our catalog also includes a wide variety of books by contemporary theoreticians and clinicians including Richard Hycner, Lynne Jacobs, Violet Oaklander, Peter Phillipson, Erving & Miriam Polster, Edward W. L. Smith, and Gary Yontef.

In 1976, we began publication of The Gestalt Journal (now the International Gestalt Journal), the first professional periodical devoted exclusively to the theory and practice of Gestalt therapy.

Our collection of video and audio recordings features the works of Frederick (Fritz) and Laura Perls, Violet Oaklander, Erving & Miriam Polster, Janie Rhyne, and James Simkin.

The Gestalt Journal Press, in conjunction with the University of California, Santa Barbara, maintains the world's largest archive of Gestalt therapy related materials including original manuscripts and correspondence, published and unpublished, by Gestalt therapy pioneers Frederick & Laura Perls and Paul Goodman. The archives also include more than six thousand hours of audio and video recordings of presentations, panels and interviews dating to early 1961.

TEACHING A PARANOID TO FLIRT

The Poetics
of Gestalt Therapy

MICHAEL VINCENT MILLER

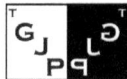

A Publication of The Gestalt Journal Press

Published by:
The Gestalt Journal Press, Inc.
P. O. Box 278
Gouldsboro, ME 04607

ISBN # 978-0-939266-70-8

In Memory of Anatole Broyard, close as a brother, who taught me to trust my voice, and Isadore From, mentor and dear friend. And for Joe Wysong and Molly Rawle, who always supported my writing over the entire thirty years covered by this book.

Contents

Part Two: Commentary

Part Three: Founders and Shapers
Introductions and Elegies

∫ Introduction

It has been more than forty years since my friend, Cindy Sheldon, a well-known Gestalt therapist, who was in a training program with Frederick Perls at the time, got a green light from him to bring me to one of her training weekends with him in San Francisco. She thought that I would be fascinated with the extraordinary work this innovative therapist was doing. Little did she know how important the experience would turn to be for me — or perhaps she had a premonition. At the time I was a doctoral student in the English department of the University of California at Berkeley, an aspiring poet just beginning to publish some poems, and a teacher of American literature and creative writing at Stanford University. My only experience with psychotherapy at that point had been a year and a half or so spent with a psychoanalyst during a period when I was nursing a broken heart. The therapy had been extremely valuable. But that weekend experience with "Fritz," as he was called by everyone in the group, was the beginning of a change in my thinking about what I wanted to do with my life. The training group was working on dreams, its members were psychiatrists, psychologists, and clinical social workers, and I was an oddball outsider. I came away from it with a sense that here was something astonishing: a powerful method of exploring people's inner lives that took metaphor and character out of the classroom and off the page and put it to use in ways that freed people to live more vibrant, fulfilling lives.

After Stanford I went on to teach at the Massachusetts Institute of Technology in Cambridge. Perls showed up in Boston just before he died in early 1970, and I joined a four-day training group he conducted that introduced Gestalt therapy to New England and left behind a lasting influence. It turned out to be the next to last workshop that Perls led; within a matter of days he was dead in Chicago from pancreatic cancer. The loss for me was hard and confusing. I had decided to leave M.I.T. and follow Perls to Cowichan Island in British Columbia where he had recently established a residential training program. I was now intent on becoming a psychotherapist and, I was already quite certain, a Gestalt therapist. Eventually I left teaching and went back to graduate school a second time to get a doctorate that would enable me to become licensed as a psychologist. During the same period I completed an eighteen-month-long training program through the Gestalt Institute of Cleveland directed by Erving and Miriam Polster when they still headed the faculty there. Somewhat later I spent several years in supervision with Isadore From, whom I, along with many others, came to regard as the master teacher of Gestalt therapy.

I describe this background because it accounts for the major themes that initially drew me to Gestalt therapy, that have continued to influence my view of psychotherapy through the entire course of my professional life, and that weave their way throughout the essays in this book, giving them whatever unity they may possess. Like the founders of Gestalt therapy, I came to it from a background in the arts and humanities that preceded the decision to become a psychotherapist. For Frederick Perls, it had been the theater; as a young man in Germany he had studied to be a director under the great Max Reinhardt even before he went to medical school. For Laura Perls it was her involvement in music and dance, as well as her studies with the existentialist thinkers Paul Tillich and Martin Buber while she was completing graduate work in psychology. Paul Goodman published poetry, novels, and plays in addition to social and cultural criticism both before and after he joined Frederick Perls in the writing of the central text on Gestalt therapy in 1951. And when he met Perls, Isadore From was studying philosophy at the New School in New York. From was also a serious reader of literature. He told me once that he had learned as much about human conduct and what to look for in psychotherapy from Henry James and Proust as he had from Freud.

This inclination toward artistic or humanistic pursuits showed up in the early Gestalt therapists' teaching, writing, and their very methods of practice. Frederick Perls created a theater of symptoms with his empty chair technique and, always the director, guided patients through an enactment of how they maintained self-defeating behavior in their present lives. In the therapeutic dramas that unfolded, he helped people discover the bottled-up energy in their symptoms, such that they could choose release from them. Laura Perls and the Polsters, like good literary or art critics, help people revise their own experience in ways that brought out new and surprising possibilities from the stale, monotonous ways of locking themselves in that brought them into therapy. In both his psychotherapy and supervision, Isadore From brought a philosopher's keen eye to the incongruities, discrepancies and contradictions that gummed up the lives of patients, and he taught theory with the care and precision with which philosophers analyze the nature of our knowledge of ourselves and our world.

From my association with these founding figures, I arrived at a conviction that psychotherapy could best be understood on a foundation that resembled aesthetic and philosophical principles more than a scientific outlook. (This was not colored by any refusal on my part to take scientific method seriously; my bachelor's degree was in mathematics and physics.) An underlying premise of Gestalt therapy is that experience is always in a process of being made; it's never just given. That is why Gestalt therapy insists that the most effective work comes from paying the closest attention to what is unfolding moment to moment in the present situation of the therapy session itself. The therapy session could thus serve as a tiny theater or classroom or laboratory for staging, inquiring into, reflecting upon, and experimenting with the shapes and meanings that patients assigned to their experience. By becoming aware of how they form their experience and playing with the possibilities of making it differently, people could take more command of it and reconfigure it for a better life.

This fundamental perspective — that psychotherapy by its very nature is an activity that resembles both the making of expressive forms called works of art and the investigation philosophers do of what is taken for granted by subjecting it to critical reflection — has dictated just about all of my own teaching and writing. My outlook was fortified when I went back to the writings of Otto Rank and John Dewey, both of whom, along with Freud, had influenced the development of Gestalt therapy. They helped me see how a person's everyday life itself — where it failed and where it succeeded — could best be understood through the lenses of what we learn from the close observation of making art. To put this as simply as possible: The healthy or good life had the character of good art — a shaping of experience into a vital representations that were fluid and resilient enough to keep up with present circumstances. I thought of this as something like the poet Ezra Pound's definition of poetry as news that stays news. Neuroses, on the other hand, as well as the other illnesses and disturbances of mental life, resembled bad art in that they tended to be ill-formed and awkward remakings in the present of responses to vanished or obsolete past circumstances. Thus they were fixed and repetitious to the point of monotony and imposed like a hallucination over the liveliness of present actuality.

Much later I found this point of view to be compatible with the thought of phenomenological philosophers such as Husserl, Heidegger and Sartre, Merleau-Ponty and Levinas, whose works I began reading intensively. From them I gained an understanding that human experience is not best understood as a lone self confronting a world of otherness "out there," but that we are already in the world, and the world is in us. Recent psychoanalysis and Gestalt therapy have both developed theory and practice that places emphasis on the relationship between the patient and the therapist. A serious encounter with phenomenology carries us well beyond relationship between persons to a much deeper and more basic sense of our inextricably embedded involvement not only with each other but our entire event-laden world.

My career-long concern with bringing psychotherapy, which is to say Gestalt therapy, more in line with art and philosophy — not only as technique but as fundamental theory — is quite old-fashioned in some respects, even though I believe that it moves psychotherapy forward from where it has ended up for the past few decades lodged in medical science. During the nineteenth century in the United States psychology was still considered a branch of philosophy, and two of America's foremost philosophers, William James and John Dewey, were also among our most innovative and far-reaching theoretical psychologists. For that matter Freud's theorizing, despite his early hopes that psychoanalysis would eventually find its scientific basis in neurology, was often philosophical in character and also drew on the tradition of German poetry and literature. Early in the twentieth-century, however, psychotherapy and the psychological theories that informed it, especially in the United States, broke off from philosophical speculation to borrow its method from the natural sciences, fastened with a vengeance on the medical side of Freud, and moved away from humanistic concerns in an attempt to construct a science of behavior, cognition, and emotion, initially based on stimulus-response conditioning and eventually on biological theories of brain functioning. In recent times the academic and medical mainstream has, if anything, more fully embraced this outlook, although some schools of contemporary psychoanalysis have separated themselves from it and as of late have been rapidly approaching Gestalt therapy to the point that it seems likely the two may eventually merge.

II.

If the treatment of psychology and psychotherapy as science has its roots in the analysis of empirical data, Gestalt therapy, insofar as it takes its cues from humanistic pursuits, has its roots in the phenomenology of conscious experience. This leads rather naturally from positivistic and empirical philosophies to phenomenology, which is a branch of contemporary philosophy that has been much less widely received in the United States than in Europe and South America. For me, a phenomenological outlook has a number of implications that govern themes of the essays that follow in this book.

I have always been committed to the development of psychological theory as a foundation for clinical practice. In my writing and teaching, however, I tend to be less concerned with the search for universal assumptions that lead to grand theory, or what in psychoanalytic thought since Freud has been called "metapsychology," than with a level of conceptual thinking that the sociologist Robert Merton calls *theories of the middle range.* [italic his.] Merton defined these as "theories that lie between minor but necessary working hypotheses that evolve in abundance during day-to-day research and the all-inclusive systematic efforts to develop a unified theory that will explain all the observed uniformities of social behavior, social organization, and social change"(Merton, 1967, p. 39). He felt that the attempt to reach for a universal theory that would explain all social phenomena would become too remote from the observable particulars of social experience. On the other hand, not going beyond the common-sense intuitions that inevitably come up in what he called "day-to-day research" left one mired in the particulars themselves with insufficient guiding principles to find relationships among them.

There is a story that Freud tells from his student days about a classroom exchange with his teacher Charcot. When one of the students [apparently Freud himself] objected to a comment of Charcot's on the grounds that it violated the Young-Helmholtz theory, Charcot replied, "Theory is good, but it doesn't prevent things from existing" (Cited in Bromberg, 2006, pp. 1-2). To Charcot's succinct point that one limitation of our theories is their inability to account for everything that exists, I would add that they all too often posit existence of things that don't exist. One of the main ways that psychologists have tried to keep their favorite theories intact is through reifying the theoretical concepts themselves. By treating them as thing-like phenomena, they can be manipulated to fit causal formulations. Thus we get *the* unconscious, the *self, an* object-relation, *a* harsh superego, etc. Such concepts have valuable uses as metaphors through which to look at experience and make sense of it. But once the grammatical articles, such as "the," and "a," of individual separate existence are placed in front of them, psychology and psychotherapy are on their way to a pseudo-empirical materialism.

Clearly some degree of generalization and abstraction is necessary if we are to have any sort of compass to help us navigate in the teeming world of particulars which go into the making of our experience. The danger is too much generalization or abstraction. Finding the right balance between the general and the particular is a matter of maintaining theory in good contact with practice. It's like taking someone's pulse: If you don't touch the wrist, you feel nothing. If you squeeze down too hard, you shut it off and feel nothing. What is required is getting close enough to feel the actual throbbing rhythm of life, but too hard a grip shuts it down. Merton's notion of the middle range was his hope of creating theory that would keep the social science researcher in touch with empirical observations but also prevent getting lost wandering among them. My comparable wish has been to work at developing a level of theoretical thinking that guides the therapist's work in the psychotherapy session without losing the immediacy of direct observation and intuition.

Psychotherapy at is best, in my view, is an improvisatory art; at least this is the only kind of therapy that interests me. The relation of theory to practice in psychotherapy can also be likened to how jazz musicians work. Serious improvisation in jazz is far from a free-for-all. Although the individual musicians in a jazz group may be fully absorbed in spontaneous creation during the heat of performance, that spontaneity is grounded in structure that combines innumerable hours becoming virtuosos on their instruments with learning theories of harmony, counterpoint, modulation of chord progressions, and the jazz tradition itself. That body of background knowledge is a coherent foundation that both guides the individual improviser and ties the band together. Without it everybody on the bandstand would be at sea. Theory gives form, structure, and continuity like this to the moment-to-moment give-and-take of the therapy session.

Such is the general point of view that informs most of my writing about Gestalt therapy and related matters, although I have also written a good deal about the historical development of Gestalt therapy, comparing and contrasting it with other schools of psychotherapy. And I have written about the founders of Gestalt therapy as well as supplied introductions (which are included in this collection) to several of their seminal books. However, I would also like to point out something extremely important to me about my writing style itself.

Adam Phillips, one of the most literate, wise, and far-ranging writers among contemporary psychoanalysts, has proclaimed that "Psychoanalysis does not need any more abstruse or sentimental abstractions — any new paradigm or radical vision — it just needs more good sentences" (Phillips, 2001, p. xvi). Unfortunately, there have not been a great many writers of good sentences in psychology after Freud (who was himself an outstanding writer, and won not the Nobel Prize for science but the Goethe Prize for literature). I would include Donald Winnicott, Michael Balint, and Ernest Schactel, besides Phillips himself, among the best writers of good psychological sentences. The problem is that so many writers in the field simply settle for the language of their particular school, which means that they communicate among one another in jargon specially designed for that school. Or they cook up new jargon, which leads to the overproduction of (what appear to be) new paradigms. Such writing may come off as scientific memoranda that may speak to a professional elite, but it makes for unsatisfying (and unnecessary) obscurity for the rest of us. And it often violates a principle called Occam's Razor (after the medieval philosopher William of Occam), which commands the thinker not to multiply entities beyond necessity. Ideas do not gain in power from such writing. A number of important philosophers in modern times, following the lead of Wittgenstein, made a turn from a specialized obscure language of metaphysical speculation in order to examine carefully and write in the ordinary language of spoken conversation. I believe that psychology serves us best by doing much the same thing. The best and most communicative prose is a carefully heightened and edited version of our ordinary talk.

This goes for Gestalt therapy as much as any other school. Its particular terminology — the contact boundary, retroflection, id, ego, and personality functions of the self, and confluence, for example — at first served to open new ways of looking at human nature, but they are already in danger of becoming reified — a situation in which a name comes to replace the object or quality it points to — in much of the Gestalt therapy literature. Even the present moment, beloved of Gestalt therapists, which William James among others has argued can never be found, often gets treated as though it actually exists. Although I cannot altogether avoid discussing those concepts that have become enshrined in the tradition of Gestalt therapy, whenever possible I try to write in the language of our common understanding. And that is why I choose

16

to write about topics such as curiosity and disappointment, the familiar and the unknowable, "I" and "you" and "we," love and hate.

Beyond my own personal interest in such topics (In the essays collected here, which range over a thirty-year period, they both preceded and came after my book, *Intimate Terrorism*, where they are more fully elaborated), they serve to protect me, Gestalt therapy, and psychological theory from the tendency toward reification that I allude to above. Reification solidifies ideas, giving them the appearance of permanence. As Edgar Levenson, another among the writers of good psychoanalytic sentences, points out, "The analyst convinced of the immutable relevance of his position may find himself, like a penguin, drifting out to sea on a melting bed of premises" (Levenson, 1995, p. 13). Most of our theories and therefore our therapies have treated their basic concepts as though they exist in space, which makes it easy for them to take their place among an array of things. But love, hate, and the other emotions that make up our psychic lives express themselves in waves that rise and fall over time. The temporal dimension of the human dimension has come to play a larger and larger role in my recent work.

New York City
December 7, 2008

References

Philip Bromberg. 2006. *Awakening the Dreamer: Clinical Journeys.* Mahwah, New Jersey: The Analytic Press.
Edgar Levenson. 1995. *The Ambiguity of Change: An Inquiry into the Nature of Psychoanalytic Reality.* Northvale, New Jersey: Jason Aronson.
Robert K. Merton. 1967. *On Theoretical Sociology: Five Essays, Old and New.* New York: The Free Press.
Adam Phillips. 2001. *Promises, Promises: Essay on Psychoanalysis and Literature.* New York: Basic Books.

Part One:

Themes, Clinical and Philosophical

∫ Notes on Art and Symptoms

The theory of Gestalt therapy draws heavily upon categories we usually associate with art. This is more than a matter of fashioning analogies or metaphors from the arts to illustrate psychological principles. As Laura Perls insisted in a recently published interview, "Gestalt is an aesthetic concept." [**] She and Paul Goodman are chiefly responsible for bringing a concern with the nature of art to bear on Gestalt therapy. One finds this concern in her writings, which unfortunately are scattered and few; but she has also transmitted it consistently and widely through her teaching. For a comprehensive written account, one must turn to Goodman. In his half of the book that he wrote with Frederick Perls

---

[*]From *A Festschrift for Laura Perls*. Edited by Daniel Rosenblatt. *The Gestalt Journal* Vol. III, No. 1 (Spring, 1980). Reprinted with permission.

[**]Edward Rosenfeld. 1978. "An Oral History of Gestalt Therapy, Part One: A Conversation with Laura Perls," *The Gestalt Journal*, Vol. I, No.1. p. 26.

and Ralph Hefferline, [*] Goodman plants Gestalt therapy firmly in a context of aesthetic values as well as psychological ideas, and it is still the most important theoretical statement we have.

Why did art figure so prominently in the development of Gestalt therapy? For one thing, Gestalt therapy was conceived by thinkers and clinicians who were, to varying degrees, involved in artistic disciplines. In addition to making important theoretical contributions to this new approach to psychotherapy, Goodman wrote poems, novels, plays, literary and social criticism. He was to become a distinguished man of letters. Laura Perls, during her early years in Germany, studied music and modern dance, which led her to an abiding interest in the body's rhythms and gestures in her work with patients. And in his youth, Fritz Perls got training in the theater from Max Reinhardt. Fritz Perls did not contribute directly to the aesthetic orientation in Gestalt therapy; his interests lay in other directions. His early fascination with the theater though, certainly colored his therapeutic style and his teaching. It gave rise to his "hot seat" approach and his love for staging a production of the patient's neurosis. But Laura Perls and Goodman, who worked together closely for a time and influenced one another, found in the arts a vision of ideal functioning, which they extended to all human activity. This vision became their measure of health and pathology and their guide to the practice of psychotherapy.

There are more specific reasons why the arts provided the most useful model for conceptualizing Gestalt therapy. The principles that Gestalt therapy learned from experimental Gestalt psy-

---

[*] F. Perls, R. Hefferline, and P. Goodman. 1951. *Gestalt Therapy: Excitement and Growth in the Human Personality.* New York: Julian Press.

chology suggest that much of human experience has properties that might well be described as aesthetic. In their studies of perception and cognition Gestalt psychologists such as Kohler, Koffka, and Wertheimer had demonstrated that people tend to make experience into wholes characterized by form, structure, and unity. Gestalt therapy took this notion a step further and emphasized the creative autonomy of healthy activity. Hence the assumption in Gestalt therapy that people best fulfill their natural capacities when allowed to regulate their lives with a minimum of interference. Herein is a source of Gestalt therapy's radicalism, an anarchist position opposed to liberal ideologies that promote manipulation of the individual by experts, whether children by parents, citizens by social engineers and the welfare state, or psychotherapy patients by behaviorists and medical authorities.

Radicalism of this kind, anarchistic, motivated in part by the values inherent in art, should probably be more familiar to Americans than Europeans. Fritz and Laura Perls came from a European milieu of psychoanalysis, Gestalt psychology, and existentialism. These were intellectual and clinical developments that Goodman knew well. But thanks to Goodman, Gestalt therapy was also strongly influenced by a native American tradition of radical social criticism that has always posed an ideal of art against the evils of established society. Emerson, Thoreau, and Whitman, Veblen and Dewey to some extent, Randolph Boume and Lewis Mumford belong to this tradition, and Goodman was perhaps its chief modern spokesman.

Through their mutual exchange, Goodman and Laura Perls, in particular, made a fruitful synthesis of these European and American intellectual tendencies. The following notes present some reflections on what their understanding of art implies for the theory and practice of psychotherapy.

TEACHING A PARANOID TO FLIRT

Art and psychotherapy have been compared often enough, but rarely in ways that shed much light on either. It is hardly illuminating to say that both are "creative" or that expressing oneself is therapeutic or that therapists are more like artists than scientists.

But art and therapy do share underlying features which point to their common source in a peculiarly human tendency to form and transform one's given relation to the world. Both make use of formal structure and artifice to achieve their effects. They both enclose experience in some kind of frame or medium which lifts it out of the stream of everyday life. To accomplish this, they edit, choreograph, dramatize, condense, revise, in other words, reorganize life. But toward what end? In art, at least, the creation of a formal object in itself might be the purpose. That would not be very true of therapy, although the artifact could be said to be oneself.

There is another purpose that they have in common: to bring something novel into the foreground, to cast the overly familiar, well-worn arrangement or habit in a new light. Thus both present new information. Great works of art, in fact, seem to contain an inexhaustible supply of it. We can return again and again to a masterpiece and come away refreshed. This is what Ezra Pound meant when he said "poetry is news that stays news." How it manages to do so remains mostly mysterious.

However Rudolf Arnheim, a psychologist and philosopher of art, offers an intriguing clue to part of the mystery. He points out that "the word 'information,' taken literally, means to give form; and form needs structure." * Only at first glance, then, does the question of new information in art and psychotherapy look like a separate matter from their formalism. Both bring about new information through a transformation of the familiar. They create a new form that fuses the past with the present, old routines or conventions with new possibilities (in this sense, Wordsworth's principle of poetic creation — "emotion recollected in tranquillity" — is something like Freud's interpretation of free associations). Through such means, they can provide occasions for discovery, making it more possible to bring out what has been forgotten, never attended to, or repressed.

Consider dreams, fantasies, and the like from this standpoint. They are creations but in themselves neither works of art nor automatically therapeutic. One makes one's dreams, but it is the remaking of them that is important for art and therapy. Yet there are times when this distinction gets overlooked in the programs and, on occasion, even the practices of both professions. For instance, certain surrealist poets and painters in the early twentieth century, under the influence of a romanticized Freudianism, assumed that free association opens the unconscious and art pours out immediately. The turn-of-the century French writer Lautreamont once announced: "Beauty is the chance meeting on an operating table of a sewing machine and an umbrella." At best that is a whimsical but not very far-reaching definition; still it was adopted by many surrealists as a theory of art.

---

*Rudolf Arnheim. 1971. *Entropy and Art: an Essay on Disorder and Order.* (Berkeley: Univ. of Calif Press, 1971), p. 18.

Thus the surrealist program mistook the kind of material that dreams release for the finished work (even so, great surrealist writing and painting transcended its programs and achieved an intense formalism). This resembles in principle some modern tendencies in psychotherapy which prescribe the discharge of raw emotion or flights of ideas called "fantasy exercises," as though these in themselves would constitute the therapy. Like good artists, good psychotherapists treat dreams, memories, emotions as incomplete. When a psychoanalytic patient brings in a dream, the analyst completes the meaning by interpreting the symbolism of the dream's content and the patient's accompanying associations. A Gestalt therapist might coax the patient to stage the dream himself as a new experience, in order to integrate its links to the past with what is alive in the present situation. The difference between these schools of practice is a little like the difference between a seminar in literary history and a creative writing workshop.

What can be said, then, of a person's living of his or her everyday life? It is not a work of art nor a therapy session. Psychotherapy is to life as art is to life: Both are specialized pursuits, structurally and qualitatively different from ordinary life. But their value springs from a deep common source in human nature — the power to give form, to transform experience in a manner that leads to a new integration. This capacity is so thoroughly embedded in human consciousness and activity that it must be close to the root of virtually all learning, growth, and change.

That is why an understanding of art can be so useful for psychology and psychotherapy. For Gestalt therapy, it is summed up in the conception of "contact," a somewhat awkward and now overused technical term that describes a person's ability to meet and interpenetrate his or her surrounding world and to gain something new from it. Contact is no mechanical adaptation of self and external world to each other, precisely because humans are form-making and integrating animals.

Gestalt therapy has no "truths" in the sense that it teaches a right way of behaving and communicating to its patients. But it does hold the following conviction: When people move or talk in the ways that are right for each of them, their activities exhibit those qualities by which we judge art — economy and gracefulness, necessity and flexibility. In other words, contact obeys the dictum "truth is beauty."

It follows that the good life (or, now that the therapeutic, for better or worse, has mostly replaced the moral dimension in our culture, we would call it the "healthy life") is shapely and satisfying to contemplate. Yet the good life would hardly be an untroubled existence. That would be too far from nature to hold our interest for very long. Like a work of art that absorbs and provokes us, a life worth taking seriously contains elements of struggle and reconciliation, challenges met and obstacles overcome, pain and difficulty as well as beauty and pleasure. It is too complex to reduce to Eden. Medieval and Renaissance theologians sometimes spoke of "felix culpa" — the "happy sin" — for it got us out of the mindless stasis of the Garden and introduced challenge into life.

I want to stress that this is no art-for-art's sake view of human existence. I believe there is something fundamentally moral in the vision I have just described, which I take to be inherent in Gestalt therapy. Too many so-called humanistic psychotherapists, including many Gestalt therapists, in their rush to overturn the oppressive residues of Puritanism, sneer at all judgments of good and evil. Granted that a moralism of do's and don'ts and shoulds used for purposes of controlling others ought to be attacked. But the outlook I am presenting is not that sort of doctrine; rather, it

27

respects the nature of things and concerns itself with the use of human resources and qualities that best preserves the fit between self and nature. It perceives an elemental reality behind the care for the shapes and forms of experience that one witnesses in the work of every serious artist, scientist, and philosopher.

————

We might do worse than to judge pathology from this perspective as well. For if truth that somehow seems natural and whole is beautiful, what is missing in neurosis is that its "truths" are frozen into one-sided, dogmatic caricatures that are fundamentally incomplete. The chronically depressed person, for example, feels ugly, and rightly so, for depression is ugly. Depressed people deny themselves the dignity of feeling and knowing their grief or sadness or anger clearly and allowing these to consummate their purposes.* Since these emotions in depression are locked up with fragments of unresolved past experiences, no integration occurs. They contaminate one another, conflict with each other, and do not become freely available for the person's present life. As in all neurosis, there is exhaustion without completion; there is neither catharsis nor epiphany.

This does not mean that health comes from an angelic side of the personality and pathology from a demonic one. On the contrary, they both proceed from the same creative impulse, the innate momentum in the human organism to define itself and shape its relationship with the environment.

---

*This point was suggested to me by my colleague Richard Borofsky.

28

People tend to look upon babies as totally helpless and dependent. They are certainly dependent but not as helplessly so as it may seem. They go about meeting their needs with the faint beginnings of motoric elegance and capacity to give shape to interaction. If this sounds like too much adult projections in the opposite direction from attributing helplessness, consult the careful research studies of Barry Brazelton and his associates. They have discovered a good deal about the artful characteristics of healthy newborn behavior. For instance, their research has shown that infants only three days old take some charge of their relations to their environment and display rudiments of individual style in doing so. Each one begins to make his or her own distinctive patterns of curiosity and absorption, acceptance and rejection.

Newborn babies even develop stratagems for coping with demands on them from others. When adults become unwanted intrusions, one infant tunes out and pretends sleep; another throws a tantrum (just like the adults do in more complicated ways). These are not passive responses. They are sequences of yeses and noes by which these tiny beings make a boundary between themselves and the world, like a prelude to identity. Such are the beginnings of self-definition that go into the making of contact. A beloved pet can stare at you with devoted intensity but never with that searching for the give-and-take of a relating that includes elements of self-expression. Yet one sees this in infants who are only a few weeks old.

Many developmental theories in psychology have stressed the part that the child's sense of danger in the family environment plays in the forming of his or her character. From the standpoint of Gestalt therapy, children's innate creative powers can be diverted by the presence of such danger from making contact into the construction of defenses. Or to put it more precisely, where there is real danger, the defense is the child's way of making the appropriate contact to meet its needs in that circumstance. If, for instance, a parent gets too anxious and typically withdraws or rages whenever a child cries or becomes angry, then the child will probably learn to stop its tears or yells so that it can continue to get the care it must have. To keep crying or having the tantrum and lose the parent could result in serious deprivation or, in extreme cases, even death. Children diminish their range of self in these situations in order to survive. There is artistry in building defenses, but if they become chronic, they inhibit growth, contract the personality, and narrow the resources available for making contact in other situations.

Neurotic symptoms are an instance of what the economist Thorstein Veblen called "trained incapacity." Veblen was referring to a kind of cultural ossification that sets in when people learn skills and styles of behavior all too well. Then they become blind and paralyzed in certain respects — unable to respond to, or even perceive new developments as new. When the British Redcoats[*] marched in neat ranks and files into the eighteenth-century New England wilderness to put down a colonial rebellion, they were easily destroyed by snipers hiding behind trees and rocks. These

---

[*]I borrow the Redcoats from the art critic Harold Rosenberg, who used them to indicate how certain periods in the history of painting got bogged down in narrow conventions. [*The Tradition of the New* (New York: Grove Press, 1961), pp. 13-15].

highly skilled British soldiers, trained to perfection on European parade grounds, could make no sense of, much less cope with, the bullets coming at them from all directions.

Symptoms are like this well-oiled British fighting machine. They represent skills tuned and tuned on the battlefields of childhood, skills that have become a liability. If revolutionary art makes war on the cliché, overthrows entrenched conventions in its quest for new consciousness, symptoms are at the conservative end of the creative spectrum. Symptoms rely on already perfected techniques for meeting emergencies in order to control anxiety. Thus they cannot meet the new emergency or even the new situation. The original crisis has long since passed, but its shadow remains in the personality now as anxiety, fueling the same defensive action over and over. Symptoms are repetitive and stale, like bad uninteresting art.

Thus we get the vicious circle of neurotic character — a form of witchery, incantation, life lived in a tense, boring trance. One salient characteristic of neurosis is its monotony. The capacity to improvise is lost. Yet it is essential that psychotherapists remember that symptoms, like art, originate in a human talent — the ability to make something by modifying reality. The artist of his or her own neurosis may need as much passion and discipline, originality and cunning to make a symptom as a painting or poem.

———

The idea that one is an artist of one's neurosis is not just a metaphorical turn of phrase. Otto Rank called the neurotic an *artiste marque*. He believed that the artist and the neurotic were similarly driven by an intense longing for immortality, a desire to transcend the limitations of ordinary creaturehood. Such would be

31

their escape from the anxiety of being a separate individual. The difference — and it is equivalent to the difference between health and pathology for Rank — is that the artist as artist (for he might be neurotic elsewhere in his life) ultimately accepts his individuality and copes with the anxiety by recreating his sense of self in art external symbolic medium. Thus the artist can function productively, which means finishing a project and moving on to risk the uncertainty of the next creative task. The neurotic, on the other hand, perpetually manipulates his own actual personality in an effort to gain control over uncertainty and anxiety through making his life predictable. By thus turning to himself, he ends up turning on himself, since his task can never be completed. The neurotic is therefore led to practice incessant self-criticism, makes impossible demands on himself for perfection, and constructs a personality crippled by guilt and dissatisfaction.

creativity ~ uncertainty
~novelty ~ ...

––––

Every psychotherapy has its roots in a view of human nature. Psychoanalysis tends toward a tragic view. It depicts the individual, buffeted between Eros and death, needing civilization yet always chafing at its restrictions. The ego tries to navigate on a stormy sea of instincts and scarcely remains afloat. The "cure" in therapy entails an understanding and an acceptance of these inescapable difficulties and the limitations they impose.

Gestalt therapy also aims toward an acceptance of the limited and the imperfect, but it introduces a note of comedy into the proceedings — in the classical sense of comedy (like the *Divine Comedy* or a Shakespearean comedy) as consisting of errors, misunderstandings, pride, and stubbornness that, once brought into the light, lead to resolution and integration. This outlook follows from the insistence in Gestalt therapy that the individual largely creates his own circumstances. Tragedy implies that character is fate; comedy that it is will.

We need both perspectives. Keeping the tragic and comic sides of life in some balance with each other is one function of irony. In art, especially in literature, irony serves as a powerful device for synthesizing diverse sides of experience. The ironical perception hints at multiple realities: For every meaning one gives an event, irony finds another, often opposed to the first, and keeps these different meanings in view as an integrated whole. Among the blessings of irony is that it discloses options.

Therefore irony can be an extremely valuable tool in psychotherapy. Once you see things in an ironical light, it becomes more difficult to carry on as though your unhappiness is destiny.

An account of a therapy session with a playwright seems appropriate to illustrate what I mean. At our first meeting, he tells me about the crisis that prompted him to call me. He and his wife are on the verge of divorce. Their evenings are consumed by bitter quarrels. I listen but I also watch him closely, trying to take in his presence as well as his presentation. A wiry, athletic-looking man, he nearly groans under the weight of his depression. No doubt this burden is partly due to his marital crisis. But it is not hard to tell that he has always been pretty much like this. His dead voice and slumped shoulders, his victimized look and self-deprecating talk come from years of inward sadness and preoccupation.

He says that the battles with his wife leave him paralyzed with guilt and frustration so that he is unable to work for days afterwards. Amidst a blow-by-blow description of one of these fights, I also learn that he fears becoming like his father, whom he

portrays as a stiff, withdrawn man who treats his family with indif-
ference except when he has something to complain about. An
outwardly successful businessman, the father had become obsessed
with the idea that he had wasted his life. The resulting collapse
into depression was severe enough to require periods of hospital-
ization. The playwright is afraid that his own fate will be similar:
His marriage will fail and it will have been his fault; he will be
unable to write; life will become meaningless.

Self-pity, obsessive guilt, and a sense of doom are the
grand themes my client brings in. This is the stuff of tragedy, or at
least melodrama, so I am prompted to ask him about his plays. To
my surprise, it turns out that he writes satires. When I hear the
note of pride with which he tells me this, I wonder if he has acted
in any of his own plays and find out that he never has. So I suggest
that he present me again with his latest marital blowup, but this
time I will be the audience, and he is to stage it as though it were
one of his most cynical satires. Moreover, he is to play both the
leading roles, taking first one part, than the other. At first he objects to this silliness, and I urge him on. After stumbling around
for a few minutes, he begins to get into it and enjoy himself. He
becomes a very funny man, full of antic gestures, as he discovers
the predictability of their argument — how he knew perfectly well
that a certain comment would set her off, and it did, right on
schedule; how she tried to bite his arm when he grabbed at her
while both of them were delivering pompous ultimatums — it all
begins to seem inflated and contrived. Then a sadder amusement
at the spectacle overtakes him. And from this new distance, he is
more responsive to their mutual plight; his sorrow now extends to
her as well as to himself. For the moment, at least, his depression

34

has changed into something more generous and useful to both of them.

When my playwright-patient becomes a ham, he begins to free himself from the endless cycles of his self-involved mournfulness. He cannot avoid seeing what thin partitions sometimes divide the tragic from the absurd. Depression is a case where absurdity helps restore some flexibility. If, for example, people who are addicted to the miseries of childhood can discover something ridiculous in the whole business, they may have taken the crucial step toward becoming adults.

In a study of nineteenth-century French politics, Marx claimed that all important episodes in history occur twice — the first time as tragedy, the second as farce. The protagonists, of course, take themselves just as seriously the second time around. We might stretch a Freudian point to show that something similar happens on the smaller historical stage of the individual personality. For Freud taught us through concepts such as transference and the repetition compulsion how the history of the child is reenacted by the adult. If the original tragedy was the child's fall into anxiety, the later farce is that so much of what makes the adult anxious involves shadow-play and unreality, a projection of past players and obsolete stage sets, a tragicomedy of ghosts. Once again the protagonists take it all too seriously and lose themselves in it. One task of psychotherapy is to help them discover the absurdity of unnecessary anxiety.

This patient happened to be a practicing artist. In his art he had learned to revise his experience to include humor but, like his father, had sentenced himself to misery in his life and marriage. I gave him a slight nudge that enabled him to make the translation from art to life. That sort of translation is useful not only to artists; it is open to everyone and, Gestalt therapy would say, is a necessary step toward further growth.

———

Of course Gestalt therapy is by no means the first psychological theory or clinical method to address itself to the question of art. I do think, however, that it may be the first (except for Rank) to deal with the strictly aesthetic as well as the psychological elements in the arts.

Most psychological interpretations of art have treated it as though it occupies a borderland between madness and exaltation, now using it as a kind of Rorschach for diagnosing disease, now putting it on a pedestal as the highest human achievement. Freud exemplifies this kind of ambivalent attitude, which wavers between romanticism and a scientific rationalism. He proclaimed repeatedly that artists, especially poets, had anticipated many of his own insights into unconscious processes. On other occasions he attributed the display of unconscious material in art not so much to insight as to a narrow escape from regressive breakdown or to tabooed fantasies disguising themselves in order to win social applause. A man of cultivated taste, Freud responded to the ennobling quality of masterpieces; yet he published "The Moses of Michelangelo" anonymously, one suspects, not just because he thought himself inexpert, but also because he felt it was unsuitable for a man of science to write such a rhapsody to a piece of sculpture.

Works of art, according to Freud, result from sublimations of instinctual conflicts — conflicts between forbidden pleasures and the demands of social reality. This is an intriguing explanation, but it seems somewhat beside the point when you are in the presence of a great masterpiece. One reason Freud may have tended to reduce art to pathology in his theory, if not his personal response, is that he mostly ignored form and concentrated on content, as Richard Wollheim has argued.* This approach is similar to his method of dream interpretation, which hunts for symbolism masking hidden conflicts and desires. Many modern literary and art critics have borrowed Freud's method, so we now have a lot of intriguing gossip about artists, along with some fruitful new insights, though just as often these seem to have little to do with the works themselves. And many psychological thinkers after Freud have continued to treat art like a particular kind of nineteenth-century patient — a beautiful mysterious creature, hysterical even if gifted, who looks charming draped around a theoretical point.

————

Nowadays, the roles have frequently become more or less reversed: Some clinicians and counselors have plundered the arts for therapeutic techniques and called the result "art therapy." Here the emphasis is on the tools rather than the interpretation. The art therapists have come up with suggestive experiments but no more than the psychoanalysts do they concern themselves with the integration of form and content, the lyrical or powerful wedding of experience and medium. Even Janie Rhyne, a leading art therapist with a Gestalt orientation, seems to misunderstand the nature of

---

*Richard Wollheim. 1974. "Neurosis and the Artist," Times Literary Supplement, March 1, 1974, pp. 203-4.

both art and Gestalt therapy when she writes "aesthetics is irrelevant when we are working for self-discovery, and judgments of good or bad are eliminated as irrelevant. The question asked is 'What are you finding out about yourself?'"[*] Most art therapy tends to boil art down to something that is good for you — self-realization through recreation and calisthenics. This approach suits our preoccupation with the technology of self-improvement, which includes self-help manuals, Masters and Johnson, and biofeedback. Dismissing the aesthetic dimension of human activity on grounds of its irrelevance to therapeutic insight contradicts the essence of Gestalt therapy.

According to another popular modern notion, both art and psychotherapy are above all supposed to put you in touch with your feelings. A partial truth is thereby taken for the whole. Feelings are brought into the foreground of experience as though they are ends in themselves. The artist is then used somewhat like a pornographer to stimulate emotions, and the psychotherapist becomes a conductor, urging the patient on to ever greater crescendoes of emotional expression.

It is not difficult to see how our culture, originating in the relentless inward scrutiny of its Puritan forebears, might arrive at this formulation — especially now that it rebels against itself and directs its self-absorption away from sin to the consumption of

---

[*]Janie Rhyne. "The Gestalt Art Experience" in *Gestalt Therapy Now*, edited by Joen Fagan and Irma Lee Shepherd (Palo Alto: Science and Behavior Books, 1970), p. 275.

pleasure. So we listen to music in order to focus on the emotions it arouses or pound pillows in encounter groups to gain back our anger (as if it were a possession). People become fascinated with their own sensations in a kind of foreplay and, clinging to these (this was Freud's definition of perversion), do not get on to the real business of contacting what is next to and outside themselves.

Yet there is a possibility of meeting between oneself and a work of art or another person that the sensations and arousals of emotion can move one toward, even as they enhance the reaching. Emotions help one obtain nourishment through contacting something or someone other than what one already knows and is. Without this contact, no growth is possible. In other words, emotions connect us to our surroundings in very specific ways: They inform us about ourselves in relation to what is out there (or what is missing, in the case of grief, for example) in the landscape, telling us what we need from it or want to do about it or to it, whether it be to draw it closer, push it away, destroy or possess it. But this central purpose of emotional life is passed over in the claim that feeling itself is the fulfillment.

Feelings thus play a part in forming the self's world-view at a given moment. For instance, feeling hungry involves a world-view in which sources of food thrust themselves upon one or are conspicuously absent. This may be a world-view only briefly for most of us, for it disappears or is transformed into another feeling when the hunger is satisfied. But if hunger becomes chronic, it continues to color all one's entire orientation to the world and the tone of one's existence in it. During a period in the Middle Ages, when a substantial portion of Europe lived near starvation, jokes about food had the same kind of titillating effect that sexual jokes do on us. And all of us by now are familiar with the impact our own obsession with sexual feelings has had on our cultural world view, from cosmetics advertising to automotive design to psychoanalytic theory. The chronic dominance of the personality by one emotional tone is always a sign of pathology either in the self or in the environment.

If such be the case, psychotherapy ought not to be so concerned with the intensity of emotions (like certain modern Reichians tend to be) as with their quality, degree of flexibility, and precise direction in relation to the environment. Then they serve not only to deepen one's experience but also to make one's knowledge of it more lucid. An excellent drama coach told me that he cannot bear actors who work themselves into a frenzy trying to express their emotions in order to work them into the characters they are depicting. He gives his students exercises in which they are to describe an object or person to someone else in as many ways as they can invent. He believes that the appropriate emotions will then arise naturally, get expressed as part of the ensuing contact, and then modulate to meet the next thing that matters.

a poetry

Compare the following two statements:

> . . . . conversion of resistance and tensions, of excitations that in themselves are temptations to diversion, into a movement toward an inclusive and fulfilling close. [*]

Could there be a better definition of psychotherapy?

---

[*] John Dewey. *Art as Experience* (New York: Capricorn Books, 1958), p. 56.

. . . . manageable experiences is realized only at the point where the means for its interpretation and transformation become available. [*]

This would be an apt description of what goes on in making a work of art.

The first statement is John Dewey's definition of the aesthetic. The second is Laura Perls' description of the therapeutic process, which she, in fact, explicitly likens to "the creation of a work of art (the highest form of integrated and integrating human experience)."[**] In both — and their similarities are indeed striking — there is an emphasis on organic fusion of an already existing content, which tends toward disintegration or fragmentation, with a new form that converts it into something more coherent, complete, and satisfying.

In psychotherapy, the fragmentation represents bondage to the past and symptom-formation. People come into therapy like failed artists who are wasting their talent and misdirecting their passion. Having made a self based on the regulation of anxiety, they produce works that are repetitious, fragmented, and unconvincing. In the therapy session I described earlier, both the playwright's depressive character and his plays are creative compositions. But in most areas of his life this creative impulse is governed

---

[*] Laura Perls. "Two Instances of Gestalt Therapy" in *Recognitions in Gestalt Therapy*, edited by Paul David Pursgove (New York: Funk and Wagnalls, 1968), p. 45.

[**] Ibid.

by anxiety, although one area, his art, gives evidence of having mastered anxiety.

Thus it is the patient, not the therapist, who is the artist, no matter how unsatisfactory his or her works may be. Symptoms and their manifestation in therapy, usually called resistance, are still passionate strategies for living and deserve respect. The synthesizing transformations described in the passages I just quoted can free an individual from symptoms and the past without throwing either away, for the latter would amount to repression once again and probably result in little more than an exchange of symptoms. Such a synthesis then becomes a way of recovering the vital resources imprisoned in an attachment to the past and to symptoms, so they can be used as wisdom and skills in one's present life. Unfortunately, psychotherapists too often have acted like surgeons, donning rubber gloves to remove a diseased organ or limb. But you cannot amputate a neurosis without diminishing the patient's personality even further. As Laura Perls once pointed out, the psychotherapist functions less like a doctor on one hand or an artist on the other than a critic, concerned to restore a person's sense of choice and discrimination about his or her own productions. *

*Laura Perls. "The Psychoanalyst and the Critic," *Complex* (Summer, 1950), p. 44.

∫ Curiosity and Its Vicissitudes

I.

For several years after I began a private practice of psychotherapy I wore a rather thick beard. One morning I woke up with an impulse to make a change, so I went into the bathroom and shaved it off entirely. Not surprisingly, it wasn't easy at first to recognize the new face I saw staring back at me from the mirror.

None of my patients had ever seen this version of my face before. Over the next few days at work in my office, I found that they had an intriguing variety of reactions to the sudden transformation in my appearance. A number of them said with a bit of shock in their voices, "You shaved off your beard! Looks good (or not). What prompted you to do it?" Then there were patients who gazed at me a little searchingly, and asked "Isn't something about you different? Have you lost weight? Or did you get a haircut?" But some came in, sat down, and immediately began telling me what was on their minds without appearing to notice that anything about me had changed, whether they looked at me

*From *The Gestalt Journal* Vol. X, No. 1 (Spring, 1987). Reprinted with permission.

or not. A few just seemed unaware that I was not quite the same as the week before. With others, it was hard to tell whether they noticed a difference but felt it was not permitted to become too personal and question an authority figure, such as a therapist.

It was this event that first got me interested in the possibility of using curiosity, its variations and disturbances, as a diagnostic tool. When new patients came in for a first therapy session, I found myself paying a good deal of attention to the degree of free play in their ability to be curious. To what extent did they look around and take in the surroundings — the furnishings, the décor, the whole setup? How did they go about checking me out, if at all? Did they size me up and feel free to ask me questions? It struck me that curiosity plays an important role in how people orient themselves in a new environment. When an animal roams into new territory seeking shelter, among its first activities might be checking out the food supply, the safety from predators, and the whereabouts of potential mates for procreation. In the case of the human animal, curiosity is an essential response for getting oriented, a necessary supportive capacity for making good contact with one's changing world. If you can't be curious, you don't know much about where you are or what is there to meet your needs.

Beyond the first session, I now tend to evaluate from session to session the continuous workings of my patients' curiosity and their relation to it. Can they examine with interest, investigate critically, question in detail and keep on questioning what I am like, how they are with me, how I respond to what they say? For example, Gestalt therapy teaches us that if patients are talking to you and not looking at you to see your reactions, they are talking to a blank screen onto which they are projecting. Contact, like nature, abhors a vacuum, and projections rush in to fill it. Or if they are not questioning the therapist's comments, interventions, and interpretations, they are very likely just introjecting the therapist.

The value of a person having free and independent curiosity seems unmistakable. Babies appear to be born with it. Yet society does a lot to discourage its further development. Parents often tell the children, "Don't ask so many questions," especially if the parents have something to hide. Culture since Victorian times has admonished us that curiosity killed the cat. In societies ruled by dictatorships, the citizens learn to lower their gaze and not raise questions about institutions, bureaucrats, or elections lest they wind up in prison or worse. From family life to the whole of social life, curiosity openly exercised can become a revolutionary force.

In the pre-relational days of psychoanalysis, when the therapist sat behind the couch, his or her remaining a blank projection screen and offering interpretations of the unconscious (which tend to be introjected) were considered to be technically desirable — thus surely limiting curiosity about a lot of what is going on in the session itself. A patient who became too curious about the therapist, for instance, was likely to be charged with resistance. I am by no means denigrating the Freudian discovery of unconscious motives nor the recent evolution of psychoanalytic practice, which has much in common with Gestalt therapy. But it's the more embracing issue, the forward thrust of curiosity toward the world and the equally aggressive tendency to block it, that I want to emphasize here. Through investigation, curiosity seeks to dismantle the world and know it for what it is. Curiosity in full bloom takes little for granted. My patient's ambivalence about this sort of knowledge ("After such knowledge, what forgiveness?" as T. S. Eliot put it) reaches as far back as human history. Whether to preserve the father's rules, the social conventions, the sexual mores, the religious dogmas from undergoing too much scrutiny is a question fraught with conflict that began with Adam's and Eve's disobedience in the Garden. It gives rise to speculation about what is first repressed in human development — forbidden sexual impulses or forbidden curiosity.

According to Freud, the adult's drive for knowledge originates in an infantile sexual impulse, a kind of voyeurism and urge toward sexual investigation, eventually repressed in the course of development. Freud makes much of this notion (Freud 1947), as do subsequent psychoanalytic theorists, such as Melanie Klein and Harry Guntrip. Infantile sexual curiosity comes to a bad end in Freud's account. Judging from his case histories, nineteenth-century Viennese babies characteristically woke up in their cribs at the foot of their parents' beds, witnessed violent movements, overheard animal cries, and thought that a murderous battle was in progress. In the midst of the fray, they caught a glimpse of the female genital and were terrorized by their first dose of castration anxiety. This scenario, Freud's "primal scene," would hardly leave them very much at ease with their sexual curiosity.

From transformations and sublimations of the mostly repressed infantile sexual curiosity, Freud claims, all subsequent curiosity derives: the artist's lust for beauty, the scientist's quest to penetrate the secrets of nature. But if you consider the order of events in Genesis to reflect human development, Freud did not go back far enough. The original taboo, the only one in Eden, was the taboo on knowledge of good and evil. It was Eve's intellectual curiosity, her desire simply to know, not her sexuality, that plunged both her and Adam into deep trouble. The anxious mixture of lust and shame aroused by looking at one another's genitals, which led Adam and Eve to hide them, did not surface until after the Fall.

I do not find it altogether convincing to locate the origins of so far-reaching a human trait as curiosity in an infantile sexual instinct. Of course children are curious about sex, a subject filled with wonder and terror, but they are curious about everything else as well. Nor am I satisfied with the idea that all artistic and scientific pursuits, along with most other human interests, result from a kind of sublimated or spiritualized lust. To make sex the root of all later curiosity is a Victorian projection, one that tends to reduce our excitement in finding out about the world to a disguised obsession, an urge that lingers because it was tabooed and left unsatisfied during childhood. Granted that Freud and his followers performed a valuable service, given the Victorian era, by showing us that in both the noblest and crudest personalities, in the highest as well as the most vulgar products of culture, the animal is always lurking. There is drama in Freud's insistence that Eros, the drive for pleasurable union with others, has a part in all our doings. But nowadays we can accept and affirm this without reducing human development, culture, and psychotherapy to sex. D. H. Lawrence, who certainly didn't slight sex, claimed in his *Fantasia of the Unconscious*, a polemic against psychoanalysis, that creativity is a more primordial impulse than sexuality in human development. Otto Rank suggested much the same thing in his writings.

But I think that curiosity has at least as much claim to be an elemental shaping force in human development as creativity or sexuality. What if we were to construct an account of human development and its problems, in which curiosity usurped the place of Freud's key term, the libido? Such a theory would be of immediate use to Gestalt therapists, who have long needed a developmental perspective congruent with their practice. Treated as a fundamental theoretical concept, curiosity fits readily into the phenomenological basis of Gestalt therapy, for it is an "intentional" concept; that is, it combines awareness with aggression in the sense that Gestalt therapy uses these terms, reflecting the subjective experience of a self directing its meanings and purposes toward the world. One major implication would be that disturbances in the patient's freedom to be curious would assume a prominent role in psychotherapy.

Therapeutic concentration on a person's style of being or failing to be curious attends to the observable without sacrificing the subjective, making it possible to avoid the reductive determinism to which both psychoanalysis and behaviorism fail prey in different ways. It takes the individual's capacity to be deeply interested in his or her world as the sign of health and addresses lack of such absorption as the problem to be treated. Curiosity can be a rich theoretical category: it can connect self and other, emotion and intellect, the empirical and the innate, the impact of early personal history and the immediacy of present contact. It represents active desire without being overly sexualized, and it is cognitive without being overly abstract and intellectual.

II.

Infants can't tell us directly if they are curious (our assumptions about what they perceive and feel can only be based on adult projections), but we can make some informed guesses from studies of how babies direct their attention, since that at least is behavior we can observe. Robert Fantz and Sonia Nevis, among others, did research into the nature of infants' attention between 1958 and 1971. In one of his experiments, Fantz presented pictures in pairs to infants between the ages of one and six months for ten successive one-minute intervals. Each pair consisted of a picture that always remained the same, while the other was constantly changed. It turned out that babies older than two months preferred to look at the novel picture, a result that has been confirmed by later investigators conducting similar experiments. Infants younger than two months apparently don't have mature enough central nervous systems to form a lasting image of what they have seen or heard (Pick, Frankel, and Hess, pp.4-5). If you can't remember anything, nothing is familiar, and there is no difference between the known and the unknown.

Fantz, Nevis, and other researchers have consistently found that beginning around eight weeks of age infants display a "developmental trend toward preference for novelty" (ibid., p.5). This conclusion points to the dawning of a rudimentary curiosity. It is difficult to see how a preference for novelty could be attributed only to the sexual drive, which at this early stage, according to psychoanalytic theory, attaches the infant to the most familiar objects — namely, itself and its mother treated as an extension of itself.

The pediatrician and researcher T. Berry Brazelton, who carries out his experiments in natural settings whenever possible, argues that although lab studies indicate that a two month old does not yet have the visual capability to follow a moving object six or eight feet away, a baby in its family can prove them wrong. "When the object is invested with the libido that his siblings have for him," Brazelton writes, "he will use all his capacity for vision, attention to cues of all kinds, head-turning and concentration in order to keep them in sight. A testing object in a sterile laboratory setting is hardly likely to interest him in the same way — hence inaccurate test results" (Brazelton p.75).

Brazelton's example, its Freudian terminology aside, suggests not only attachment, but a surprising capacity in an eight-week-old infant for differentiated interest akin to curiosity. As Brazelton describes it, this sort of primal fascination is deliberate and selective, supported by arousal, mobilization, and motoric action. It is certainly not the passive, global fooling that many theorists have attributed to newborns. In the language of Gestalt therapy, it would be evidence of an early ability to form figures, an innate capacity for Gestalt formation already beginning to show itself.

Further support for the view that curiosity plays an active and affirmative role in early growth comes from a revisionist position within the psychoanalytic movement itself. In his important book *Metamorphosis*, Ernest Schachtel criticizes Freud's theory of pleasure as inadequate to account for the exploratory and inquisitive nature of children's play. Essentially, Freud defines pleasure as relief from excitation through reducing tension, bringing about a quiescent state approximating sleep or death. Pleasure, for Freud, heads in a negative direction; it moves toward withdrawal from life. His conception of the pleasure principle leads him to formulate a death instinct. Schachtel, by contrast, insists on the *"joyful* encounter with reality" inherent in stimulation and activity for the child. The pleasure for children in exploratory play, he claims, resides not in "the reduction of a want tension nor the abolition of an intruding stimulus, but the maintenance of the relation to the object and continuation of the ongoing activity itself with its fluctuating and enjoyable tensions." What comes from such activity is "positive, joyful expansion of relatedness to the new and rapidly enlarging environment" (Schachtel 1959, p. 64). In other words, psychological growth occurs through the excitement of contact — through active, creative meetings, characterized by novelty, curiosity, and uncertainty, between the self and its world.

According to psychoanalytic developmental theory, curiosity is a secondary phenomenon arising from early transformations of libido. In the view I'm proposing here, curiosity is itself a primary force linking the evolving infant to its environment and playing a central part in deepening and enriching this relationship. An important corollary of this difference for psychotherapy follows from how each of these views regards the origins of consciousness. In Chapter Seven of *The Interpretation of Dreams*, Freud claims that the infant strives to satisfy its needs first by hallucinating, drawing upon memory traces of former perceptions of need-satisfying objects. Only when this process fails does the infant turn to the actual environment to seek satisfaction (Freud 1955, p.565-7). Consciousness begins as an elaboration of this tendency to hallucinate; it arises from turning inward. But a theory predicated on the primacy of curiosity has the infant going to the environment from the beginning. It locates the origins of consciousness in the relationship of self and other.

If anything, the consciousness of psychoanalysis, at least in theory, seems deficient in aggressive curiosity about its surroundings (although analytic practice depends on the patient being curious about himself). It behaves like a passive observer of the self's incessant activities and flow of feelings. As Paul Goodman explains it in *Gestalt Therapy*, "Consciousness is still taken, in psychoanalysis and most of its offshoots (an exception was Rank), to be the passive receiver of impressions, or the additive associator of impressions, or the rationalizer, or the verbalizer. It is what is swayed, reflects, talks, and does nothing" (Perls, Hefferline and Goodman, p. 219). A prone position on the couch is an appropriate posture for such a consciousness as it drinks in the therapist's interpretations. This is in contrast to the roused awareness, busily probing and inventing, that Gestalt therapy describes as engaged in forming figures.

In considering the curiosity of young children, we have to imagine their experience of a world that is everywhere fresh and strange because seen for the first time. I remember reading an article about fatherhood, in which the author describes coming home from work one day and greeting his three-year-old son with the question, "What's new?" To which his son replied, "Everything!" This could be an exciting way for an adult to live as well, but it would require one to remain open to the unknown, the unpredictable, the unfamiliar, the mystery inherent in what one has not yet assimilated. At beginning of her adventures in Wonderland, when strange things start happening, Alice cries out to herself with more fascination than anxiety, "Curiouser and curiouser." Alice and a three-year-old boy apparently can enter the realm of wonder and become absorbed, but most of our patients — or most adults, for that matter — would find it difficult or impossible to tolerate for very long. What has happened along the way?

Adults have always been uneasy with children's curiosity and worked to constrain it to safe, predictable channels in the family and schools, even though they often idealize childlike openness and innocence. The message to children is "curiosity killed the cat." When you look up the word "curious" in Webster or the O.E.D., you find that its very definition has negative connotations. The synonyms given are "inquisitive" and "prying," with the implication, according to *Webster's New Collegiate Dictionary*, of "being interested in what is not one's personal or proper concern." It seems that we are still struggling with Eve and the snake.

There are a number of reasons why this so. Organized society depends in large measure on its ability to impose order, control, and predictability. But curiosity directs itself toward the unknown and unpredictable. Whereas exploring new territory may create the pleasurable excitement that accompanies an expanding sense of self for children, it also gives rise to anxiety. Being openly curious depends on how much anxiety one can tolerate or, to put it conversely, how much excitement one can support. One of the main obstacles to curiosity is possessing a "strong character," something we venerate in this culture, but which, as Michael Balint, a shrewd psychoanalytic theorist, puts it ironically, implies rigidity as much as strength. People with strong characters, Balint points out, tend to travel along one track in life, having severely limited, as a defense against anxiety, their capacities to experience varieties of pleasure and love (Salim, pp. 160-2).

Social and family life have always propped up their authority through mystification. In Victorian times a source of mystification was the taboo on sex; in our own day we have created mystification through masking power as love. But the child's uncensored, probing curiosity threatens to expose the underlying truth, holding up the emperor's nakedness to our embarrassed gaze.

III.

I have already suggested that a developmental theory of curiosity could provide new diagnostic possibilities for psychotherapy. To take it a step further, I believe we can gain fresh insight into the problem of neurotic character by looking closely at pathologies of curiosity. When a child's native curiosity is interfered with and becomes inhibited, characterological disturbances are the likely outcome. Edward R. Shapiro, a Boston psychoanalyst who works with families, has pointed out that "families whose members manifest major character pathology demonstrate a striking lack of curiosity about one another. Instead, these family members are often extraordinarily certain that they know, understand, and can speak for the experience of other family members without further discussion or question" (Shapiro, 3:69). Whatever the difficulties that lead them to enter therapy, most patients come in with a limited or constricted ability to be curious.

For instance, some years ago a new patient, who had been in a few sessions of Gestalt therapy in Los Angeles before moving to New England, appeared in my office for a consultation. Upon sitting down, he began directing emotional remarks not so much to me, but to another chair in the room. Then to my astonishment, he lept up, switched seats, and began answering himself. I was too stupified at this spectacle to do anything for a moment; so I just sat there watching as he went through a couple of additional rounds of changing chairs and working himself up into what seemed to be an angry stare. This was Gestalt therapy as a masturbatory technique.

I might as well not have been there; he ought to have just sent a bill to himself. However after a few moments, I asked him, "Who am I?", and he answered, "A Gestalt therapist." I came to realize that there was terror beneath this man's self-directed activity, terror of anything much outside of himself. Living with little awareness of his surroundings, he could make only the most minimal and abstract reality available to him. He had grown up with an extremely authoritarian father, a career Naval officer, as I recall, and a clinging, overprotective, rather seductive mother, the kind that nowadays it's fashionable to call symbiotic. A family such as this is very close to the Victorian paradigm exemplified by a father who tends to be a tyrannical patriarch and a dependent, engulfing mother. In that era hysterical symptoms were rampant, and indeed this man's diagnosis in traditional terms would be something like "hysterical personality disorder."

But what I would underline is the nearly complete lack of curious concern this man displays about the novelty and strangeness of the situation he is in, about who I am and how I might be different from his previous therapist or some general notion of what constitutes a "Gestalt therapist." The free play of aggressive curiosity over one's field of awareness enables one to participate in and give shape to the world, to know what is is, and to discriminate in it what is nourishing and what is not for the continuing growth of the self. This patient's predicament stems from his having know it all in advance, to have the answers prematurely, to get his information about the environment precisely from the wrong place, namely from himself.

Indeed, there are many people who walk into a therapy session for the first time and start reeling off their most intimate worries and darkest secrets without having any idea who they are talking to. They seem to be convinced that a psychotherapist must be automatically worthy of their confidence. Such people are promiscuous with their trust in love and sex and everywhere else in their lives. The therapist can grow a beard, change the entire decor of his office, and they won't notice. On the other hand, there are others who interrogate the therapist endlessly — about credentials, techniques, motives, etc., until it is clear that they cannot surrender enough to begin therapy in a serious way. Everything they say is merely prefatory, a trial run that continually declares their doubt and dissatisfaction. Although both types of response treat the therapist indiscriminately, they do so in opposite directions: In the one case, he is always measuring up; in the other, never. Both represent pathologies of curiosity. The first kind of individual is unable to be curious at all; the curiosity of the second is trapped in one dimension.

These are only two possibilities along a continuum of failings to be appropriately curious. When a patient first comes into therapy, it is useful to gauge how curious he or she is about the surroundings, about the therapist, about the circumstances of his or her own life. How flexible or finely tuned, how wide-ranging or penetrating is each person's curiosity? The more severe the disturbance of curiosity, the more limited and narrow its range, the less a person can be in contact with or discriminating and selective about the particularity of the actual. Absence or fixation of curiosity can lead to a repetitious, trance-like existence. If curiosity is sufficiently perturbed, there is a loss of the central thread that connects people to reality.

To take another example, I recall a patient whose eyes virtually never left my face. But they were chronically narrowed in a look of suspiciousness. He appeared to weigh everything I did or said but none of it seemed to make any difference. One day I said something to him that I thought was rather startling, and his expression didn't change a bit. After I got over the discomfort of feeling like someone at a party who told a joke at which nobody laughed, I asked him if he would deliberately change his expression by widening his eyes in surprise. I finally startled him and myself as well: He simply, try as he might, couldn't do ir. Since the relevant muscles were frozen, he was unable to register feelings such as surprise or awe. You can't play music with much emotion on a cello made of plywood. Among other things, he would have to spend some time working at loosening his eye muscles.

This patient could be said to have one kind of insatiable but rigidly fixed curiosity — the over-mobilized paranoid curiosity that is usually called vigilance. He sought the negative in the environment and, of course, through projection, he always found it. His body, as well as his psyche, were by now dedicated to not being taken by surprise, which for him was synonymous with danger.

Sameness prevailed also in the case of an obsessive man for whom curiosity had been drowned by worry. In one way or another, he would tell the same story over again week after week. At some point in every therapy session, he would issue a complaint that took the form "I'm thirty-four years old, and I haven't found a girl I'd consider marrying," or "I'm thirty-four years old, and I don't really know what kind of work I want to do," or "I'm thirty-four years old, and I still haven't accomplished anything." It seemed like the only news was going to be eventually, "I'm thirty-five years old, and . . . " I planned on a long-term stable income from this patient.

Not only was he unable to do anything to change his circumstances; neither could he readily alter his way of thinking or talking about them. His ritualistic repetitions amounted to practicing a technique he had inherited from his family. As he was growing up he learned from his parents that the world was an alien and chaotic place. But staying close to home could provide safe shelter, if everyone did his or her part to keep things smoothly following the same course. The family cultivated routine and conspired to eliminate conflict, novelty, anything that might rock the boat.

All neurotic symptoms involve a problem about being curious because healthy curiosity is receptive to uncertainty, whereas neurosis is a strategy for creating an illusion of certitude in a contingent universe. For example, the relationship between parent and child is relatively certain — neither as a rule can leave — whereas in adult intimacies, either partner has the radical freedom to choose to depart. But people often try to make this seem not the case. A woman in her thirties looks and talks like a little girl. She reports feeling as though she is merely acting adult roles, like a kid dressed up in her mother's clothes and make-up. Yet she has a Ph.D., lives with a man, holds an important university teaching job. Despite her childlike qualities, instead of a child's curiosity about the world, she experiences exaggerated fear of the forces in it that could overwhelm her. Thus she suffers from phobic and hypochondriacal anxiety hysteria symptoms, such as continual fear that her moles are changing, that she will contract a fatal illness, that her boyfriend will abandon her at any moment, that she will lose control of her car if she drives alone. Her symptoms attempt to push her back into a condition of childhood certitude under the protection of caretakers — doctors, boyfriends, parents.

Generalizing from the instances I've portrayed, we can glimpse some common patterns of disturbed curiosity. The obsessive personality can only be curious about what he or she already knows. The feeling of wonder, an essential ingredient of curiosity, has been narrowed into unresolvable doubt. For hysterical personalities, curiosity is blocked in general, so that these individuals are constrained to act as if they understand or know the answers to questions they have not been able to ask. The sources of wonder are experienced as terrifying. In the case of the paranoid character, there is a kind of relentless curiosity that has become locked into operating on one channel. Whatever in the environment might give rise to wonder takes on for the paranoid individual the aspect of threat. For all three, innocence has disappeared. I am not referring to the unquestioning Eden-like innocence of infants, which has to be lost, but to a mature innocence that registers and explores what is, a spontaneous, inquiring openness toward the present moment.

References

Mint, M. 1965. Character analysis and the new beginning. *Primary love and psychoanalytic technique.* NY: Liveright Publishing Co.

Brazelton, T. B. 1969. *Infants and mothers: Differences in development.* NY: Dell.

Freud, S. 1947. *Leonardo da Vinci: A study in psychosexuality.* NY: Random House.

Freud, S. 1955. *The interpretation of dreams.* NY: Basic Books.

Perls, F., Hefferline, R., and Goodman, P. 1951. *Gestalt therapy: Excitement and growth in the human personality.* NY: Julian Press.

Pick, A., Frankel, G. and Hess, V.L. 1975. *Children's attention: The development of selectivity.* Chicago: Univ. of Chicago Press.

Schachtel, E. G. 1959. *Metamorphosis: On the development of affect, perception, attention, and memory.* NY: Basic Books.

Shapiro, E. R. n.d. "On curiosity: Intrapsychic and interpersonal boundary formation in family life." *International Journal of Family Psychiatry.* 3:69.

∫ Toward a Psychology of the Unknown

"Toward a Psychology of the Unknown" was originally presented as the opening talk at The Gestalt Journal's *Twelfth Annual Conference on the Theory and Practice of Gestalt Therapy which met in Boston, Massachusetts, from April 26th through April 29th, 1990.*

Psychology since Freud has given us various ways of thinking about anxiety, perhaps our most characteristic modern emotion. Psychoanalysis, for example, defines anxiety in terms of fears of abandonment and engulfment that originate in the child's dawning consciousness of its separateness from its parents. Gestalt therapy defines it as blocked or inadequately supported excitement, which comes about when the arousal or mobilization of the self in response to needs, wishes, or hungers seems too dangerous, too hot to handle. These are extremely useful conceptions in our clinical work. But there is another definition, earlier than these historically, more embracing of the human condition, that is par-

---

*From *The Gestalt Journal* Vol. XIII, No. 2 (Fall. 1990). Reprinted with permission.

ticularly relevant to my theme. The nineteenth-century Danish philosopher Kierkegaard defined anxiety as "the dizziness of freedom."

Kierkegaard's notion may seem more metaphysical than developmental or clinical, but in fact it emphasizes a facet of human existence that ought to be a concern of every psychotherapist — the courage it takes to become a free individual in our society. To choose freedom is to resist the temptations of determinism — whether these take the form in our daily lives of dependence on authority, parental or religious, cultural or political; or of reliance in our intellectual lives on scientific determinisms, biological or psychological. The lure of determinism is that it provides us with the illusion that life is safe and predictable, that we can count on being taken care of by the environment, that everything can be known and brought under control.

To be free entails living in an unpredictable and adventurous reality rather than rooting oneself in the security of the known. As Paul Goodman puts it at the beginning of Volume II of *Gestalt Therapy*, "What is ordinarily called 'security' is clinging to the unfelt, declining the risk of the unknown involved in any absorbing satisfaction . . . The secure state is without interest, it is unnoticed; and the secure person never knows it but always feels that he is risking it and will be adequate" (p. 233). Freedom demands a willingness to make one's way through an uncertain, rather disorderly, and in some respects, mysterious universe. No one can choose freely among the possibilities in life without the capacity to tolerate contingency, including the world's own freedom to be other than oneself and therefore beyond one's total knowledge or control. It means to live not in Eden but having fallen from Eden.

Actually I don't think one falls from the Garden of Eden, so much as one outgrows it. If you stay too long in paradise, it's no longer paradise. As the novelist Edith Wharton said, "An hour of anything is long enough." Consider a patient of mine, an aristocratic woman in her mid-thirties, who went through several years of training in a particular clinical discipline with the aim of going into private practice. She came from a wealthy New England family, which had established a trust fund that made it possible for her to live without a job. But she felt committed to developing a career working with people nevertheless. A year after she had graduated from the training institute, however, she still had no clients, despite several referrals from friends and colleagues. She had spent thousands of dollars fixing up her basement into a home office, which was ready and waiting. But when someone called, she always managed to find some excuse to put them on hold. One evening during the week, she went to a supervision group, even though she had no clients to present there.

She was unhappy and bored with herself. But she just could not manage the step into uncertainty if she were to go out on her own into actual private practice. She had plenty of supportive resources obviously. Out of them she had designed a life of unending preparation for life. She dwelt in the known territory and kept trying to take in more and more knowledge without risking the treacherous footing of negotiating the unknown. Perhaps she thought she might eventually arrive at an endpoint, where she would finally feel safe enough to face that awkward, uncertain encounter with her first client. Of course she would never get there by her current route.

I had occasion to see her and her husband together for a few sessions of couples therapy during a period of marital crisis. He complained that their sex was never spontaneous, nor would

she allow him initiative in their lovemaking. He said that she always insisted on choreographing the show, telling him what felt
good or bad each step of the way. He felt stifled by this to the
point of threatening divorce, but she was unrelenting about it. The
connection to her inability to launch her career is evident, even
though in the one situation she is all initiative and in the other
appears unable to exert any. In both cases, anxiety overwhelms her
need to surrender to novelty, surprise, spontaneity, error, exploration. She dared not flounder; she had to remain in control at all
times.

Her family background was characterized by the immense
protectiveness and thoroughgoing organization of every detail of
daily life found in certain powerful New England families. She
never saw her parents at a loss or at odds so far as she could remember. Her father was a captain of industry, a man of terrific
enterprise and momentum, her mother an eminent socialite, landscape designer, and hostess. What she mostly recalled was that
their daily life never seemed to have a hair out of place. It seemed
perfect, and perfectly in control.

Prospero, in Shakespeare's *Tempest*, composed an environment like this for his daughter Miranda — a controlled environment of nearly total support on an island. But then he gave her a
wonderful gift. He roused, through his sorcerer-like powers, a
storm that caused a shipwreck and landed a number of adventurous men, both good and evil characters, on its shores. He introduced beings from unknown lands — unknown to Miranda, at
least — and let the drama unfold. My patient had not yet been
able to exclaim in delight as did Miranda in the *Tempest* "O brave
new world that has such creatures in't!," for nothing very new,
nothing rich and strange could occur in my patient's world. For
her the unknown wore the aspect of chaos and disintegration, of

64

potential failure or catastrophe, and the risk was too much to bear.
We had to work hard at disheveling her life a little, of enabling her
to enjoy a misplaced strand here and there, at teaching her the
virtues and possibilities of improvisation, serendipity, of making
interesting mistakes, of feeling tentative but alive.

You can readily see the resemblance of this woman's situation to obsessive-compulsive fixation. The obsessive turns all his
attention to what he has already digested and thus already knows.
It is a profound act of constriction, of fencing oneself off in the
familiar. Obsessives do this in a peculiar way: They treat the obvious, the self-evident, the certain as though in fact it remains unknown to them, and therefore worthy of their unending delibera-
tion. They can only be curious about what they already know.
They are committed to a quest for a perfect or absolute knowledge, a knowledge free of error, that can never be achieved. This is
how they avoid the terrors of the actual unknown.

The contact boundary, as Gestalt therapy describes it, is
where one goes through the gate of the known into an unknown
landscape. How much anxiety can one tolerate in order to stay
with the excitement and accomplish something? A person needs to
feel some anchor in the safety of support — that which is known
because it already belongs to the self — to venture into the unknown. A good therapist works with a delicate touch at the point
where the patient's anxiety has a slight lead, because in order to
grow one needs to be a little overextended. When people resign
themselves, out of fear and loss of faith in either themselves or
their environment, to living amid what they already know too well,
the outcome is stagnation, boredom, and deadness. It is life without any vitality or excitement, life as a fixed stare at a portion of
one's world, subjecting it to stereotyping and projection. The disturbances of contact as Gestalt therapy views them — introjection,

[handwritten: of what is 'safe', cf shame experiences]

projection, retroflection, confluence — represent anxiety at work substituting the known for the unknown. *[handwritten: or potentially shameful/excluding]*

[handwritten margin: X]

This kind of monotony is a central feature of all neurosis. The neurotic finds himself imprisoned in a stale, unchanging reality, as though there can be no options. The paranoid is trapped in a hostile, spying world; the depressive in a lonely twilight; the obsessive in an eternal *deja vu* laced with doubt. These prisons are their shelters from the "dizziness of freedom." One male patient of mine is married to a woman who bores and plagues him, but he feels safe with her. He talks constantly of leaving her, but he makes no moves to do so; in fact, he assents to her wishes to buy a bigger house together and have a child. He derives gratification of his need for novelty from fantasies of running away, fantasies of sexual encounters with strangers, sometimes from fantasies of strangling her. Another patient hates his job and has continually made elaborate plans to resign and get another one for the last ten years. These are like shipwrecked people huddling on a raft even though the shore might just be a short swim away. But who knows what sharks lurk in the waters in between?

All neurosis resembles addiction in being fixated on something that the person can't give up — a palpable, even if painful, familiarity, to substitute a more tolerable reality for what must seem an unbearably anxious reality — the void of unknowing, the dizziness of freedom. It is not easy to convince anyone to relinquish this when all you can promise in return is having to face uncertain prospects. What is greatly dimmed in the fixation, however, is the quality of life. The neurotic is like a consumer who shops in the bargain basement of life and buys something he doesn't really want just because it's on sale.

Neurosis is like bad science — it's a reductionism that offers oversimplified causal explanations for the complexity of life.

[handwritten left margin: including competence / losing (self, other, context, etc.); not shame]

66

Or to turn it around the other way: Some of our sciences, our psychologies, our clinical methodologies, have come to resemble neurosis in their deterministic fixation on cause and effect explanations, in their falling back on mechanical determinisms. In the sixteenth century the Baconian and Cartesian revolutions in western culture succeeded in splitting the subject and the object. Science, especially applied science or technology, subsequently became the means of repossessing the object through conquest and domination of nature: This was knowledge as power. It is by no means the only scientific attitude, but it is the one that has been the most deeply institutionalized in western society, and for all the discoveries it has made possible, and all the control over our circumstances, it has also brought us some of our most towering misfortunes. Neither nature nor social life may survive the consequences. *also, then, in relationship — not necessarily power, but control*

Like Baconian science, neurosis is riddled with cause and effect, which it translates into a language of guilt and blame. It, too, regards knowledge as power, the power to eradicate anxiety. It functions by constricting the scope of variability, editing out complexity, isolating factors. Of course, scientists do this when they build a model. The creative scientist uses the model as a hypothesis, an approximation of reality, which then provides a base of support to take on the next unknown phenomenon. The neurotic fixes his model in place, and treats it as though it is reality. Of course, it is by no means only our patients who subject reality to such a diminishing. Psychoanalysts do it when they refer everything unknown in human conduct to an Unconscious with a capital "U," as though it were some kind of thing; politicians do it when they design housing projects and proliferating bureaucracies to rid the world of social evils and leave out the obstinate irrationality of human impulses; teachers when they use curricula that

for allostasis) or weather forecast!

force every student to learn in the same way at the same pace. All these knowledge experts tend to replace the idiosyncrasies and the unaccountable in human nature with a plastic image molded to fit their theories. As the art critic Harold Rosenberg once put it, "People carry their landscapes with them, the way travelers used to cart along their porcelain chamber pots."

So-called "scientific" psychiatry and psychotherapy strike me as especially neurotic because they are indeed fixated on an unchangeable past. They construct their models of human behavior on a mechanistic philosophy of science that the true "hard" sciences, such as physics, have long regarded as obsolete. I ran across the following passage recently in the introduction, written by Herman M. Van Praag, Chairman of the Albert Einstein College of Medicine, Montefiore Medical Center Department of Psychiatry, to a new monograph series on Clinical and Experimental Psychiatry. "Psychiatry is moving," writes Dr. Van Praag, "still relatively slowly, but irresistibly, from a more philosophical, contemplative orientation, to that of an empirical science. From the fifties on, biological psychiatry has been a major catalyst of that process . . . In addition, it forced the profession into the direction of standardization of diagnoses and of assessment of abnormal behavior. Biological psychiatry provided psychiatry not only with a new basic science and with new treatment modalities, but also with the tools, the methodology and the mentality to operate within the confines of an empirical science, the only framework in which a medical discipline can survive . . . In other fields of psychiatry, too, one discerns a gradual trend towards scientification." We have been hearing such claims at least since Freud's ill-fated "Project for a Scientific Psychology."

"Scientification," as Dr. Van Praag so inelegantly calls it, may serve to eliminate the clinician's anxiety, but at what cost, this claim of conquest over illness of the soul? Dr. Van Praag's viewpoint seems to me quite at odds with that of the man after whom his college was named. Albert Einstein proclaimed in 1930 in an article titled "What I Believe," "The most beautiful thing we can experience is the mysterious. It is the true source of all art and science." I'm not saying that there hasn't been any progress in understanding the biological involvement in human psychological misery, or that Prozac doesn't provide real relief. But no chemical that prevents the reabsorption of a neurotransmitter at the synaptic connections can solve the riddle of human suffering. As Wordsworth tells us,

> Suffering is permanent, obscure, and dark,
> And has the nature of infinity.

Psychiatry's Newtonian image of cause and effect lingers back in the dark ages of science, when you consider that it has already been between 50 and 70 years since a group of theoretical physicists, including Einstein himself, Max Planck, Neils Bohr, Werner Heisenberg, and Erwin Schrodinger, altered forever our vision of how the natural world is constituted and our very conception of causality itself. All of them were men who stood at the brink where the known disappears into the unknown and opened themselves to mystery. In doing so, they came up against paradoxes and contradictions that their preceding theoretical images of the universe were entirely at a loss to explain. The Newtonian world was defined by measuring the position and velocity of discrete objects. It also contained more evanescent "things," or shapes, called waves, such as temperatures, gases, light, fluids, and electromagnetic signals, whose behavior was described by sets of partial differential equations, a branch of mathematics that generated gorgeous symmetries and curves.

But physicists began to find that when you take smaller and smaller chunks of matter, down to the subatomic level, our sense of what was logically possible collapsed. Electrons, for example, as physicists like to say, behave like particles on Monday and Wednesday, like waves on Tuesday and Thursday. But what kind of "thing" could do that? What happens to our common sense notions of object or to Aristotelian logic? Moreover, the entities that were supposed to be continuous, as though they were rainbows in the sky or breakers rolling up the beach in those lovely equations I mentioned, seemed in fact to be in the grip of a devilishly mischievous impulse. Temperature, light, radio waves, etc. when you looked closely enough, increased or decreased or distributed themselves in sudden mysterious little leaps. We were left with the sense that there were tiny unaesthetic gaps in the tapestry of nature. Not only that, but these perverse two-faced creatures — particle/waves or wave/particles or whatever they were — never allowed you to get a direct glimpse of them or pin them down. You could only know them, in effect, by their absence, like the medieval philosophers' Ontological Proof of the existence of God, which defines God not by what He is but by what He is not. By the time you were able to look, you didn't see *them*, but only the footprints they left behind during their most recent departures. They were already gone! To make it all still worse, Heisenberg showed that at the subatomic level, the very process of observing and attempting to measure behavior entangled the observer in the phenomena, thus altering its behavior. We couldn't even be neutral observers of the physical world, much less of one another; it was like the old adage of nineteenth-century romanticism which claimed you half-create what you perceive. This penetration of romanticism

70

into the "hard" science of physics became known as Heisenberg's Uncertainty Principle.

So the old method of representing the world — by measuring position and velocity and plugging the numbers into neat equations that told you the next thing that would happen — was replaced by matrices. Now a matrix, as some of you may know, is a far more abstract and complex representation than a linear equation. A matrix suggests patterns of relationship, ripples in the stillness, but nothing so solid and palpable as a thing nor so predictable as a cause inevitably producing an effect. All a matrix tells you is that there are certain shapely probabilities of events occurring amid a lot of randomness. Something might happen here or there in space, at this temperature or that. But maybe not. I remember reading an article by Heisenberg in the fifties, in which he pointed out that the elusiveness and contradictory behavior of atomic particles when you tried to treat them as things left you hopelessly befuddled. Yet there were these patterns that looked more like ideas than like matter. So Heisenberg had begun to muse on the possibility of a Platonist reality: Maybe Idea was the ultimate irreducible substance of the universe, a transcendent vapor governing material appearance.

Well, all this — the birth of the Theory of Relativity, quantum mechanics, and the theory of wave mechanics — is old hat by now. But I want to mention one other event in the intellectual history of this period that in some ways was the most staggering of all. A mathematician named Godel probed mathematical logic and set theory taking their principles as far as they would go and came up with a theorem that shows definitively that the systems of logic and mathematics underlying all scientific conclusions were incomplete. Our most secure equations could be considered orderly only up to a point. Godel planted potential chaos right in

71

the middle of the mathematical certitude upon which science depended for its authority. We've learned to live with it, we've had to, just as we formerly learned to live with Nietzsche's proclamation of God's death in the nineteenth century. Nevertheless it left science and mathematics with a haunting loose end that dangles over an echoing void.

Physicists and mathematicians have gone through some wild changes — they have passed from mechanistic materialism, to a statistical portrait of a cosmos full of error and uncertainty, and on to romanticism and Platonic idealism. Recently some have even begun to look toward eastern mysticism for a view of the universe that embraces paradox and lack of clear causality. A popular spokesman for this movement, the physicist Fritzjof Capra, in his book, *The Tao of Physics*, claims that the unfathomable behavior of atomic particles or waves is nothing less than the Dance of Shiva, a seamless vibrating web in which all contradictions are reconciled. He is by no means the only eastern spiritualist among well-trained scientists. I once taught psychology at the Naropa Institute in Boulder, Colorado, a center of Tibetan Tantric Buddhism. There was a sizable group of distinguished physicists, biologists, and linguists visiting there that summer from all over the world, working to develop an accord between science and Tantric philosophy.

In physics and mathematics, more and more knowledge has led to more and more unknowing, more willingness to live with the anxiety of uncertainty, not only to accept but to revere mystery, perhaps even to a measure of Socratic humility among many scientists. Not so in our discipline, which I guess is not noted for its humility anyway. But then I suppose you can't have humility if you fear humiliation, as did Breuer when his patient Anna O.'s fantasies took the form of declaring she was going to have his baby, as did Freud at times when he worried about psychoanalysis being

72

dismissed contemptuously as a Jewish science, as do those modern psychiatrists who speak in the accents of Dr. Van Praag and hold their disturbingly disturbed patients at bay with a pose of scientific authority and scientific neutrality, based on an obsolete view of science.

To be sure, we also have our rebellion against Newtonian psychiatry. But alas, I fear that we, at least many of us, have not taken the time to learn the hard-won innovations and small revolutions of psychotherapists such as Rank and Ferenczi, Winnicott and Balint, Erwin Straus and Medard Boss, Paul Goodman and Laura Perls. Too many of us have leaped with a feeling of protest against scientification, to use that distasteful term, into the genteel, passive mysticism of the New Age, promoting the Tao of Therapy, where all problems and obstacles are too easily reconciled in the great ocean of oneness. In Gestalt therapy, we call premature unity "confluence." The unknown, after all, is the greatest projection screen of all. One way of projecting onto it is to treat it as a demonic force to be wrestled into submission by science and technology — knowledge as power. Another is to call it God and treat it as an icon to be worshiped. Both science and religion in their reductive forms can enslave. Originating as efforts to domesticate the unknown, they can return to tyrannize us.

There is another mode of consciousness besides mysticism, more compatible with western psychotherapy in my estimation, or perhaps more appealing to my sensibility, that also preserves the irreducible complexity, the mystery at the heart of existence. Let me call it the ironical consciousness. Physics in fact entered the realm of the ironical when it discovered the Protean elusiveness of the electron. The eminent astronomer Arthur Eddington virtually defined ironical science when he declared "To be or not to be is a primitive form of thinking." Why not an ironical psychotherapy?

TEACHING A PARANOID TO FLIRT

In an article I wrote several years ago I tried to give some reasons why irony might be valuable to psychotherapy: "The ironical perception hints at multiple realities: For every meaning one gives an event, irony finds another, often opposed to the first, and keeps these different meanings in view as an integrated whole. Among the blessings of irony is that it discloses options . . . Once you see things in an ironical light, it becomes more difficult to carry on as though your unhappiness is destiny."

Therapists such as the ones I mentioned above are among the most useful to learn from because they are able to surrender to the uncertain and unpredictable dimensions of human experience. To quote Wordsworth's great lines again: "Suffering is permanent, obscure, and dark,/ And has the nature of infinity." And suffering is the difficult, bewildering labyrinth down which the therapist has descend in order to meet his patient. If empathy is the way to another's soul, it requires a suspension of knowing the other, especially of knowing the other prematurely in one's own terms. When I was a new father, I ran across an essay of Winnicott's that discriminated among all the gradations and shades of expression that can be conveyed by a baby's crying. He could hear differences in the crying that most of us would never consider, and he suggested how parents ought to respond to each kind. Winnicott could capture the most subtle harmonies and discords between self and environment, conduct and event, because he possessed what Keats called "negative capability" — the innocence from agendas that enables one to become like what one observes rather than impose the self upon it, the patient lingering curiosity, the willingness to wait and delay knowing, that allows a person to reach into the different reality than his or her own.

Freud to a large extent had the gift of empathy, though perhaps not so many of his successors, who elevated his concepts

74

into dogma. But then Freud, after all, was a primitive Freudian. Therapists such as Winnicott and Balint are able to approach their patients as genuinely other, and therefore unknown to them, even as ultimately unknowable. Indeed, if one cannot tolerate uncertainty, not knowing, one can't allow other people to exist freely. One has to be in control by controlling them, distort their freedom to be themselves into a guarantee of who they are. One even has to do this to oneself, which as I suggested earlier is an important source of neurotic symptom formation.

Is a psychotherapy or a psychology that would appear to be so unsure of itself, so indefinite and open-ended, an art or a science? It resembles art in its willingness to proceed without very much to go on, to wait until form and meaning emerge from the shadows. But I hope that I have made it clear that this kind of patience, standing there, relatively empty, waiting to meet the unknown, is the basis of good science as well. After all, life is a kind of hypothesis. Why shouldn't science, especially a science of human nature, be tentative and incomplete? I think it should be. It should be like one of those beautiful Caucasian prayer rugs that are filled with geometrical form, yet always embed somewhere in their pattern an asymmetrical or unfinished variation, an opening that trails off into eternity.

If modern physics and mathematics have revolutionized our notions about what we can know by virtually devastating our hopes that we can know anything about nature with absolute certainty, another less widely known and dramatic but equally revolutionary attack on traditional modes of knowledge occurred in the phenomenological movement in philosophy — and it's particularly important to us because it is of course the philosophy that underlies Gestalt therapy.

Phenomenology was an attempt to reunite the subject and object that had been sundered by the age of Bacon and Descartes. The program of Edmund Husserl, the founder of phenomenology, was an attempt, in his own words, to go "back to the things themselves," and treat them as though we do not know them — that is we go back to them without trying to understand or account for them through our preconceptions about them, which is to say, without drawing on any of our general scientific or philosophical theories. Husserl's basic idea was that all theories are already abstracted away from immediate experience, and thus serve to alienate the human mind from its natural place in the world.

In other words, Husserl called for philosophical knowledge to become a kind of unknowing. He wanted it to proceed from a radical innocence, in order to eliminate the division between mind and nature, subject and object into which philosophy and science since the sixteenth century had divided the cosmos. The modern age had broken up our understanding of our place in the scheme of things, and the consequence is powerfully expressed in the words of Max Scheler, who was with Husserl the cofounder of phenomenology: "In the 10,000 years of history, we are the first age in which man has become utterly and unconditionally 'problematic' to himself, in which he no longer knows who he is, but at the same time knows that he does not know. It is only by a firm resolution to wipe the canvas clean of all traditional answers . . . and to look upon man with a radical, methodological alienation and astonishment that we can hope to gain some valid insights."

Husserl's phenomenology ultimately returned to the world as it is immediately given to one's consciousness. "Back to the things themselves" meant simply to start with our immediate perceptions exactly as they are given. You have to know something of the history of philosophy to see how revolutionary an idea this is.

Phenomenology returns us to the ordinary world that unfolds before us every waking moment of every day. And we can't go any further or deeper than this, says the phenomenologist — it is just right there, primary and irreducible. We can't even corroborate it as being true or false, because we have no access to any knowledge outside our perceptions to compare them to in order to weigh their truth or falsehood. Not that Husserl was fond of uncertainty; he was after absolute certitude, the primitive ground of all knowledge — like all philosophers, he sought by doubting everything the basis of a truth that was beyond all questioning, that would free philosophy from the terrible plague of Cartesian doubt. This was an obsessional undertaking to its very core, but I suppose if anyone is able to use obsessing productively, it would have to be the philosophers, just as poets are often productive depressives and actors disciplined hysterics. I think, by the way, it was William James who said, "I wanted to be a philosopher, but cheerfulness kept breaking in."

But if what we perceive is regarded as fundamental, and as close as we can come to truth, this does not have to lead us back into the trap of determinism. How does phenomenology conceive of what we can know? Once we insist on the primacy of the perceptual world as it is given to us — and this does not mean the physical world of the sense only, but includes feelings, ideas, values, other persons — and once we accept there is no way to evade it, nor penetrate it as though it were a mere shadow or silhouette of the real, nor to compare or measure its fit with some other source of knowledge — we find ourselves pulled toward what Husserl called the "horizon." For every structure of experience in the given situation that we perceive and describe, there is another vantage point, another possibility of being conscious of the situation next to or beyond where we are. We can never grasp everything inherent in any given; we can never, for example, see an object from every conceivable angle of vision; we are always aware of other potential angles of vision. This is what gives our reality its extraordinary strangeness and abundance. The phenomenological mood is like Wallace Steven's poem "Thirteen Ways of Looking at a Blackbird," where Stevens exclaims,

It is both seer and seen that defines an 'event'

> I do not know which to prefer,
> The beauty of inflections
> Or the beauty of innuendoes,
> The blackbird whistling
> Or just after.

For me, aware this is how I see it, and there are other ways, or relations

From the phenomenological point of view, we do know what we know, but we stand always at the boundary of the known, full of our human limitations as well as our talents, gazing off at the distantly beckoning horizon of the unknown. This is where the uncertainties of modern physics and the philosophy of phenomenology meet — and where both are relevant to and compatible with the ideal of psychological health that Gestalt therapy espouses. The horizon, shading from what we know into what we don't yet know makes life rich and fascinatingly diverse, giving it the aspect of a journey.

The phenomenological sense of the unknown does not call up a hidden realm, like the psychoanalytic unconscious, nor a transcendent one, to be scaled in states of transport. It is simply more than we can fix in a firm outline, more like a changing cloud, always becoming, always just taking shape, just over the border of the here-and-now. It is akin to what Gestalt therapy speaks of as the "forming Gestalt" or the "coming situation," which always involves both the experiencing self and its world. It is a realm deeply *and 'more than human'*

human and can never be separated from the human, no matter how foreign it may seem at times. It is resonant with excitement, dynamism, and responsiveness, both tension and gracefulness, crisis and opportunity, and the necessity of mutual respect between self and environment. Sometimes it has the character of an adventure, sometimes of an emergency, sometimes of an artistic performance. It can never be comprised by theories or explanations, such as "the observing ego," or "conditioned behavior," the "uptake of serotonin and norepinephrine," nor "cognitive premises," "paradoxical interventions," nor the "equilibrium of a system." It is both the known and the unknown. Its truth is not the certitude of causal knowledge, but an always incomplete and unfinishable truth in the process of taking a shape that includes the ever-present possibility of both wonderment and renewal.

love ??

and 'my' truth, at this time, and yours, and yours ... a knowing which alters our truths so that they are never fixed, always contingent on everything that is present — and this process is most 'fluid' — or in-formed when information is shared

∫ The Future of Gestalt Therapy: a Symposium

Participants: Laura Perls, Miriam Polster, Gary Yontef
& Joseph Zinker

Moderator: Michael Vincent Miller

The following is an edited transcript of the symposium that was presented as a part of The Gestalt Journal *'s 2nd Annual Conference on the Theory and Practice of Gestalt Therapy in Boston, Massachusetts. The symposium took place on Saturday morning, May 17, 1980. It has been edited for publication here by the moderator, Michael Vincent Miller.*

MILLER: I am very pleased to be the moderator for this symposium on the future of Gestalt therapy. So far as I know, it's the first time such a distinguished group of teachers and practitioners

---

*From *The Gestalt Journal*, Vol IV, No. 1 (Spring, 1981). Reprinted with permission.

of Gestalt therapy have assembled from different parts of the country for a common enterprise at a national conference.

An event of this kind is another among many signs indicating that Gestalt therapy has come of age. We might consider it something to celebrate, but I think we ought to do so cautiously — or at least thoughtfully. Aging is always a mixed blessing, for it entails a loss of innocence, among other things. Conferences are often occasions for telling the good news. But I would rather open our topic today with some warnings and admonitions.

The dangers Gestalt therapy now faces are the ones that face any movement when it matures enough to be considered an institution, a school of thought, an established approach, etc. Christianity began as a revolutionary movement and ended up as a wealthy, conservative, politically powerful church. A populist movement among peasants and workers swept across Russia and overturned the oppressive regime of the Czar and then hardened into Stalinist bureaucracy. A small band of radical thinkers gathered around Freud and revolutionized our thinking about human character, motivation, and sexuality; but eventually their followers came to form a wing of the conservative medical establishment.

In each of these cases, tendencies developed toward rigidity, bureaucracy, too much structure and control, intellectual laziness, and inability to remain open enough to accommodate further change. Some of the founders of Gestalt therapy were certainly aware of these dangers — perhaps for this very reason they leaned toward an anarchist social philosophy. Fritz Perls did to some extent; and Paul Goodman made anarchism the basis for his far-reaching social criticism. It is not surprising to find Gestalt therapists espousing anarchist ideas, since the fundamental principles of Gestalt therapy emphasize the healthiness of self-regulation. Indeed, I think that the anarchist spirit inherent in Gestalt therapy can help us survive the worst tendencies of too much institutionalization.

My own reflections on the future of Gestalt therapy take the form of two sets of questions, which are different sides of the same coin. First of all, we need to ask whether in fact there is a future for Gestalt therapy. Since Gestalt therapy so often appears these days as a combination plate in the smorgasbord of "humanistic therapies," can it maintain its distinctive identity as a separate discipline?

In other words, can Gestalt therapy survive the theoretical contradictions and loss of precision that result when people treat it as a bunch of techniques and then lump it together unthinkingly with techniques derived from other therapies? A great many beginning therapists nowadays go through training programs where they are exposed to a little Gestalt therapy, some bioenergetics, some Transactional Analysis, a bit of the Alexander method, a little Feldenkrais, a dose of Neuro-linguistic programming, all without any particular organizing principle. I could go on with the list for quite a while.

This is not just a question of theoretical clarity. It's much more than that. It has direct and immediate bearing on what we do with the people that we work with and on our impact on their lives.

For instance, certain modern therapies and related disciplines, such as family systems therapy, Transactional Analysis, Neuro-linguistic programming, and approaches to organizational development achieve their effects through encouraging introjection of the therapist's or group leader's model. But a consistent Gestalt therapist must look at introjection, no matter what the content, as a disturbance of the contact boundary between the therapist and the client. Any practice that cultivates introjection violates the very spirit of Gestalt therapy.

Obviously, then, careful thought has to be given to the consequences of combining Gestalt therapy with other therapies. The practice of Gestalt therapy is based on values that stress the innate capacity of human beings, when not overly interfered with, to choose what is best for themselves and accomplish their own self-transformation. The Gestalt therapist's task is to aid this process through helping people become more aware of both their native abilities and the interferences. But many of the new therapies are sophisticated versions of behaviorism, which implies that people change for the best through being conditioned by programs fed to them by outside authorities, The difference here, by the way, reflects a long-running debate during the past century between liberal social engineers who believe human nature is indefinitely malleable and can be adapted and adjusted to a social environment designed by scientific experts versus radical thinkers, more oriented toward the arts, who grant human nature the inner authority to shape its own best ends. Stripped of these distinctions, Gestalt "techniques" can be joined with behaviorism and other mechanistic approaches, but Gestalt therapy cannot.

The second set of questions arises when you look at these matters the other way around and ask whether Gestalt therapy has enough creative flexibility to absorb and integrate new developments. For I am by no means saying that we have nothing to learn from the new therapies I've mentioned and others like them. After all, Gestalt therapy began as a highly eclectic synthesis that incorporated elements from psychoanalysis, Reichian therapy, existential philosophy, phenomenology, the arts, and experimental Gestalt psychology.

And I do think that Gestalt therapy needs to continue to be eclectic in this way. But can it stretch itself enough to accommodate new developments in theory, in research, in clinical practice, and still maintain its integrity and coherence? If not it is liable to become obsolete. We have seen the difficulties psychoanalysis has encountered along these lines, for it has, until recently at least, held on to its identity too rigidly and thus nearly outdated itself. On the other hand, bending too much can make a stew out of both self and other — we call this confluence. It's like the problem that comes up in intimate relations: two people must remain fully realized individuals if they are to merge in a way that makes contact and not confluence. In the task of furthering theoretical understanding as well, meaningful new integrations best occur at a boundary where what is useful can be absorbed and what is not can be rejected.

Finally, I want to raise briefly a third issue which I see as being of crucial importance to our future. Gestalt therapy began in the nineteen forties and fifties as a movement which concerned itself seriously with culture and social life as well as the self. Anyone familiar with the thought of the original New York circle, especially that of Paul Goodman, knows that to be the case. But many Gestalt therapists got caught up in the "me decade" of the late sixties and the seventies. There was too much emphasis on getting in touch with *my* feelings, on taking responsibility for myself. However, times have changed.

Now, in the nineteen eighties, we've become aware of the depletion of natural resources and of energy, of ecological dangers to the environment, and of the possibility of facing a sinking standard of living. It looks like we can no longer afford a certain kind of narcissistic indulgence. Some amount of self-sacrifice and cooperation is necessary if we are to survive. We have responsibility for each other, not just for ourselves, even responsibility for the entire planet.

What, then, will Gestalt therapy look like in this new climate? Well, I believe that the requisite creative adaptability is to be found in the principles underlying Gestalt therapy. A moral vision concerning the unity of human life with nature is the truth that Gestalt therapy embodies. As Paul Goodman said, paraphrasing the Eastern philosopher Chang Tzu, "To have an environment and not take it as an object is Tao." This is the view of Gestalt therapy. It is a deeper truth than the one expressed in the Gestalt prayer, which says "I'm not in this world to live up to your expectations." I think that the message of the Gestalt prayer is an important one for children (or adults) who are still separating from their parents — it may help them avoid or heal a neurosis — but it is not the ultimate vision of health that Gestalt therapy has to offer.

The vision it does offer is one of respect for nature, and of the best use of nature's resources, and of the native capacities and resources in human nature to create what is necessary for growth. So there is inherent in Gestalt therapy a vision that will fit the change in the times.

PERLS: Well, you have actually already made most of the points that I intended to make. I can perhaps reemphasize a few things and perhaps clarify some.

You speak about the confusion of theoretical models. I would add that many people who call themselves Gestalt therapists are so ignorant of theory that they don't even, know what the word Gestalt means, where it comes from, and how the concept of Gestalt therapy has developed. This is, in part, a consequence of the anti-intellectualism of the '60s and '70s. They simply can't or won't talk in a coherent way about what they are doing. They don't really know what they are doing. Yet they are doing it, and sometimes very well.

Moreover to the extent they have not done so, Gestalt therapists have to take part in and learn from the general discourse about psychotherapy that is going on all the time. Since the development of psychoanalysis, there has been a continuing debate, and Gestalt therapists need the nourishment from participating more fully in it.

For the purpose of this discussion, I would like us to think of Gestalt therapy as our client with whose future we are concerned and whose future depends on what this client has now and what it doesn't have; that is, the supports that are available now and also the blocks which are in the way.

I would like some suggestions from all of you about what support you think is available for the ongoing development of Gestalt therapy. The aim for Gestalt therapy, as for any of our clients, is to support and heighten the ongoing Gestalt formation so that what is of greatest interest and therefore most useful for growth comes into the foreground. What then, we need to ask, is really the greatest interest for Gestalt therapy right here and now?

YONTEF: In recent years people have been asking whether there is a future for Gestalt therapy. The first time I heard that question I dismissed it. But now I think it is time to look at this question and this panel is a perfect opportunity not to dismiss it but to examine it. I have no doubt that there is a future for Gestalt therapists. There will always be a need for good therapists. Nor do I have any doubt that there will be a future for the principles for which Gestalt therapy stands and upon which it is built.

I believe those principles are rooted in some basic human needs, but I do have questions about the future of Gestalt therapy as a whole. I believe that the way we put these principles together into a whole system of psychotherapy is in danger. I think we are in an identity crisis or a developmental crisis. Our future will depend upon how we define ourselves now, how we decide who we are and who we are not. Similarly, our present is in some way dependent on certain developmental tasks that we did or did not work through some years back.

Fifteen years ago, when I got into Gestalt therapy, we had the illusion that defining Gestalt therapy was easier than it is. It seemed enough to say: We know who the analysts are, they're the uptight guys who wear the jackets and ties and have the patients call them doctors. And we know who the Rogerians are — they're those passive nice guys that don't get anything done. And we know who the encounter leaders are. They're not *us*! They're the wild men. And we are the good guys.

Well, times have changed. The analysts may be recognizable but not by that description. They are talking about empathy — at least some of them are — about human relationships instead of just transference — and some are even talking in the language of process. Eclectic therapists have adopted many of the things that we pioneered and fought for in Gestalt therapy.

Furthermore, the number of Gestalt therapists has proliferated. And this includes people who are doing horrible things under the name of Gestalt therapy. Those of us who think we're not doing those things go about our business as if we can just ignore those therapists who are exploiting people, being incompetent, and using Gestalt therapy and Gestalt principles as an excuse.

My favorite horror story used to be about the person who came to a weekend workshop and the next morning declared himself a Gestalt therapist. Now I'm worried about that person fifteen years later, still no better trained, still calling himself a Gestalt therapist and probably training people to do the same thing he wasn't trained to do in the first place.

There have been a number of attempts, both explicit and implicit, to define what Gestalt therapy is. One view defines Gestalt therapy as a technique or set of rules. Some people accept this definition and go along their narrow, unchanging way. Others accept that narrow definition of Gestalt therapy but chafe under its yoke. Then whatever they believe has been left out, they simply add on, rather than integrate. So they come up with Gestalt therapy plus everything else — the long list. "Gestalt therapy and . . ." Another group that I hear and read about say that Gestalt therapy is a set of narrow techniques and that they "used to be" Gestalt therapists, but Gestalt therapy is dated. For example, some of these people claim that Gestalt therapy is the use of your senses and feelings, but not your mind. And then they discover, lo and behold, people have minds! So Gestalt therapy becomes dated for them.

Now, obviously, the ego boundaries of these definitions are too narrow. They substitute a part for the whole. But the reaction against that narrowness also worries me. One reaction proclaims that Gestalt therapy is what Gestalt therapists do. On the face of it, that's no definition at all. At a minimum, we have to ask: Which Gestalt therapist? The answer is, "Well, obviously we are talking about what the good Gestalt therapists do." But how do you know who they are? To say merely, "I know!" is insufficient and unteachable.

And it leaves us with a definition of Gestalt therapy by charisma. Those who can capture an audience or who capture a clientele, that's what defines Gestalt therapy. I think that's intellectually dishonest. I think it's both theoretically and politically inadequate, and we've gotten by for a long time without collectively attending to this inadequacy. If we continue to ignore defining who we are in our center and what our boundaries are, I would predict a future in which we are replaced by an endless number of new techniques and in which our name is used as an excuse for poor therapy, poor training, poor discipline.

I see three overarching principles that give coherence to what we do. One is our field theory, which goes beyond figure and ground. We rarely talk about field theory, except for spending a few minutes on figure/ground. I'm not going to talk about it here either, because it is too complex to do the thorough job that I think is necessary.

The other two principles I do want to say a word about because I think they address the future and the heart of what we are if we're anything as Gestalt therapists. One of these is our phenomenology. Now the term phenomenology is sometimes used as though it were roughly equivalent to "experiencing," and in that sense I think the word has no utility at all. But considered as a discipline a phenomenological approach to psychotherapy means attending to experience in a way that allows the therapist to be impressed by, impacted by, what's obvious, with interpretation used very sparingly and in the service of seeing what is, experiencing what is. That takes the discipline of bracketing, to put aside beliefs about reality and principle and to look with fresh eyes each time you work.

I was doing a training group some time ago during which one of the trainees was acting as therapist and another trainee as patient. The patient-trainee was going into a life experience that was truly horrifying. Everybody in the group was moved by a real human tragedy, for this was not merely a neurotic complaint. The therapist-trainee had a rule in his head. The rule is: You don't say "why" in Gestalt therapy and you don't ask questions. In a moment of real anguish, basic human anguish, the patient said, "Why me?" rolling her eyes up as if to say, "God, why me?" And all the therapist-trainee could do was jump on the question of why.

The other aspect of our phenomenology that we need to mention is our use of experiment. We tell others who are not Gestalt therapists that we can do more than just sit and track the person: we can use our creative talent to create situations for increasing awareness. But then what I observe is that Gestalt therapists too often tend to convert experiments into programs to make the person more expressive, to make the person more open, to make them more creative, to make them more revolutionary, when the real point of the experiment is to clarify what is, including the blocks, and to honor the total experience of the patient, not just a part.

The other major principle that I think will determine how we survive in the future as Gestalt therapy, is our existential base. And I don't mean simply attending to human existence rather than to some innate human essence. I mean existentialism in the sense of the I-Thou dialogue. I believe it's the base of Gestalt therapy and yet we have not made its meaning clear. It we want to address those critics who distort what Gestalt therapy is I believe it will be necessary to clarify this.

Dialogue is a form of contact and I think we're relatively clear in our literature about what contact is — appreciating differences, the connecting and the separating and the movement between. But the special form of contact that is needed for the healing process, that's where I think we need to become much clearer. Dialogue includes honoring, living in, and experiencing the phenomenology of the person we're working with, and at the same time, disclosing who we are, showing our own Presence.

91

For the most part Gestalt therapists do disclose who they are but I think they often fail to honor the phenomenology of the patient.

A third aspect of the I and Thou is vital but often violated: Allowing something to happen between the therapist and patient. For example, a therapist acknowledges the patient as he is and lets the patient know who he is, but neither is affected by the other. "I am I and you are you PERIOD." I-Thou means commitment to dialogue, to Between. The dialogic attitude means to surrender to the chemistry of what's happening between. When there are differences or conflict between therapist and patient, the dialogic Gestalt therapist lets himself be affected by the patient and changed by the patient.

And the last aspect to mention and not elaborate on, (Lord knows I shouldn't have to elaborate on it), is that a dialogic relationship is non-exploitative. And, of course, it really does need elaboration since I observe exploitation by well-meaning Gestalt therapists as well as by the sociopathic exploiters. It is only because of time that I am not elaborating on this.

I disagree with what I've been hearing so far about the direction in which we need to go. I think we would mostly agree on the need for the theoretical, didactic and practical clarity about who we are. But we disagree about where we are at the level of community, the level of organization. I hear anarchy in our attitudes. Before I got into mental health, I was a graduate student in political philosophy. I studied anarchy. I believed then it doesn't work. I believe now it doesn't work. We're being very naive to think we can survive as anarchists any more than we could survive as totalitarians. I think there's a middle ground. If we don't define Gestalt therapy in terms of a national community of Gestalt therapists, then the person who just tracks and follows the patient with

no presence has just as much of a right to say, "I'm a Gestalt therapist." In this case the person who thinks dialogue just means being
nice would have just as much right to say this is what Gestalt therapy is. And worst of all, the person who uses his or her presence as
a therapist in a narcissistic way to demonstrate his or her own
power and creativity and to gather a following not only can, but
will achieve a great deal of limelight. Not all that is charismatic and
creative and called Gestalt therapy is either Gestalt therapy or
beneficial. If we continue to allow Gestalt therapy to be labeled as
a therapy in which the therapist narcissistically relates to patients
for his own characterological needs rather than for the patient's
therapeutic needs, I think our future is in doubt and ought to be.

MILLER: Gary Yontef has given a thoughtful answer to Laura's
question about what support is available. He has made it clear that
the most useful support must be discriminating. Later, I am going
to cross swords with him about the issue of anarchism. Anarchism, not anarchy. Meanwhile, I would like to turn the microphone
over to Miriam Polster.

POLSTER: When we consider the future of Gestalt therapy and,
in doing so, return to the basic tenets of Gestalt therapy, we are
confronted with the implications for the relationship of an organism to its environment. It seems to me that the future of Gestalt
therapy is going to reside in our ability to deal with polarity and
paradox. We have inherited a world that presents us with a great
many contradictions with which we are forced to live.

    Gary raised some questions about the abuses that we all
know only too well are committed in the name of Gestalt therapy.
Let me remind you that everything that has proceeded our philosophy of Gestalt therapy, every philosophy which was designed to

improve the human lot has also gone that way. Every theory that has proposed a way of life has also degenerated into some kind of abusive or sloganistic misuse. Such theories are vulnerable to that. We also are vulnerable to it. The question then arises how do we police this? Who wants to be a policeman? Short of policing Gestalt therapy which is a negative kind of approach to the problem; what can we do?

For me, the question of Gestalt therapy's future resides in a paradox: How do we keep our identity while remaining unconcerned about keeping it? Anybody who worries about having an identity, doesn't have an identity, and is compelled instead to take positions, to deal in pat phrases and set attitudes. The paradox is that the minute you begin to believe in any theory you can become dogmatic about it. The theory *becomes* the identity and stifles inventiveness and vitality. Read James Thurber, *The War Between Men and Women*, to see clearly the absurdities to which dogma can lead.

Instead of worrying about identity so much, we might consider thinking about articulation, and clarity. Figure/ground — we're back to it again. If we know what our principles are, if we also have a sense of what it is we espouse, as human beings who walk upright among the rest of the creatures on the face of the earth, and if we recognize that we are dealing with our opposite — not in the sense of opposed but in the sense of other — when we are dealing with a client, then the interaction between us, as Gary said, is dialogic.

Dialogue is in a sense the basic polarity. When you become aware of polarity, you awaken dialogue. I was talking about music the other day and what to my mind makes for excellence in music. I talk about music as much as I can. And it came to me that what you find in a good performance in music, or in a composition beautifully written, or in artistry in general, is the spirit of dialogue.

When you listen to a fine performance of a concerto, for example, what you hear is dialogue between the solo instrument and the orchestra. The solo instrument proposes an idea. The orchestra considers it and responds and the solo instrument is then affected by this, and it goes back and forth. So what I want to consider then, is how will we as Gestalt therapists carry on our dialogue with the environment, with otherness in its myriad forms, without allowing a struggle for our identity to intrude and become obsessively figural?

One of the things in the environment were going to have to enter into dialogue with is the increase in technology. We are going to have to contend with an issue which Paul Goodman raised years and years ago: we are creating a technology without a philosophy. We are creating one technologist after another who has no idea at all of the nature of man and no concern with questions which come from paying attention to human nature.

By technology, I mean, for instance, taped cassettes, therapeutic programs, handbooks on "how to," therapy via television series — these are examples of how the technological possibilities for therapy are multiplying. How are we going to make use of these possibilities — humanize them, work with them, fight against them? What we are going to be confronted with, I feel quite sure, is an increase in technology — and not merely in the hardware, although that may be its most dramatic form. Behaviorism, which was alluded to earlier, is a technology, not a philosophy. There is an implicit philosophy, but it consists of what the behaviorist says is not there. Many behaviorists will say you don't need awareness. All you need to do is to articulate your contingency schedules, your reinforcement schedules so that you program the behavior, and it occurs. Now that is a technology. You push a button and you get a result and you don't care what goes on in between. That's technology whether it produces sausages or whether it's designed to produce adjusted people.

I think we have to confront this; you and I must consider seriously what we are going to do with our increasing technological skill. We are, as we get technologically more advanced, like incredibly overdeveloped adolescents. We can do all the important adult things, only what goes on between our ears may not have reached the same stage of development. I occasionally threaten to write an article called "The Head is a Part of the Body, Too," which I think we sometimes forget.

Another development in technological hardware is, of course, the psychopharmacological drugs. We alter everything — moods, genetic inheritance — my God, we've even altered the way babies are conceived. With what more hubris can a society attempt to control things?

For another thing, I think we are going to have to deal societally with endemic catastrophic reactions.

I compare my childhood to the childhood of my children. I was optimistic. I was naive — there were things going on that I should have known about — but I was sanguine. To grow up was a good thing. The world presented me, so I thought, with opportunities. Not that I don't know about tragedy and hardship and hard work. But my attitude is still one of optimism. This is not the attitude of the generation we are going to be dealing with. I think we are going to be dealing with a society that is permeated by catastrophic reactions.

What does catastrophic reaction imply? As you may remember, Kurt Goldstein (and if you don't remember him, read him now) pointed out certain behaviors that came from the catastrophic reaction which resulted from brain damage. Rigidity, concreteness (and concreteness like any good thing can also be a bad thing); stereotyped behavior, and a tightening in general of the attitude towards the world, a wish to keep things unchanging, precisely because one doubts one's capacity to respond to the unpredictable.

Again, his was an organic population. He dealt with a group of soldiers whose cerebral integrity had been seriously insulted. You and I are dealing with a population which has been cerebrally and emotionally insulted but where the origin of these insults is often the result of societal assaults, not brain damage.

We have suffered one blow after another. The current apathy about the presidential campaign does not reside merely in the candidates. It resides in what preceded them. You and I and our children, clearly do not believe that who we vote for makes any difference at all. Now that's an incredible attitude, particularly for young people. Perhaps some stripping away of the scales from our eyes is necessary. I was too naive; our generation perhaps did not look clearly enough at certain uglinesses that we needed to see.

But the opposite is equally traumatic. So you and I are going to have to deal with a generation that lives in a state of catastrophic reaction, and we will have to open up and maintain a dialogue there, a dialogue not only between ourselves and others, but a dialogue between ourselves and the catastrophe.

In talking about paradox, I would like to finish by citing Lao-tzu who suggested that the value of an empty vessel resides in its emptiness. It resides in what will come in to fill it. I point this out as another way of saying that we do not need to be concerned so much with identity. We need to be concerned with what we put into this vessel that remains to be filled.

ZINKER: There is little question about the fact that Gestalt therapy has arrived. I was looking over Jerry Kogan's *Gestalt Therapy Resources*, and I gave myself the task of counting the number of doctoral dissertations in the new edition. Ten percent of the entries were doctoral dissertations related to Gestalt therapy! So we've arrived; our discipline is now being taught in colleges and universities, and our books are being used as textbooks.

That's both exciting and scary, as you've already heard. I would like to speak about two general categories — our future in the area of training and, secondly, our future in developing theory. It occurred to me this morning that I used the word training, and not education. This is disappointing. We do more training and less educating. Too often we focus on sharpening skills and not on educating persons. We need to re-evaluate the old apprentice system of learning and teaching. There are no more heroes or heroines to imitate; we are it.

We have to look at our students as having a unique developmental field for themselves. We look at our students as having an apperceptive mass, as coming from somewhere with a certain kind of background, whether it's in political science or philosophy, or in education, or psychology. We are beginning to realize that respect for the individual's own development is more important than feeding principles to them. What we are doing in Cleveland is emphasizing the skill of observation, rather than the skill of technique. Fritz said, "All you need to do is to see and to hear."

This is the phenomenological base of Gestalt therapy. It means we have to ask our students to see and to hear first. If you learn how to use your senses, it is much easier to use the methods we're trying to teach.

We have been intellectually and theoretically lazy in our training programs. We have made halfhearted reading assignments, and we have regarded it as old-fashioned to have arguments about concepts. But this situation is changing. We're beginning to ask our students, "What does this mean? What are you doing? How does this relate to your ideas? What is your intention with this person?"

We need to create a process for evaluating learning. How does learning take place? How do we manage to teach without giving multiple choice examinations? A creative learning experience is one in which the learner is a participant, and a creative evaluation is one in which the evaluator and the learner are active participants. It takes place when both persons leave the situation feeling *different*. So evaluation itself becomes a form of learning and teaching.

I like technology. I like this microphone. I remember fifteen years ago, or more, Fritz Perls went crazy about video taping. Cynthia Harris and I were sitting with Fritz in a little hotel room watching his video tapes. He was so excited about those tapes, and I'll never forget that particular experience because I got bored after a while and what became interesting for me was what Fritz looked like. He was beautiful. So I started drawing Fritz, and caught me. He became furious with me. I never finished my drawing. Fritz regarded video taping as the most promising method of learning the art of Gestalt therapy.

After all these years, we are finally beginning to realize the power of color video tapes for teaching. Imagine that you ask a student, "What did you intend to do when you saw her beginning to tear up?" and the student replies, "What do you mean? When was she tearing up?" With video, you can say, "Well, let's take a look. Right here, in this moment when her face is turning red, when her eyes are changing. Now, look at yourself. Where were you? Where did you go? What do you think was happening with her?" It's a very powerful technique, and in Cleveland we are spending a lot of money on this resource. Cynthia Harris and Julian Leon, who are on our staff, are working on the use of video taping. We are also using video taping in our research for purposes of understanding the awareness cycle and how it works.

I want to add my voice to those who have said that Guru teaching is impressive, mystifying, and leaves the listener stupid or, at best, uninformed. Guru teaching reinforces hero worship and stereotyped imitation. We've had enough of the Little Fritzes. Let's be ourselves.

With respect to theory, there is a lot of work ahead of us. We have all kinds of introductory texts. I think it's time we begin to have advanced texts, even though introductory texts are important. We need to elucidate our ideas with more detail and clarity; but it's also time to move forward. Here are some of the developments that I think are important for the future. Other panelists have already mentioned some of them.

We're beginning to develop a Gestalt group therapy which is based on the awareness-excitement-contact cycle and the use of experiment, but which is also based on group process and small systems theory. We now have a new book called *Beyond the Hot Seat*, edited by Feder and Ronall. It's an important book — the first volume dealing with Gestalt group therapy.

We are discovering ways to integrate small systems theory into our work. This includes groups, families and adult relationships. We are beginning to link Gestalt principles with large systems. One of the workshops this weekend will present some of this work. In Cleveland, we have a program in which we teach organizational development and examine large systems from a Gestalt point of view. Years ago, Erv Polster went into a coffeehouse in Cleveland and decided to explore the notion of community by entering into a dialogue with the folks in the coffeehouse. It's time that we begin to enjoy and celebrate the possibility of community. It's marvelous — a community in which we not only take care of ourselves, but we take care of each other.

The most important point I want to make is this: Gestalt theory is elegantly suited for integrating traditional thinking as well as new developments in psychotherapy. I'm not talking now about a sloppy eclecticism, but a thoughtful theoretical superstructure. In my view, the most comprehensive model in Gestalt theory is the awareness-energy-contact cycle. This is a cycle that begins with sensation, moves to awareness, generates excitement or energy. I like the word energy better, because it's less romantic. Sensation, awareness, energy, movement, contact, withdrawal, and then sensation again, and so on. Lately, we have been looking more at that part of the cycle where awareness and contact are connected. We have tended to overemphasize the notion of movement because we are an action-oriented society, leaving withdrawal, or the kinds of withdrawal systems like Yoga and other things, to those "crazy" Yogis.

I believe that we need to study the whole cycle, not just the active part that culminates in contact. In order to understand withdrawal, we need to incorporate insights from Yoga, TM, hypnosis, and other methods of being quietly in the world, rather than just active movement in the world. And there are certain systems which focus on awareness: psychoanalysis, Transactional Analysis, existential analysis, Jungian analysis, rational emotive therapy, for example. We need to incorporate some of their valuable insights into our cycle theory.

It's very important to keep our heads in order to experience a sense of depth. The problem of getting stuck in awareness and not moving into energy is that you develop obsessive deadness.

One of the problems with psychoanalysis is that it breeds obsessionals who then breed other obsessionals. So we need to develop a way of thinking about moving from the phenomena of awareness into energy. We need to learn to link energy and movement. Some of the systems which insert themselves in the cycle at the stage of energy are bioenergetics, which came from the Reichian point of view, and Radix, which is a system of therapy developed by Charles Kelly.

I love the notion of building a charge — an energy charge — in the person as a way of producing the full capacity for movement and for contact, and I think that we can incorporate that notion into our theorizing by linking movement and contact. Here we can learn from certain points of view which focus on the movement of the organism as a primary consideration, such as dance, aikido, tai chi, kata — which is a form of dance in karate — Zen and the art of archery. All these can help us see where movement goes in relation to contact.

We have to incorporate the notion of meditation and silences into our work. It's important to have reveries together. It's important to withdraw. Then there are systems which concentrate on the sensation part of the cycle. These ask you to feel, to move, and to see what's happening. Some examples are polarity therapy, Lomi, art therapy, and music therapy.

The point is that if we consider the whole cycle, from all these perspectives, we can develop a system of phenomenological diagnosis which enables us to say exactly where a person is stuck and where the work must take place. One person is not able to feel. Another gets excited readily and doesn't have anything in the core. The obsessive gets stuck between awareness and energy, and so forth.

A person who is full of energy and is not able to release it into movement remains somatically bloated. His or her face is red and intense, and the chest is expanded into a frozen barrel. Such a person might have high blood pressure and that sort of thing. The person who moves a lot and is not able to get in contact is clinically the so-called hysteric who experiences a lot of frantic activity — it's a form of psychological coitus interruptus — without being able to complete the experience. The person who is stuck on contact is not able to let go and has difficulty falling asleep.

It's very exciting to develop a global theoretical system which uses phenomenological language, a system that would belong to Gestalt therapy.

Finally, I want to say that the trick is to avoid psychological arterial sclerosis, by continuing to improvise, to be creative, playful, and fluid. At the same time, we can avoid getting too scattered by continuing to focus our thinking.

Thank you very much.

∫ Some Historical Limitations of Gestalt Therapy

Three years ago, I conducted a symposium on the future of Gestalt therapy at the Gestalt conference in Boston. When I introduced the theme I said that it suggested Gestalt therapy's coming of age — or, at least, its passing into adolescence, that time of life when we dream about the future. Now, we're beginning to concern ourselves with limitations, which is, perhaps, an expression of Gestalt therapy's reaching middle age. For the psychologists who study "adult development" tell us that limitations are one of the chief worries during the mid-life crisis, as we discover that the ideals and dreams of youth are not, alas, ever going to be wholly realized.

If this sounds like a pessimistic note upon which to begin a symposium, let me point out that it's healthy to shed illusions, accept limitations, and consolidate energy for a commitment to what's possible. In fact, you could consider awareness of one's

---

*From *The Gestalt Journal*, Vol. VIII, No. 1 (Spring, 1985). Reprinted with permission.

limitations grounds for a realistic optimism, in that it clarifies what is needed and what is available.

I think that any serious discussion of the limitations of Gestalt therapy has to consider the following issues: Gestalt therapy is based on two principles that distinguish it from every other psychotherapy. These are the contact boundary, which consists of the phenomenological meetings between the self and its world (and therefore the location of the contact disturbances that result in neurotic suffering); and figure formation — the capacity to form present experience into meaningful wholes. Do these principles somehow inherently constrict the scope of Gestalt therapy in terms of the clinical problems it can address effectively or the types of patients it can treat adequately? It is certainly true that Gestalt therapy, if one were to judge by the literature, for example, has left large stretches of the clinical landscape untouched. But is this a question of innate shortcomings — a failure of the theory — or of historical limitations due to the narrow vision of many Gestalt therapists in their approach to practice as well as in their reflections on their craft?

An analogous situation in the history of psychoanalysis points to the importance of our confronting these questions. Traditional psychoanalysis with its emphasis on directly interpreting unconscious drives was at a loss when faced with the narcissistic disorders and related character disorders. It tended to write off such patients as untreatable. Not until new theories evolved, used on the ego and on "object relations" did psychoanalysts conclude that they could work fruitfully with these problematic patients. But the new theories required something more than an extension of past orthodoxy; they came closer to a radical break with it.

Let me stake out my own position with respect to Gestalt therapy by coming down squarely on the historical side of the fence. The theory of the contact boundary and Gestalt formation leads to a therapy that, perhaps more than any other psychotherapy, preserves the differences between people and the quality of their actual experience, views them in relation to one another and their environment, and respects the individual as the shaper of his or her own reality. I don't think that Gestalt therapy contains intrinsic limitations that call for a radical revision of its foundations. Everything that the psychotherapist needs to understand, both psychopathology and healthy functioning, is potentially available in the theory of Gestalt therapy.

I say potentially because I think that there are rich implications in the theory that have not been put to use. The sense that Gestalt therapy is a limited approach derives from the fact that the growing numbers of those who practice it have not carried the insights of its founders into new territory in a way that remains consistent with its principles. They have tended to rely on the techniques and styles of a few charismatic teachers. When they have found themselves constrained by those influences, they've attempted to supplement the techniques with methods drawn from other psychotherapies rather than by attending to the conceptual basis of Gestalt therapy itself and elaborating it from within.

For example, Gestalt therapists need to address themselves more urgently to the problem of diagnosis. All the more so because the work of Gestalt therapy involves staying so close to the patient's moment-to-moment experience. Present moments can become random and discontinuous unless they are grounded in a larger perspective that includes the past and the future, which is to say a view of human development, and a way of understanding how people make their experience, which is to say a theory of character.

Improvisation is the heart of the therapeutic enterprise, but even jazz musicians build their flights of imagination on some given structure of chord progressions or motifs. Or to use a more homely metaphor: Even a driver with the best nose for directions finds it useful to consult a road map when traveling through unfamiliar terrain. In this respect at least, we look with some measure of humility at modern psychoanalysis, which has thought longer and harder than any other psychotherapy about human development and neurotic character. It thus provides its practitioners with considerable (in some ways too much) guidance and support for making sense of what comes up in the therapy session.

Not that their view would do for us. I'm not making a plea here to reduce Gestalt therapy to still another variation of psychoanalysis. But Gestalt therapy has thus far had surprisingly little to say in its own distinctive language and thought about either character or development. I think that the material is there in the theory but that it has been mostly overlooked. To take an instance: It seems to me that in their haste to keep up with the mutability of life in the here and now, Gestalt therapists have not lingered long enough over the neurotic constructions that we call "fixed Gestalts" as a basis for thinking about neurotic character. To formulate these more thoroughly would not be tantamount to setting up diagnostic categories in which to shove people and freeze their experience. On the contrary, the idea behind the notion of the fixed Gestalt is that what appears fixed is actually what is repeated — it has to be made over and over again, and that's why one can create the possibility of changing it by concentrating on how it is being made in the present situation of the therapy session.

I stress this because we all know that diagnostic categories have been used abusively to overpower. Or dispense with people's experience. There's some feeling of dread attached to the very idea

108

of psychological diagnosis as a result — rather, I imagine, like what people in certain primitive cultures must feel when they refuse to allow themselves to be photographed. The value of a diagnostic approach in Gestalt therapy, however, has much less to do with placing people in categories than with enabling the therapist to sense more precisely, to articulate, and to help the patient become aware of the particularity of his or her own reality.

∫ Teaching a Paranoid to Flirt

I.

In Gestalt therapy, insight often occurs closer to the beginning of each session's story than the end. Of course, awareness, which Gestalt therapists work with intensively, is always a continuing part of the process. Awareness is a necessary though not usually sufficient condition to bring about change. Where there are long familiar habits of conduct and being, thoroughly entrenched in a patient's self-definition, not only are new insights on his or her part generally required but also new actions followed up with ongoing practice. The deeper part of psychotherapy has to engage character, not only the relief of symptoms. Without steady practice it is not so easy to metabolize new experience to the point of making it truly part of oneself.

---

*"Teaching a Paranoid to Flirt" originally appeared in French as "Apprendre à flirter à un paranoïaque" in La poétique de la Gestalt-thérapie by Michael Vincent Miller (Bordeaux, 2002: l'exprimerie). It was translated and revised for publication here by the author.

For this reason Gestalt therapy has always had a built-in "coaching" dimension long before coaching became a popular term in the self-improvement culture. The Gestalt therapist functions most effectively like a combination of meditation instructor, relational psychoanalyst and piano teacher: A piano teacher can help the student with the fingering, pedaling, and expressive dimension of a sonata, but those guidelines to performance won't turn out a pianist. In a similar vein, without regular practice in between the sessions, therapist and patient are likely to just keep repeating the same piece over and over, sometimes for years. This may make for low market turnover, but it's not good therapy.

Why would it be useful to teach a paranoid how to flirt? What kind of practice would that amount to? I will come back to these questions, but first it is important to understand certain characteristics of paranoia. Freud gave us the earliest explanation of paranoid symptom-formation from a perspective within the individual. By 1911, in his discussion of Schreber's memoir about his own paranoid psychosis, Freud already regards projection as the internal dynamism in paranoia. He analyzes there how delusions of persecution arise from internal conflicts that have been expelled into the environment, from whence they come back at the person as though they were slights, humiliating responses, or threats of injury from the outside world (Freud, 1950).

Paranoia leads the person under its spell to confine himself to a relationship with the social environment that is at once complicated and reductive. The German philosopher and sociologist Georg Simmel defined the stranger "not . . . as the wanderer who comes today and goes tomorrow, but rather as the person who comes today and stays tomorrow" (Simmel, 1950). One could apply this formulation equally to the paranoid, who stays in a troubled relation to another or a community of others. Like the stranger, the paranoid is always nearby yet at the same time far away; in that very proximity one discovers his distance and vice versa.

This apparent paradox is not really a paradox. The paranoid, like everyone, must discover how to be himself and at the same time to be involved with others, including the search for how to find a balance between identity and intimacy. Every individual has to contend with this dilemma, which is crucial for human development, but in the case of the paranoid person it has become sadly derailed. The particular form anxiety takes in paranoia stems from a conflict between a longing to join another in intimacy or to belong to a collectivity and the terror of dissolution or fixation that such unions give rise to in him. For if he comes too close to another person or a group he feels in danger of losing himself through being overexposed and then trapped in the other's definition of who he is. The gaze of the other for the paranoid is like the gaze of the Medusa: It threatens to render him powerless and turn him to stone.

Thus he feels compelled to move increasingly outside every relationship until he feels alone and cut off, even when he is among others. Yet the need for connection persists. Such conflicting fears and desires are the bottom line of paranoid anxiety. His belief that others are conspiring against him, scheming to betray him, intending to humiliate him or do him wrong results from the conflict. As odd as it may seem, that belief becomes his way of experiencing a very limited and painful kind of belonging. It's as though he is isolated and at the same time the main object of the group's attention because he imagines that every intimate conversation among others conspires against him, every joke is on him. Being at the center of things in that way is not a fun place to be.

The presence of fixation and impotence in the life of paranoia accounts for why flirtation — specifically, helping the paranoid learn how to flirt — can play a telling role in the psychotherapeutic treatment of paranoid personalities. People who are paranoid are obsessed with certitude and the lack of it. Uncertainty for them is filled with fear of that others are about to seize control of them and overthrow their precarious, unstable sense of themselves. Above all they depend on certitude to protect themselves against the unknown of the future. Into that unlit unknown that none of us can know, the paranoid projects a special brand of absolute knowledge, which consists in the certainty that what the others are up to is going to be hazardous to his well-being. He can rely on no one except himself and even there only on what he believes he knows for sure. If he lets his guard down, he will be unsafe, unprotected, and unfree. It follows that a person who is paranoid cannot play, and flirtation can be a safe way to play with uncertainty. *or is always playing on his own!!*

The paranoid character's imagination, which is in fact a powerful instrument, operates within a narrow corridor. For him social life is an extremely serious concern, an issue, one could say, of psychological life or death. He cannot entertain the perspective that society might be a game or a theatrical production, a matter of masks, costumes, and roles in the sense, as Shakespeare put it in *As You Like It*, "All the world's a stage, / And all the men and women merely players." To deal with the dire seriousness of the social enterprise, the paranoid turns into a kind of scientist of interaction, although a rather mad scientist. He gathers evidence in an effort to discover the laws of cause and effect underlying social motivation. His madness takes the form of rigidity or even fundamentalism, because he is not open to anything that might disprove his theory that people getting together in his vicinity is bad news, namely for him. What he does not see is that his own defensive behavior, whether withdrawn or aggressive, before the fact — that

114

is, in anticipation of the coming blow — contributes to confirming what he believes he already knows.

Nevertheless he tends to be very skilled at taking account of everything, noting every move, gesture, every nuance or undertone of conversation around him. Nothing is lost on him, and in this he also resembles a scientist or perhaps a novelist. It follows that his perceptions (except perhaps in the extreme case of psychosis) typically contain at least a grain of truth. The trouble begins when he interprets what he sees and hears. He looks upon these partial truths as the whole story and fixes them in mind as though he had uncovered a scientific law. For example, it is true that very little intimacy is based on pure love; power relations almost always get into the picture. For the paranoid person, this perception is likely to become an equation: love equals power. Searching for absolute truth under each surface appearance, the paranoid person refuses to accept much of anything at face value.

The demand for certainty in dealing with life's complications is a symptom-forming theme not only for the paranoid character, but for virtually all neurotic character. From this standpoint, one can think of neurosis as resembling a religious quest, although unlike the true religious pilgrim, the neurotic never finds peace in an act of faith, because the capacity for faith, especially in the intimate environment, was usually lost in childhood. For example, an obsessional character bites off a morsel of experience, tears it up, and then keeps on mentally chewing into smaller and smaller pieces, as though in this way he will finally arrive at an indisputable conclusion. Like the paranoid, he craves certitude, but what he experiences is unending doubt. So he keeps repeating the same process with the same bit of experience, trying for a clear resolution, but at every conceivable stopping point, doubt is renewed.

Obsessing is the attempt to arrive at the end of uncertainty without faith. He can never arrive at the notion that enough is enough. If the paranoid is a kind of mad scientist, the obsessive is like a mad philosopher. Descartes built an epistemology around doubt, and the obsessive personality is a Descartes run amuck, who can only get to "I think . . . ," but not to a final determination that anything exists. The paranoid's variation on the Cartesian cogito is "I'm right, therefore I am." Whereas the obsession is never sure of what he knows, the paranoid knows everything in advance.

∵ projection

II.

Flirtation at its best, as a social art form, is a mode of play, specifically, the play of the imagination. It involves two people (sometimes more) playing with fantasy together about what could happen between them without either insisting that he or she knows exactly what the other has in mind. You could also define flirtation as people playing with the projections going on between them. Flirting is an absorbing means of making contact, sometimes fleeting, sometimes prolonged, that leaves the mysterious unknowability of the other intact. It is at once provocative and respectful. And there are reasons to think that those who are paranoid could be quite good at it.

Again, Freud gives us the hint of why this might be true. In one of his late works, *Inhibitions, Symptoms and Anxiety*, dating from 1926, he wrote that "The delusional constructions of the paranoiac offer to his acute perceptive and imaginative powers a

116

field of activity which he could not easily find elsewhere" (Freud, 1961). Why not easily elsewhere?

The paranoid is unaware that the loss of self he fears has already occurred. Because he projects painful, unintegrated aspects of himself onto the environment, from whence they seem to return to attack him, he feels less than he is — and thereby far too small in a world that seems too big to cope with or navigate in. Since you can only go in two directions in life — toward others or away from them — the paranoid chooses away, though not so far away that he cannot watch or listen in order to keep tabs. Social life for him is like being alone and afloat on dangerous waters in a boat with no sail or paddles. So the paranoid person sees the playfulness of others around him, hears their jokes and laughter, as a sham or mockery, usually directed at him as part of a conspiracy to shame or otherwise harm him. The others are in the know; he is out of it.

Flirtation can be a way of testing one's projections as though they were merely hypotheses — that is, without depending on knowing the outcome in advance. There is considerable artfulness in the imaginative projecting of the paranoid, as Freud intimated. In the passage just cited, Freud already recognizes the creativity released through projecting. Paranoid projections, he points out, are the constructions of a gifted imagination, not unlike the psychological making of new forms or ideas that underlie artistic or intellectual work. The creative power of projecting is involved in the expressiveness of art, in the making of myths, in the building of philosophical systems, and, for that matter, in all human communication. We cannot think the thoughts or feel the feelings of one another, and that is why we have to project ourselves in building a bridge to what we can know of another person.

TEACHING A PARANOID TO FLIRT

Psychotherapists all too often seem to think they are in the business of correcting projections, as though this will help eliminate them in the name of reality. Whose reality? As Isadore From used to point out frequently to his supervisees, the central question is not whether projections are right or wrong — to interpret them as wrong violates the patient's experience — but to attend to what part projections might play in disturbing the quality of contact. Gestalt therapy, of course, has learned much of what it knows about projection from Freud and supplemented it with Otto Rank's notions about the artistry, that is, the individual expressiveness, inherent in projecting. A good Gestalt therapist conserves the individual expressiveness while aiming to help the paranoid patient expand his or her repertoire beyond negative themes.

At the poles of engagement with another, projecting tends to gravitate toward expressing and perceiving hostility or empathy. Often the therapeutic work consists in helping a patient loosen up too much inclination to stick to one pole or the other in order to develop the flexibility to move between them as the situation merits. The poet John Keats understood the creative potential of empathic projecting; he implied that in order to write a convincing poem about a Grecian urn or a nightingale, first you have to become a Grecian urn or a nightingale. He called this "negative capability," which had nothing to do with negative feelings, but with letting go of oneself enough to identify fully with the other. One apparently finds a similar idea in the Zen approach to teaching archery. According to Eugen Herrigel, who studied with a Buddhist archery master, becoming a great archer in this tradition has less to do with how one aims the bow and pulls the string then in developing a mental identification with the target.

The ability to leave the self behind, like a Keatsian poet or like Zen archers, for the sake of identifying with or joining the object of one's interest, is precisely what the paranoid, despite his talent for projecting — or because of it — is unable to do. The paranoid's projecting carries him toward his destination, which is the other, but something blocks him en route. Such a trip is never an innocent one for him. It is a reminder of past relationships that were traumatically invalidating, and he feels he can't again afford to be taken by surprise. To enter into the sphere of influence of another feels to him tantamount to surrendering to the will or power of the other and becoming imprisoned there.

This is where learning to flirt can become a valuable tool for the paranoid. As a mode of making contact with others or the environment, flirtation is a gentle art, a playful one, in which you can take risks step by step. You can put your toes in the water and then move in deeper if it's not too cold. You can flirt with danger, you can flirt with seduction, and you can flirt with other possibilities. You can cut loose and set sail but turn around at any moment if the wind becomes too strong to handle. The real point here is that flirtation gives the paranoid a way of initiating contact, rather than feeling buffeted by the initiative of others and defending against it. Flirtation has the advantage that you don't risk rejection and humiliation or the feeling of being trapped through overcommitting or overexposing yourself. You can take the initiative in joining with another, but at any moment you can extricate yourself without either you or the other losing face from a prospective sexual encounter or business deal or whatever just by changing the subject or saying something along the lines of good-bye, let's have lunch soon. The art of flirtation for the paranoid is

119

the art of navigation in an uncertain world. It can provide him with a method to steer his way through a sea of contingency.

III.

Here is an example of how I attempted to teach one patient of mine at least some beginning steps in the art of flirtation. He was a middle-aged man, quite attractive except for the rather narrow-eyed, tense expression he usually wore. When he was in elementary school, he had been overweight and athletically awkward. His peers, who are not generally graceful about such matters, taunted him regularly. On one occasion, he told me, he came home in tears, and his mother took one look and said, "I always hoped for a daughter, and now I've got one." His father was a strict, rule-governed man and an evangelical Christian who made it pretty clear that women were predatory, opportunistic, and used sex to gain their own ends.

My patient's principal complaint was that he lived in depressing isolation, which he felt powerless to do anything about. He had married in his twenties and divorced a few years later when he discovered that his wife was involved in an affair. Since the divorce he had had one other important relationship that also had ended badly. Since then he had renounced women and had never made any close male friends. He had to some degree followed his father's lead in religion, but seemed to derive no comfort from his faith.

Although depression was his presenting symptom, it became clear that this was fueled by an underlying paranoid structure. I've often noted that there are, roughly speaking, two kinds of depression — wet, somewhat histrionic ones, streaked with tears

120

of self-pity, and dry, paranoid ones, parched like a desert where the rain never falls. This man's was as arid as they come, thanks in part to the lessons he learned from both his parents.

For the first several months, his therapy focused to a large extent on moment-to-moment self-awareness — sensations, thoughts, feelings. This is often an important way to begin with a patient like this who is paranoid, because such an individual typically projects his experience, including his motivations and initiative, onto the others around him. He feels particularly small and unsupported because so much self has been displaced through propelling it outward into the environment. It seemed especially important for this man to regain a sense of his agency in the making his own experience. So we worked for quite some time to reach an understanding between us of how he contributed to creating the very solitude that he felt victimized by.

Since he assumed rejection a priori, he tightened up around anyone whom he felt attracted to and frequently fled from an encounter. If someone interesting approached him, he responded with an impression of being aloof and cold. He told me that on one occasion he went to a party where there were a number of women who were attractive to him, but when dancing started he immediately went home. He was sure, he said, that no one would be willing to dance with him. Most weekends he stayed in his apartment, wishing he had an intimate partner.

Every projection that a patient can become aware of and recapture can be empowering: Working toward this end is a basic process in Gestalt therapy — it was the core of Frederick Perls's empty chair technique — that increases one's base of self-support, helps the release of pent-up, unexpressed emotions about past events, and strengthens one's sense of agency in the shaping experience. However, it still rarely brings about much change, given the

of course! ✳

conservative, and in its way, protective, force of habit. Eventually I coaxed my patient into getting out of his apartment on weekends, where nothing was going to happen, and going out on the town — hitting the museums, concerts, and jazz clubs, staying longer at parties or dinners and taking the risk of engaging in conversations. I worked with him, as though therapy could become a kind of finishing school, at developing some skill at telling interesting or amusing stories about his life. We even had a brief course in witty one-liners, including ones with a touch of sexual innuendo for use when the listener might be a woman he was drawn to.

I discussed with him the difference between feeling demanding, which is the child's way of trying for what it wants and usually gets repressed in the adult, and being commanding, which is an adult way of getting others interested in you. People with unexpressed demands tend to walk into a social scene, slink off to the margins, and sit there silently waiting to be invited to take part. When no one pays attention, they grow resentful. If they are paranoid in addition, they assume any attention that does come their way will be threatening.

So that he would learn what it means to become more commanding, I suggested that he find out what might happen if he tried walking into a social gathering and looking around with bold curiosity (first I had to work up his curiosity in place of his assumption that he always knew what was going on). Next he was to use his curiosity to get responses from people who intrigued him, especially women. His being the one who does the looking was particularly important, because people who are paranoid tend to either glare at others or watch what's going on out of the corners of their eyes, both of which readily make a screen for negative projections. I was intent on helping him become the agent of his social contact, thus feeling that he was in control of its dosage and direction, rather than remaining the passive recipient either of neglect or other people's (threatening) approaches.

Convincing him to risk this took quite a bit of doing. And that is why I put it all in the context of learning how to flirt. Flirtation is a game of inquiry, the art of being playfully curious. It makes for social engagement, but it also can be a generous and face-saving game. It's generous, because you bring yourself to it without insistent expectations as an offering to the other person. But it is also face-saving, as I suggested above, because, as in all games, either player can bow out at any moment, by either letting it deepen into something serious if that is where it's heading (then it's no longer just a game); or by simply changing the subject or saying goodbye without it being embarrassing, rejecting, or otherwise endangering to either party. It's the right game for the paranoid, who has such a deep fear of finding himself a captive at the mercy of the other. *or rejected?*

One major effort in psychotherapy, especially from the standpoint of Gestalt therapy, is to identify and preserve every resource that the patient brings into the consultation room, and then help the person discover new pathways and forms for putting them to use. Such work with paranoid patients entails turning their imaginative and interpretative talents from their insistence on pessimistic certitude — and the consequent making of negative and self-defeating repetitious projections treated as absolute truth — into fluid projections that preserve life's uncertainties and remain open to surprise and renewal. Teaching a paranoid to flirt can provide a valuable social skill that paves the way to this transformation.

References

Freud, Sigmund. 1950. *Collected Papers*, Trans. by Alix and James Strachey. London: The Hogarth Press. Vol. III, p. 452.

Freud, Sigmund. *1961. Inhibitions, Symptoms and Anxiety*. Trans. by Alix Strachey. Revised and edited by James Strachey. London: The Hogarth Press. p. 13.

Herrigel, Eugen. 1968. *Zen in the Art of Archery*. N.Y: Pantheon.

Simmel, Georg. 1950. *The Sociology of Georg Simmel*. Trans. and ed. By Kurt H. Wolff. N.Y: The Free Press. p. 402.

∫ Transference and Beyond

In "The Fairy Godfathers," one of his disquieting short stories about our failures at love, John Updike brings together two definitive modern experiences — divorce and psychotherapy. The story concerns a pair of lovers who are in the midst of leaving their marriages in order to be together. In the past they had traveled with their former mates in the same suburban circles: among couples who play tennis and attend early music concerts together; among husbands who borrow each other's tools on weekends and wives who go barefoot in summer, displaying shapely, dancer-like arches. Eventually they had begun an affair. Now, picking their way through the debris of their ruptured families and their own guilt and vacillation, each of them sees a psychotherapist.

They meet regularly at his new fourth-floor walk-up apartment. During these encounters they carry on a rueful courtship, approaching one another with self-deprecating irony which mixes

---

*This essay originally appeared in *Intimate Environments: Sex, Intimacy and Gender in Families* edited by David Kantor and Barbara F. Oken (New York: Guilford Press, 1989). Reprinted with permission.

doubt and reassurance, desire and pathos — the emotions of people still haunted by the marriages they have abandoned. But above
all, they discuss their latest therapy sessions, which stimulates their
desire for each other. Just as being in love can become an obsession, so can being in therapy. Psychotherapy acts upon them like
an aphrodisiac; poring over its intricate probings of motive and
impulse turns into a sort of spiritual foreplay that overcomes their
conflicted feelings. Steered by therapy away from their previous
marriages and toward each other, as though this were the passage
from neurosis to health, they eventually get married, buy a house,
and terminate therapy — whereupon they discover that they have
virtually nothing to say to one another! It is as if their romance
were little more than an artifact created by the two therapists.

As its title suggests, Updike's story is a modernist fairy tale,
a kind of grotesque new version of "Cinderella." (In case the title
isn't enough to make sure we catch the allusion, Updike nicknames
his heroine "Pumpkin.") It also resembles those ancient Greek
myths in which gods and goddesses, operating from dubious,
all-too-human motives, interfere in the doings of mortals who have
managed to arouse their interest or hatred. In "Cinderella" the
heroine is delivered by supernatural intervention from poverty and
familial oppression to a wonderful fate — marriage to a prince.
But in "The Fairy Godfathers," hero and heroine are both delivered to the emptiness of modern marriage. Instead of nineteenth-century fairies or capricious Greek deities, Updike gives us
psychotherapists who cast their spells disguised as psychological
insights.

"The Fairy Godfathers" reminds us of a danger in the cultural phenomenon that the sociologist Philip Rieff once called "the
triumph of the therapeutic" (1966). The avowed purpose of psychotherapy is to help people live better lives. But all too often it

manages to insinuate itself so thoroughly into patients' attitudes that it becomes a substitute for the real thing. Has the therapeutic triumphed by defeating life? There is a poignant innocence in our hope that benevolent experts or wizards can purge us of uncertainty and confusion. But as Updike warns, we are not likely to be saved from the pitfalls of love — its illusions, compulsions, and dependencies — by becoming more psychologically sophisticated. Love was probably better off when it was still blind.

Therapy's Influence on Marriage

In case one is tempted to write off Updike's little fable as poetic exaggeration, let me turn to a research project currently in progress. The Harvard psychologist Carol Gilligan has been interviewing couples with children who are suffering through marital crises, in order to explore how they arrive at decisions to separate or stay together. Gilligan found that a large number of couples in her sample head for therapists' offices before they wind up in those of lawyers.[*] This is hardly news to me or my colleagues who practice a lot of marital therapy; we depend on this unfortunate turn of events to make a living. Judging from Gilligan's account, the therapeutic results for these couples were not uniformly impressive. Although some of her couples were very satisfied with what they learned from therapy that might help them resolve their problems, others were left awash in ambiguity, and some were even plunged into further turmoil over the therapy itself. Gilligan's preliminary findings confirm my own less systematic clinical hunches — name-

---

[*] C. Gilligan (April 12, 1988), personal communication.

ly that all too many patients who turn to therapy desperate for help with marital distress come away feeling that the therapist has somehow maneuvered the rescue or breakup of their marriages, leaving them bewildered and uncertain about their own real wishes.

There are active therapists who move in with a heavy hand, advising, provoking emotions like cheerleaders, criticizing the husband or wife who is unwilling to change, supporting the one who more readily accepts the therapeutic agenda. Such therapists are busy playing the role of savior or parent and mainly succeed in infantilizing their patients. But therapeutic interference can also be much more subtle; it doesn't take a deliberately active or directive therapist to confuse patients or come between intimate partners. There are plenty of therapists who seem to think that by doing nothing except listening attentively or providing "mirroring feedback," they are assuming postures of neutrality and objectivity, leaving everything else to their patients' imaginations. (Updike's story is all the more convincing because we don't know how much of what the lovers report about their therapists' opinions is real and how much is imagined.) They influence their patients nevertheless. After all, *someone* is there listening, and being heard may be precisely what is missing from a patient's marriage. Even silent therapists can end up caught in triangles as though they were rivals for a husband's or wife's affection.

There are also the therapists in whom love and sex seems to bring out the worst, as psychosis does. These therapists tend to rely on clinical technique and professional formalism, which makes them rigid and abstract. They approach their patients with arrogance instead of tenderness, coldness instead of empathy, and dogmatism instead of open-mindedness. Maybe they manage to avoid the anxiety that their patients evoke in them, but this is a peculiar goal when you consider that sex and madness are the very topics upon which they are consulted as experts.

Of course, there are excellent therapists of every persuasion, and good and bad therapy is conducted along the entire continuum from overt meddling to limp inertness. The point is that therapists have real impact on their patients' lives, whether they behave like psychological athletes or circumspect statues. In either case, they can only be responsible for their intervention to the extent that they both know themselves and are conscious of their effect on others, in addition to recognizing their patients' actual concerns. Passivity may look at first glance like evidence of responsible therapy, but it can turn out to be only a more insidious form of interference. It is no wonder, then, that so many accounts of marriages subjected to therapy are deeply disturbing. Whether or not such therapy serves the best interests of patients in unhappy marriages, whether or not the therapists' roles are accurately perceived, one impression comes through consistently: Psychotherapy is capable of having massive influence on the fate of marriages.

The social implications of this influence are terribly unclear. How are therapeutic decisions about marriages being made, and what values are they based on? Does therapy tend to support or even create a culture in which gratifying oneself is praised and marital ties are disparaged? Are the therapists fighting the last vestiges of Victorian patriarchal tyranny or are they fostering narcissistic self-indulgence? Are they wrecking families through what used to be a civil offense called alienation of affection, or are they helping free men and women from pathological bondage? Has the neighborhood marriage broker of old become a marriage breaker? How much projection occurs, where the therapist's neutral interpretations are distorted by wishful thinking in the case of some patients and by bitterness, fury, or melancholy resignation in the case of others?

That so much is left open to question does not serve this strangely unaccountable profession nor its clients well. It suggests that psychotherapy is not exempt from our general confusion about love, sex, and marriage. More specifically, ambiguities arise from a gap or an incongruity between the theories that psycho-therapists espouse and what actually goes on in their practices. The traditional analytic view reduces the intimate, erotic, and other powerful, elemental feelings that arise between therapist and patient to transference and countertransference. This theory im-plies that the therapist is a neutral bystander, a mere catalyst, the vague object of inflamed regressive feelings on the part of the pa-tient. But at least it does acknowledge the passionate nature of the attachment, akin to falling in love.

Another influential viewpoint, rooted in modern ob-ject-rela-tions theory, places more stress on mutuality and empa-thy, which leads it to suggest that the development of intimacy in therapy may in itself have a curative effect. This theory acknowl-edges the immediacy and reality of feelings between therapist and patient, although usually in a rather mild and uninspiring way. A third conception, held by many practitioners of family therapy, concentrates on the structure of interaction in therapy and virtu-ally edits out both the therapist as a person and love as a subjective phenomenon. None of these approaches to intimacy in the clinical situation does justice to the demonic complexity that can envelop therapist and patient when powerful emotions, especially erotic ones, are set loose in the close quarters of a therapy session. The impact of the therapist's personality on the patient in particular remains largely unacknowledged and unarticulated. Most of the theories that psychotherapists use to explain their role seem designed to preserve their innocence. *and goodness?*

We are not flourishing in our intimacies. My own feeling is that psychotherapy has not yet been very successful in helping men and women grapple with the anxieties of loving one another. Perhaps there is not enough psychotherapy (with the exception of certain existential and phenomenological approaches such as Gestalt therapy) that focuses on the actual quality of contact between people. Most psychological theories have little to say about how we can surrender to intense feelings for each other and yet keep our differences intact in the struggle to know both ourselves and another man or woman. If anything, a great many couples have found that their bouts with therapy lead them further into self-absorption and away from their marriages. I know of at least three situations where husbands or wives became so steeped in the therapeutic culture that they left their marriages and went into training to become therapists themselves.

Where can a husband and wife turn when their marriage begins to come apart? In the seventeenth-century Puritan village, when it became known that a married couple was helplessly stuck in a severe quarrel, the governor sent in a representative to mediate. This illustrates how important the family's well-being was to the life of the early American community. Since we can no longer depend on much assistance from organized religion, the surrounding community, the extended family, or other traditional bolsters of married life, psychotherapy may be all we have to fall back on.

But the kind of dilemma that Updike portrays with satirical clarity may have been built into the very origins of psychotherapy, and it continues to plague most contemporary therapies. From the beginning, even as it struggled to teach people the liberating power of intimate and sexual speech, psychotherapy developed a peculiar one-sided silence of its own — a technical and methodological silence — to which it gave the name "transference." The concept of transference has proven to be a mixed blessing, because it has been at once a powerful diagnostic instrument for discovering how love can fail and a frustrating obstruction to learning how to love more fully.

Sex and Transference

Despite Freud's quest for a science that could explain mental and emotional life, his theories remained on more familiar terms with passion than have most subsequent psychologies. He was still only a generation away from the Romantic era, whereas we have tended to bury much of our romantic idealism in an era where sex, marriage, and divorce all verge on becoming technicalities. And perhaps the forbidden sexuality of Freud's times made him more sensitive to the alluring urgencies and tensions of the erotic.

Fin-de-siècle Vienna smoldered with sexual desire and sexual sickness. Based on instinctual repression, the social order of Freud's time seemed about to explode. Its erotic contradictions were "like a dark underground vault over which rose the gorgeous structure of middle-class society with its faultless, radiant facade," wrote the Viennese novelist and critic Stefan Zweig (1953, p. 82). When Freud looked underneath the ornate scaffolding of Viennese life, he discovered lustful fantasies and yearnings, including grotesque ones, lurking everywhere — among both children and their parents, psychotics, mobs, dreamers, mystics and priests, artists and poets, aristocrats as well as laborers. This was certainly a cultural setting that would tend to produce ripe specimens of Eros in neurotic disguise.

Freud became occupied, even preoccupied, with the sexual issues that led him to develop the concept of transference before the turn of the century. During the 1880s he collaborated with Breuer on experiments using hypnotic suggestion to treat hysterical symptoms. Not only did it become apparent to them that repressed sexual urges and related emotions might produce these symptoms, but there was increasing evidence, bewildering but unmistakable, that their work itself awakened strong erotic longings in their patients, most of whom were women.

One evening Breuer received an urgent call to go to the home of his patient Anna 0. Upon arriving he found her suffering from phantom labor pains. Writhing in her bed, she announced that she was about to give birth to his baby. Breuer, a married man, fled in panic and abruptly ended her treatment. His colleague Freud had a less exotic but equally unsettling experience: As Ernest Jones describes the incident, when Freud leaned close to hypnotize a certain hysterical patient, she suddenly flung her arms around his neck "in a transport of affection" (1953, p. 250).

These were among the more blatant incidents. A few years later Freud concluded that the feelings stirred by analysis could also appear in much more subtle and subterranean forms, which included hostility toward the therapist as well as desire for closeness to him. Much to his dismay, Dora, the sexually pent-up and suffering adolescent of his most famous case history, quit therapy at the point where he thought that they were on the brink of success. Not until it was too late did Freud realize that she might have been prompted by a blend of secret love and vindictiveness.

If Freud's scientific curiosity was provoked by these events, one can imagine that he must have felt anxious and defensive as well, given the dim official view of sex that dominated his times. He decided to step back (rather than flee like Breuer) and observe his patient's erotic overtures with detached vigilance. The resulting turn-of-the-century Viennese tableau — an attentive but objective bearded man of science and me who appears lost in thought and a female patient on a couch, inflamed with symptoms — was to have wide influence on the subsequent evolution of psychotherapy. It became the standard psychoanalytic stance for dealing with emotions such as sexual desire and feelings of love and hate, whatever the patient's personality, background, or gender.

The following is one of my favorite recent examples of this approach, because it displays such impeccable psychoanalytic decorum: An eminent analyst received a phone call one night from a female patient in a state of panic. He immediately scheduled an emergency session, and she arrived at his office in a low-cut evening gown with a fur wrap around her neck and shoulders, explaining that she had been on her way to a social engagement when she called. At the end of the hour, she rose from the couch, considerably calmed; picked up her fur from a chair; and gave it to the analyst. Turning her back, she indicated that he was to drape it around her shoulders. The analyst, a worldly man, realizing that she was assigning him the role of her escort, handed her back the wrap without a word.

One can guess that her hurt and angry feelings about the analyst's rejection might be included among the material of the next session. But this analyst, known to be a man of considerable composure, would betray nothing of his emotional response to the episode nor her reaction to it, though he might decide to remind her of its resemblance to incidents in her early life when her father had also frustrated her expectations.

Freud coined the name "transference" — it first appears in the book he published with Breuer (1957) — to describe those feelings and behaviors, overt or disguised, that kept surfacing to trouble his therapy sessions. He explained them as libidinal attachments and frustrations that patients imported from childhood and pinned on the therapist as a way to repeat the past in the present. At first he considered them to be resistances, neurotic obstacles threatening the course of treatment, but then he found that they could be extremely useful in unraveling the early history of neurotic illness. Later Freud saw another benefit for analysis in the desires awakened through transference. Only something like passionate love for the therapist, he concluded, could sustain the patient through the anxious and painful self-scrutiny necessary to achieve a cure.

There is no question that transference was one of Freud's most significant clinical discoveries or, perhaps more accurately, inventions. By linking sexual desire and infantile dependence, Freud built an entire theory of human development and behavior on the ancient Greek intuition that Cupid is a child. He added that the sexual roots of our conduct are hidden from consciousness as well. Transference lent support to the theories of infantile sexuality and the unconscious and provided the clinician with a concrete means to implement them in therapy. It would not be an overstatement to say that transference made psychoanalysis feasible.

In its initial formulation psychoanalysis emphasized the regressive and pathological facets of love, rather like those ancient cultures which considered falling in love akin to madness or spirit-possession. It ignored the possibility that strong emotions between a therapist and patient, especially those aroused in the therapist by the patient, could in any constructive way be regarded as an end in themselves. In psychoanalysis, such feelings are allowed to flow only in one direction — from patient to therapist. Transference theory is, as John Shlien put it, "the analyst's proclamation of innocence" (1987, p. 28). ... goodness, psychoanalysis, detachment

Is the analyst somehow invulnerable to arousal? It is said that Freud was obliged to conceal an erection at the end of a therapy hour spent with an attractive female patient. If this were true and had become generally known, the theory of transference as a regressive sexual attachment of the patient to a neutral therapist might have been amended. Freud's erection is not easily reconciled with the canon of analytic objectivity. Its exposure would have weakened the authority of those patriarchs of analysis — medical doctors explicating in "dry and direct" tones (Freud's characterization of his manner of talking frankly about sexual acts to innocent young girls) the unconscious, forbidden desires of their patients (Freud, 1963, p. 65). Transference, among others things, was a brilliant tactic which enabled Freud to avoid Breuer's terror, so that he could stay with the patient when sexual feelings started to heat up the therapy office. It wasn't that Freud was blind to the therapist's own longings and fears, but he regarded them as dangerous to the course of treatment. Subjugating the "counter-transference," as he called it, became a crucial part of every analyst's training.

If we hold the psychotherapist more responsible for the effects of his feelings on the patient, we soon begin to burst the confines of transference. From this perspective we can discover in transference theory a thinly cloaked politics, a therapeutic ideology or myth in which the therapist figures as absent hero, and we find ourselves increasingly uneasy about the psychotherapist's cultural role.

Sex as Power: the Politics of Transference

[projection]

The question is not whether transference exists or whether
it is useful, but whether psychotherapists mistake it for the whole
of intimacy in therapy. To the extent that they do, they offer a
reductive vision of love — one that leaves out both its complex,
terrifying politics and its almost religious yearning for transcendence.

Even at their best, intimate relations exist in a precarious
balance. They are always on the verge of being pulled in two directions at once — toward union and toward conflict — because they
are continually buffeted by the competing claims of love and
power. The contradictoriness makes intimacy vulnerable to anxiety-ridden, even violent turbulence. As though it were not hard
enough, love and power have a way of disguising themselves in
each other's clothes. For instance, "surrender" can describe an ec-
static loosening of the self or a capitulation to another's will.
"Bonds" can refer to a freely chosen close and persistent attachment or to the bondage of enslavement or imprisonment. "Commitment" can mean a voluntary, enduring loyalty or a miniature
version of what society does to people it defines as criminals or
insane. Our language for describing erotic experience reflects the
mixture of freedom and determinism that makes love difficult and
ambiguous. Updike's story plays on such difficulties: It dramatizes
how confusion of love and power can occur between patients and
therapists as well as between lovers. Therapists presumably ought
to help us disentangle the sexual from the political when the confusion damages our intimacies. We hardly need them to add more
complications.

Insofar as therapists veil themselves and their procedures in
mystification, they promote further confusions of love and power.

I don't think that this is a satisfactory way to help people deal better with their intimate lives outside of therapy. For example, the classical transference model reduces the therapist to a silhouette, a projection screen dispensing occasional insights. One could argue that the shape of love and power in the transference situation — the yearning sexiness of the needy patient and the detached neutrality of the distant therapist — parodies a patriarchal social order with its emotionally unavailable, power-wielding fathers. Freudian analysis may have succeeded in freeing people's sexuality from neurotic symptoms by clarifying their origins in childhood, but it left them in the grip of patriarchal authority. It is not surprising that so many analyses ended in so-called transference cures, where patients gave up symptoms to please or spite the therapist and then returned to their lives eventually to develop new ones. The political structure of transference has as much to do with the maintenance of patriarchal authority as with the protection of patient and therapist from each other. This is probably why psychoanalysis, which began as a radical enterprise containing an implicit critique of the established order, gradually became a therapy of adjustment to that same order.

Psychoanalysis returned its patients to the danger of further illness because it returned them to a social order built on a foundation of sexual repression and male domination. Feminist historians have shown how the Victorian era's severe, inhibiting attitude toward sexual desire was tied to the oppression of women as a class. For all its usefulness in gaining insight into the patient's history, transference can also be viewed as an ideological instrument of male domination in psychotherapy. Recent developmental theorists, such as Nancy Chodorow and Carol Gilligan, have explained why women seek interdependent intimacy, whereas men tend to detach themselves from it. Transference denies the mutuality of intimate feelings between the therapist and the patient.

The dismantling and revision of classical psychoanalysis has been underway for some time. Nevertheless that part of its legacy involving a powerful, inaccessible therapist has been inherited by many of its successors, as though the invisible God of the bible still reigns in psychotherapy. New therapies have produced new reductionisms. There are behavioral therapies that rob the patient of his subjective experience and give the therapist the paternalistic task of distributing rewards and punishments. Strategic family therapy, the school founded by Jay Haley and his coworkers, scrutinizes intimacy, including that between therapist and patient, for signs of hidden power struggles with as much fervor as the Freudians searched for signs of hidden sexual desire.

Strategic therapy has been valuable in showing us how underground battles for domination figure in marital and family life, but it has let Eros slip away in the meantime. According to this school, all love is power, symptoms are tactics to gain control over others, and therapy is like a chess match in which the therapist is the superior player. Haley (1969) wrote a long essay in which he argued that Jesus Christ, the archetype of spiritual love in western religion, was a brilliant political tactician who rose to power by organizing a mass movement of the wounded and dispossessed. As far as I can recall, Haley never mentions love in this essay.

As strange as it may seem, family therapists, with a few exceptions such as Nathan Ackerman, Carl Whitaker, and R. D. Laing, have simply ignored love and sex as serious subject matter. They interest themselves in the forms of intimacy — patterns, structures, systems, and cybernetic loops — and hardly at all in its content. Their tendency is to equate the therapist with his tech-

139

nique for altering dysfunctional patterns of behavior in individuals, marriages, and families. As a result, the person of the therapist is not just neutralized, as in psychoanalysis, but virtually eliminated. These therapies are perfectly in tune with the era of technology and information processing. So austere is their perception of intimacy that they make transference and countertransference seem in comparison like an operatic duet.

Sex as Language

"There is no sex without talk," wrote the psychiatrist Leslie Farber (1976, p. 167). Erotic love always contains the option of revelatory conversation, even though it may choose to be silent. But sex without self-disclosure is no more than lust. Neither the silences nor the conversations of lust are eloquent; they echo down the stark corridors that reflect the participants' absence from each other. At least such encounters are often mercifully brief. But what about the hopelessness that afflicts unions like that of Updike's adulterous lovers after they marry? These marriages may resound with superficial chatter or interminable complaints or violent quarrels to disguise the deeper silences. Modern marriages too often recall Ford Maddox Ford's description of a troubled marriage in *The Good Soldier* as "a long, silent duel with invisible weapons" (1951, p. 123).

It is perhaps worth reminding ourselves that self-expressive talk is also the primary medium of psychotherapy. Through its work with hysteria, classical psychoanalysis stumbled on the deep, inevitable connection between desire and speech. The repressive sexual morality of the Victorian era tried to make sexuality nearly mute, so that it remained almost unknown and incommunicable.

Perhaps this speechlessness was the true meaning of the unconscious. Hysterical symptoms, so widespread during those times, were themselves a kind of language — a distorted, wordless language of sexuality, especially the sexuality of women painfully confined to the wrong parts of the body. Psychoanalysis made an important contribution to the relief of human suffering when it learned to use the give-and take of free association and interpretation as a method for transforming the unconscious language of symptoms into explicit sexual speech.

The failure of modern psychology to do justice to love and sex is in part a failure of language. Our problem is not that we labor, like the Victorians, under the tyranny of secrecy — certainly not in this age of overflowing information. If the nineteenth century suffered from too much sexual repression, it may be that the twentieth century suffers from too much random sexual expression — which may yet accomplish what repression failed to do: Kill off sex as a passionate and transcendent experience. The formula that has dominated our times — sexual freedom plus social science used as a basis for moral values — however liberating at first, has ended up playing a part in draining the erotic of vitality and mystery. In trying to be scientific, our current psychologies and psychotherapies have contributed almost as much as pornography and narcissism to the waning of sexual love.

Contemporary psychiatrists and psychologists writing about love have produced a pretty uninspiring reading list and, if anything, could improve things by introducing more pornography. Neither the language of object-relations theory, nor the stimulus-response accounts of behaviorism, nor the cybernetic categories of systems theory contain any passionate utterance or imagery. In general, the social sciences have not provided us with a rich vocabulary for understanding intimacy. For example, one of the most flattening (and most inescapable) words we use in talking about intimacy is the word "relationship." In a college math course, I learned that a relationship is something that exists between two variables that affect one another, which can therefore be d scribed in an equation. Lovers affect one another, but variables do not make love (or go through struggles at failing to make love) nor is the act an equation.

What would a behaviorist or a systems therapist make of the scene in *The Magic Mountain* where Hans Castorp passionately celebrates Madame Chauchat's x-ray? For Castorp, her x-ray is a metaphor, a blueprint of his beloved's soul; it's as if he can still see her radiance through it. Sexual love is the poetry of contact. It involves the discipline of connoisseurship, an aesthetic appreciation of another's being. As long as psychotherapeutic theory and practice continues to be dominated by mechanistic thinking, all we are left with is the x-ray.

The best writing on love and marriage comes not from social scientists but philosophers such as Plato, Kierkegaard, and Ortega y Gasset and novelists such as Thomas Hardy, D. H. Lawrence, and Virginia Woolf. Freud admired poets and novelists and thought of them as his precursors.

He came as close as any psychological theorist has to understanding the complexity of erotic life, yet he seems to have had a sense of his own limitations. He backed off from portraying the subjective experience of love and sex in his writings, just as he backed off in therapy through the use of transference. Instead, he presented a theory of the preconditions in mental life which cause love to succeed or fail. When psychological writers come up with "empathetic communication" and other such empty abstractions in their quest for operational definitions of intimacy, one wishes they would back off too.

"pedestrian language does not capture the field"... projection is? serving someone to be... worship it was so?... make it so?-

Psychological theory does not have to be mechanistic. In his book *Thalassa* (1968), Sandor Ferenczi described sexual inter-course as though it were a mixture of paradise and catastrophe. He went on to link sexual desire with a primitive instinctual urge to return to the sea-life from which we came. This may be more imaginative than scientifically accurate, but at least it gives Eros the kind of cosmic scope that D. H. Lawrence always reached for. At times Ferenczi almost managed to adapt the ideas of biological science and psychoanalysis to the unruliness and unpredictability of human passion.

Not all the signs of our times are discouraging. There is a shift away from mechanistic conceptions in modern psychoanalytic practice as well as in other modern schools — Rogerian therapy and Gestalt therapy, for example. Some practitioners insist that therapists can make valid use of their feelings — that it is not enough to view the patient's emotions through a one-way mirror; that awareness or insight heals mostly when the patient feels sup-ported by not only close but affectionate attention. And what is love but close, appreciative attention?

I am not saying that the intimacy of psychotherapy is the same as the other intimacies in our lives nor that it represents any substitute for them. The therapist's job is to pay attention to the patient's needs and not the other way around, whereas husbands and wives or lovers ought to be aware of each other's needs. The asymmetry of therapy is part of what patients pay for. You could say that psychotherapy is to life what a painting of a landscape is to an actual landscape — a carefully edited and condensed version of the real thing. Like a painting, the therapy session exists within a frame that lifts it out of the everyday flow and sets it apart, making it more simplified and finite than life. The idea is that when spectators leave the museum or patients the consulting room, they will walk outside and see the world (and themselves in it) differently.

What intimacy and psychotherapy have in common is that both are emotionally charged, difficult enterprises, demanding persistence, courage, discipline, and self-knowledge. William Carlos Williams wrote that "The business of love is cruelty *which*, by our wills we transform to live together" (Williams, 1962). There's always pain in therapy, as there usually is in love. But the outcome of contending with the painfulness can be a more satisfying human existence.

In many cases, the psychotherapist is the only person that the patient is free to love. That sad truth is among the reasons why people come to therapy in the first place. Maybe only the therapist sees the patient truly naked. Even lovers do not really see each other naked; they are usually still clothed in self-protection. We don't know how to show our souls to each other, and we try to learn in psychotherapy. How can therapists not help but feel intimate when they are being given something close to the total knowledge of another that most of us only dream of? How could they not feel a poignant affection wash over them at such revelations of the human condition?

Freud pointed out that love for the analyst enables the patient to tolerate the anxiety of therapy. We might add that only love for the patient enables the therapist to tolerate therapy without taking refuge in mechanistic theory and technique. Whatever relief it provided from Victorian neurotic symptoms, the formal, studied neutrality of analytic transference is out of date in our day. Yet many influential attempts to go beyond the transference model in psychotherapy seem at least as unsatisfactory. We need to develop a psychology that is more lyrical and ironic, richer in the phenomenology of erotic experience, one that can make the psy-

144

chotherapist a more daring, compassionate explorer and teacher amid the tragicomedies of love and sex in the modern world. Such a theory might help bring the therapist to life in the therapy session. If it is to speak with real conviction to our anguished, faltering, still persistent willingness to risk loving one another, psychotherapy may well demand more emotional communion between therapist and patient than anything psychological theory has yet suggested.

References

Breuer, J., & Freud, S. (1957). *Studies on hysteria*. New York: Basic Books

Farber, Leslie H. (1976). *Lying, despair, jealousy, envy, sex, suicide, drugs, and the good life*. New York: Basic Books.

Ferenczi, S. (1968). *Thalassa: a theory of genitality*. New York: W. W. Norton.

Ford, F. M. (1951). *The good soldier: a tale of passion*. New York: Vintage Books.

Freud, S. (1963). *Dora: an analysis of a case of hysteria*. New York: Collier Books.

Haley, J. (1971). *The power tactics of Jesus Christ and other essays*. New York: Avon Books.

Jones, E. (1953). *The life and work of Sigmund Freud*. New York: Basic Books.

Rieff, P. (1966). *The triumph of the therapeutic: Uses of faith after Freud*. New York: Harper and Row.

Shlien, J. M. (1987). A countertheory of transference. *Person-Centered Review, 2*, 15-49.

Williams, W. C. (1962). *Pictures from Brueghel and other poems.*
    New York: New Directions.
Zweig, S. (1953). *The world of yesterday.* London: Cassell.

The Emptiness of Gestalt Therapy

Originally delivered at the first international Gestalt therapy conference, "A Global Vision: Taking Gestalt Therapy into the 21st Century," which met from November 6-10, 1996, in Cambridge, Massachusetts. Cosponsored by the Boston Gestalt Institute, and The Gestalt Journal, the conference brought together presenters and participants from a global scale to explore views of Gestalt therapy from a broad spectrum of cultures.

The subject of this conference is "taking Gestalt therapy into the 21st century." My talk represents both a lament and a new departure. The lament is that my beloved, idiosyncratic, and aging profession of psychotherapy, as I have known it for twenty-five years, seems to be dying, like a close relative who grows weaker by the day. For a number of reasons, the era that the sociologist Philip Reiff in 1966 named "The Triumph of the Therapeutic" is coming to a close. At least this is true in the United States — and

---

*From *The Gestalt Journal*, Volume XX, No. 2 (Fall, 1997). Reprinted with permission.

perhaps in other countries as well. The therapists themselves, caught up in survival of the fittest amid conditions of scarcity, may be helping kill it off. If so, Gestalt therapists are by no means exempt from this charge. It is true that the scarcity is increasingly real and, in some respects, beyond our control. But our traditional ways of thinking about theory, practice, and even professional organization are helping bring about a decline. Here is the first emptiness that occurs to me, a negative emptiness, a sense of decline and loss.

Do the changes — both the large-scale social changes and the ensuing changes in the status of the profession — that are taking place at the end of the century represent the potential death of psychotherapy? (When I say psychotherapy here, I mean the process of reflective discovery and transformation that includes Gestalt therapy. I am not talking about the ten or so sessions of behavioral-cognitive consultation plus a prescription of antidepressants that characterizes treatment under the new insurance bureaucracies.) Or is it rather that these changes imply the need for a reinvention of psychotherapy as we have known and cherished it? I mentioned a new departure. The new departure I have in mind is a way of reinterpreting the meaning and practice of psychotherapy, particularly Gestalt therapy, that, I believe, can help renew its soul and may point to some fruitful possibilities for a new definition of its role in society. And this, as I will try to show in the course of this talk, involves the conversion of negative emptiness into a positive emptiness.

In an atmosphere of scarcity people's conflicts over differences grow especially bitter and desperate. One can see this in a troubled marriage, for example, where an artificial scarcity tends to get created, as though there's only enough to serve one person's needs — especially the need for self-expression and recognition.

Then a disastrous shift takes place. Given scarce resources, imagined or real, bids for power and domination replace the appreciative respect for differences that is a necessary ingredient of love. The important aspect of this that I want to bring out here is that each party to the now conflicted relationship puts forward a view that he or she claims is the whole truth.

In a bad marriage, each person's claim to truth is an account of the relationship that aims to prove that the other person is at fault. In the profession of psychotherapy it's the narrowing of theory or technique used to prove that one party has the true psychoanalysis or Gestalt therapy or what have you. Karl Marx, now an almost forgotten figure, taught us more than psychology has about a group's or subculture's insistence that its beliefs have a hold on the Truth. Marx argued that all theories and intellectual systems are ideologies, which means that they are abstract constructs assembled by intellectuals and professionals to shore up their position in society with respect to social class or wealth or authority. I am not trying to reduce all psychology to mere ideology; the theories and techniques within each discipline, as well as across them, offer valuable tools for understanding and guiding one's work. But I am arguing for tolerance of pluralism and curiosity about other points of view. The more ways in which one can construct various frames, perspectives, and narratives for making sense of phenomena the better.

When theory is used reductively to exclude differences and to bolster superiority, it becomes ideology. The great virtue of pluralism, which gives rise to fluidity and development of vision through cross-fertilization, is lost. At their worst, the quarrels in our profession turn ad hominem, which shows how much they are about power, ego, and market-share. People who have something to say to one another — and who could build strength through complimentariness and counterpoint — no longer speak to each other. Their silence plays a large role in creating a negative emptiness.

The entire history of psychotherapy, like the history of modern marriage, is fraught with factional disputes — perhaps because, besides economic considerations, like marriage the profession of psychotherapy entails such fundamental issues of identity and intimacy. The original Freudian circle, as you know, was filled with backstabbing, competition, and excommunications. Freud rid himself of his disobedient disciples, and some of his followers worked hard at doing each other in. Jung was thrown out for dissenting views. Then Ferenczi and Rank, two of the most inventive minds in the early psychoanalytic movement, were exiled for straying too far from the party line. A. A. Brill, who at one point headed the American psychoanalytic organization and who translated several of Freud's major works into English, once introduced Otto Rank's speech to an international congress at Madison Square Garden with the warning that Rank was psychotic. Later, in France, Jacques Lacan was tossed out of the chief Freudian organization, whereupon he founded his own.

Similarly Gestalt therapy was marked by cleavages from its beginnings. The two figures mainly responsible for the brilliant definitive early text, *Gestalt Therapy: Excitement and Growth in the Human Personality*, Frederick Perls and Paul Goodman, ended their good will toward each other not long after its publication. Perls hardly ever referred to this book again, as he went on to California to develop his own Gestalt approach, a mixture of psychoanalysis and existentialism, psychodrama and Buddhism. Goodman remained till his death a New York intellectual, a "man of letters" as his book jackets always put it. He eventually left psychotherapy behind and became one of America's greatest social and culture critics. Yet all his writings continued to be saturated with the principles of Gestalt therapy, which led to penetrating insights that are still extremely useful for us to draw from. With respect to the theory and practice of Gestalt therapy proper, it remained for Isadore From, along with the steady contribution of Laura Perls, to carry on from where Goodman left off. I had the good fortune to study with or know as friends every one of these people, who are now all dead. I also learned from some creative teachers who are still very much alive and are here tonight — Erving and Miriam Polster and Joseph Zinker — when they were still together at the Cleveland Institute. Their wide spectrum of differences enriched me in viewpoint, sensibility, and skills. Emptiness, for me, in the negative sense is an ideological state of oppressive reduction, where certain differences are condemned and ruled out.

Is it that Perls and Goodman had nothing more to say to each other? Don't you believe it! The tragic thing is that those people who often might have the most to say to each other are the ones who stop talking or worse. Freud gave us a valuable concept for understanding this phenomenon: He called it "the narcissism of small differences." The more intimate, the closer in spirit and outlook two parties might be, Freud pointed out, the more cruel and barbaric the conflict over their differences can become, because in competitive circumstances they have to go so much further to distinguish themselves from each other. What else could explain why neighbors who use to live and work together were precisely the ones who inflicted the most barbaric rape and mutilation upon each other's families in Bosnia? What else could explain Freud's and Brill's devaluing treatment of Otto Rank, who Freud once looked upon as his heir apparent? What else explains our periodic bouts of incivility toward one another, boycotting each other's Gestalt therapy conferences and journals?

Can you imagine the further development that might have occurred if Frederick Perls and Paul Goodman had continued their collaboration, along with Laura and Isadore and others, throughout the 1960s? Instead we ended up with — and still have — Perlsians versus Goodmanians, East versus West, the "hot seat" and psychodrama techniques versus theory, feelings against intellect. Not only in America: I've have seen similar splits in nearly every country in which I have taught; in addition there are all the ones I have only heard about.

This recurrent balkanization of Gestalt therapy, as far as I'm concerned, is one of the most boring things about it. It tends to produce stagnation and impasse. It's not that there is a lack of excellent Gestalt therapists and teachers both here and abroad; it's not that there is a complete absence of forward motion of achievement in Gestalt therapy. It's that a great deal of useful energy gets squandered, leaving Gestalt therapy much more impoverished than it needs or ought to be — "The expense of spirit in a waste of shame," as Shakespeare put it. Let me list just a couple of the lost opportunities. The important contribution to Gestalt therapy of the pragmatism of William James and John Dewey via Paul Goodman, who was much shaped by these thinkers, has hardly been noted, much less explored (with the exception of some hints from the late Ernest Becker). Then, even though the word phenomenology is tossed around often enough, mostly by people who know little about it, the crucial relation for Gestalt therapy of phenomenological intentionality to the concept of gestalt formation is barely understood, except, so far as I know, by a few Gestalt therapists in Europe who make it a point to concentrate on such matters. Yet this relationship is spelled out in great detail in the work of Maurice Merleau-Ponty and Aron Gurwitsch.

I do think that things are going to get worse, as we head toward the year 2000. I mentioned that we are presently in circumstances of increasing real scarcity. In this country — and I'll have to let each of you from other countries adjust the following description to fit your own social conditions — we are in the midst of what can only be called a second industrial revolution. It's called "managed care," one of the most grotesque Orwellian oxymorons yet to come along. With respect to mental health, managed care is supposed to distribute treatment more broadly and cheaply. What this really means is that the same sources of capital who made the most of factories and mass production in the nineteenth century are at it again. The first industrial revolution was about the efficient production of goods; this one is about services. The bankers, big insurance companies, and major pharmaceutical corporations know that there are of billions of dollars in profits to be made from health care.

Just as in the first period of monopoly capitalism, these forces have to institutionalize and rationalize production — this time around, the production of health care services — for the sake of economic efficiency, that is, to cut their costs. So it becomes necessary to put psychotherapists on the assembly line. In a very few years, the fate of the solo private practitioner will resemble the artisans of old who left their home workshops for the factory assembly line or went broke. Private practice will serve only a few wealthy people who are willing and able to pay for therapy as though they are purchasing a beautiful handcrafted cabinet made from fine wood. The rest will shop for mass-produced bedroom suites in a discount department store: ten sessions of cognitive therapy or behavior mod and a year's supply of Prozac. There's going to be less to go around for private practice and training institutes. Factional disputes and claims to possess the truth will intensify in virulence.

By the way, you may think I am speaking against psychopharmacology. I'm not. I think that the debate between psychotherapy and psychopharmacology is mostly stupid and pointless — or rather it misses the real point. These are not substitutes for each other. Arguments about which is better are irrelevant, and the most thoughtful and informed therapists and psychopharmacologists know this very well. I participate every week in an interdisciplinary seminar right here at Cambridge Hospital. The director of psychopharmacology, the head of neuropsychology, several distinguished psychoanalysts and other therapists, along with a theologian, an accomplished painter, a writer of biographies, an anthropologist, and a famous philosopher of science attend this seminar. I am the group's token Gestalt therapist. Our discussions take place on the cutting edge of several fields. One thing has emerged clearly. Everything one can learn about the human brain and everything one can learn about the human will and imagination is fascinating, valuable, and has interactive possibilities.

The head of psychopharmacology puts the relationship between selective serotonin reuptake inhibitors and psychotherapy this way: Imagine you have a map showing all the routes for getting to your destination. Imagine you full of purpose about where you want to go and how to get there. But the automobile you own has faulty spark plugs and will barely limp along. How good will the trip be? This is a vastly oversimplified analogy, of course, but it makes the essential point. Prozac and its relatives can tune the biological engine; psychotherapy fires the curiosity and will, provides the map (and perhaps the tour guide). In the terms of Gestalt therapy, the one might be said to relate more to support, the other to contact, though no doubt each involves matters of both support and contact. There is nothing in what I am going to discuss next that precludes the potential usefulness of psychopharmacology.

* * *

Given the pressures to rationalize and medicalize therapy — to turn it, in effect, into a prefabricated mass treatment for the lowest cost relief of symptoms, what else is there for patients and therapists alike who look to psychotherapy for something more? Of course, therapy can help relieve symptoms, which is a crucially important benefit, but that is only one of its functions, and medication probably does it at least as well. What, then, of Gestalt therapy, with its rich aesthetic and phenomenological basis?

I submit to you that the real power of psychotherapy, beyond its usefulness for the relief of symptoms, has been its radical and dramatic insight into the nature of human reality. Psychotherapy, from its beginnings, has offered us liberation by showing us that reality is made through our own construction, even though certain constructs become collectivized or universalized and treated as a kind of solid thing. Thus it may be that there are any number of realities potentially available to human experience. Freedom, from this perspective, means that life is a theater and one is both playwright and an actor on its stage, an agent who composes existence like an artist. The idea of so fluid an existence is sufficiently threatening to most cultures such that families and social institutions quickly strip it from us when we are still children. It tends to stay lost, since society continues to be in charge of the definition of reality. And society has a huge arsenal of weapons at its disposal to enforce its will. For example, the great psychiatrist Harry Stack Sullivan pointed out that every culture socializes us, which entails forcing a particular reality upon us, by grabbing us where it hurts — that is, by our most primitive anxieties of being abandoned.

Psychotherapy can help us learn that life is a theater because therapy itself is a form of theater. It always has been. Let me begin with Freud, since as you might have guessed from my comments yesterday, I am out to vindicate at least some of Freud against his present-day hordes of detractors. Psychoanalysis supposedly works through interpretation, specifically through interpreting the patient's present difficulties in terms of underlying causes in his or her early childhood. Now what exactly are these interpretations? They do not merely specify the causes of later effects based on the model of natural science. It is true that Freud stressed this aspect of psychoanalytic theory in his metapsychology, probably for several reasons. Among them: It was the currency of innovative thought during his age. And given his position as a Jew in an antisemitic society, he no doubt had an understandable desire to couch his revolution in terms of scientific and medical legitimacy.

When you think about them, Freud's actual interpretations are often drawn from the eternal motifs of high theater. They are filled with the stuff of melodrama, ritual, and tragedy. The infant's development, as he depicts it, is no mere unfolding of neat biological and psychological phases but is fraught with incestuous wishes, violent pornography, which Freud called the "primal scene," a secret urge to overthrow God the Father, fears of castration, a brotherhood of barbarians, which Freud called the "primal horde," and the like. Where did Freud learn all this? From the ancient Greeks, from Goethe, from Shakespeare, not from the enlightenment rationalism of Newton, Galileo, and Francis Bacon. Perhaps the latter emphasis served as his cover.

The psychoanalytic unconscious behaves like a playwright who casts on the little stage of the nuclear family combinations of Gothic horror tales and Greek tragedies. Then the ego steps in, along with its guardian at the gates, the superego, and in accord with society's dictates, lays on a thick patina of mundane social reality. Yet the buried subjective reality with its extraordinary themes and motifs remains the driving force. But all that peeps through now are residues or hints called neurotic symptoms.

What seems implicit in Freud's view but eventually got lost through a variety of factors — his own ambivalence, the desire to make psychoanalysis a respectable science, later commentaries, and translations of his works — was the notion that psychoanalysis explores the creation of meaning, even if such creation is left too much in the therapist's hands and not enough in the collaboration of patient and therapist as we would emphasize in Gestalt therapy. This is something quite different from the kind of interpretation that tends to narrow the patient's experience to causality.

Viewed in this way, psychoanalysis becomes a method to help loosen and shift the patient's neurotic determinism into the blend of distance and identification that theater has always provided. It places the patient in the position of audience or observer of his or her experience as well as author of it, to a substantial degree at least, which holds out the promise that he or she can change it. Granted that Freud had an authoritarian side that tended to force the issue; granted that his own projections, which ranged from Greek tragedy to sexual soap opera, probably became too involved. When he tried to cure Dora's hysterical symptoms by confronting her with this stuff, she would have none of it and fled. But something very radical and intriguing was going on in all this. You can find further developments of it in certain subsequent psychoanalytic thinkers. Herbert Fingarette, a British philosopher, argued several decades ago in a book called *The Self in Transformation* that psychoanalytic interpretations had little or nothing to do with recovering anyone's actual infantile history, which could never be truly known. What they offered instead was the possibility of nudging patients toward new frames of meaning that enabled them to make more sense of and take more control over their present productions. More recently, Donald Spence, a well-known psychoanalyst, wrote a book in which he put forward much the same viewpoint with respect to dreams, suggesting that one never interprets the actual dream but rather makes a new aesthetic creation based on the dream as reported in the present situation of the therapy session.

When you add to such outlooks the growing number of modern psychoanalysts who insist on making their therapy a task of collaborative reconstruction with the patient, we are not very far away from Gestalt therapy.

Here, it seems to me, is where we need to go to resurrect the radical soul of psychotherapy. We have to look into the heart of Freud's work — and into Ferenczi's, Rank's, Wilhelm Reich's, Winnicott's, Michael Balint's, Milton Erickson's, Jay Haley's and R.D. Laing's, as well as into the work of Frederick Perls, who was nothing if not a dramatist, that of the anarchist Paul Goodman, and that of Isadore From, the phenomenological philosopher of Gestalt therapy. All of these psychotherapists and thinkers held out the dream of freedom among fluid and pluralistic realities, in which one could influence the shape of one's existence. All of them taught modes of transcending one's blind and apparently fixed circumstances through a kind of non-attachment. Such psychotherapy is truly the Buddhism of the West. But to follow in its path we need now to empty psychotherapy of a great deal of paraphernalia it has saddled itself with: aspirations to theory that, like natural science, has sweeping explanatory and predictive power, techniques or technologies for "cure," notions of normality as health, and especially the ideological tendency to believe that some one outlook has a hold on the truth. Maybe we could think of this as the beginnings of a positive emptiness.

Let me make a case for why I think that Gestalt therapy may be uniquely positioned for this restorative work to bring out the soul of psychotherapy. First, it has a basis in existential phenomenology. Among other things, this means that it emphasizes the relational intersubjectivity of our power to meet with and engage otherness in a democratic collaboration, called contact, which constructs and gives form to our experience of reality. Gestalt therapy thus collapses the distinction between inner and outer, surface and depth, appearance and reality, following Jean-Paul Sartre when he says, "The appearances which manifest the existent are neither interior nor exterior; they are all equal, they all refer to other appearances, and none of them is privileged . . . No action indicates anything which is *behind itself*; it indicates only itself and the total series." There is no qualitative distinction between the theatrical and the real. Or as the poet W. B. Yeats put it, "Seeming that lasts a lifetime is no different from reality." It is important to point out that although this is a dramaturgical perspective, it is a theater of the ordinary, one that finds sufficient mystery and richness in the continuum of everyday experience. Nothing is hidden, all is revealed, as both Sartre and Yeats tell us, yet everything is inexhaustibly mysterious, because it is so full of multiplicity and horizon, as Husserl proclaimed. Thus it keeps changing and becoming unknown. I take it that this what Perls meant when he said that Gestalt therapy is the philosophy of the obvious and then added that the obvious is the most difficult thing for us to grasp.

Secondly, the concept of Gestalt formation tells us how experience is made and how in the process it becomes impressed with the idiosyncratic stamp of a particular person's longings, interests, hungers, curiosities, tendencies, rhythms, temperament. And as these change and as circumstances change, so does the creation of reality. Isadore From used to say "A hungry rat sees food. A horny rat sees prospective sexual partners." The two rats have different realities. Given this respect for each person's different productions, we replace the normal as a criterion for health, which is a statistical concept, with the aesthetic, which preserves singularity but also says, let's see if you can create more graceful, more satisfying compositions from the materials of your life. Health, as Joseph Zinker put it in the title of his recent book, always involves a "search for good form." To paraphrase Isadore From again, the task of Gestalt therapy is to help a person make of his walking his dancing, of his talking his poetry.

Do we then require a theory of Gestalt therapy? We certainly have a number of unique and valuable concepts. Those of you who are familiar with my writings know that I have for many years called for and even tried to sketch out more solid theoretical elaboration of human development, personality, psychopathology, and so forth in the terms that are distinctive to Gestalt therapy. I don't repudiate this work by any means, but my ideas of what a theory is and what it is good for have changed considerably, especially since I have been reading not only some phenomenology philosophy but also the works of Wittgenstein. At this point I'm not so sure that we or any other psychotherapy work from what is best thought of as a theory. What does it mean to have a "theory" of psychotherapy anyway?

In physics and the other natural sciences, one endeavors to build models of varying degrees of abstraction that set forth particular relationships between variables. These relationships tell you that if certain things occur, other things are likely to happen. Such models involve definitions, which often have to be sharpened and resharpened, that specify the entities one is concerned with, and premises, often derived from hypotheses that have been empirically verified according to statistical or other criteria. One makes inferences, obeying the laws of logic, from the premises, leading to results that predict something. In part, the predictive power resides in getting the right level of abstraction. The assumption is that everyone or everything does it pretty much in the same way. There's not much room here for personal style.

I'm not sure we want a theory like this. The value in the concepts of Gestalt therapy is not in what they predict to this or that degree of statistical significance. It is that they are filled with our subjectivity, our possibilities of personal style, and a common sense view of what it can be like to be in the world. The occupational hazard of theories, as Wittgenstein knew very well, is that they require abstraction, which can lead readily to reification. Of course, abstraction is useful; the trouble comes when abstract entities are treated as though they are what really exists, as "things" that actually make up the world. With respect to psychotherapy, we have seen plenty of this in the reification of the unconscious and of object relations, as well as of the operational variables of behaviorism. Behaviorism comes closest to meeting the criteria of science, because operationalizing variables turns them into something that can be measured physically. But where does it leave us? With an empty shell.

Wittgenstein's critique of abstract entities treated as reality went very far, extending even to the natural sciences. He said, and I quote, "what a Copernicus or a Darwin really achieved was not the discovery of a true theory, but of a fertile new point of view."

By point of view, Wittgenstein intends, as he puts it, "means of representation" or even "a manner of speaking" in a language game in which everybody understands the rules. I think that the concepts we employ in Gestalt therapy, such as "contact boundary," "present moment," "awareness," "projection," and "introjection," are best understood in the spirit of what Wittgenstein meant when he said that for the most part theories are little more than "points of view." I would put an accent on both "point" and "view." The concepts that make up Gestalt therapy point us in certain directions, enabling us to view something, that is, to attend to certain possibilities that we are able to experience in a useful way.

But we have to maintain a certain vigilance. The danger of reification always looms where there is conceptual language, so that the longer terms hang around, the more they tend to harden and take on an appearance of solid existence. That's why psychological language keeps dying on the vine. It's why I tend to prefer an ordinary language psychology, which uses words like love, hate, curiosity, innocence, play, disappointment. Already ideas like "contact boundary," "present moment," and "awareness" are too often plunked down automatically in teaching and writing about Gestalt therapy and the results can be deadening, though conferences like this one are sometimes preventive medicine.

For example, there is no such thing as the "present moment," because it is not an entity that we can fix on with ontological precision, which would be the prerequisite for saying that it exists. William James once pointed out that "the literally present moment is a purely verbal supposition, not a position; the only present ever realized concretely being the 'passing moment' in which the dying rearward of time and its dawning future forever mix their lights." There is no "contact boundary" that anyone can see or measure. Show me a contact boundary. You can't. It's part of what Petruska Clarkson, speaking here, called "the Heraclitean flux." And awareness of what exactly? Of reality? Of ourselves in the process of experiencing? Can anyone describe it to me precisely and show me the mechanism by which it works?

None of these things exist, or perhaps one should say that they are a rough approximation to something we call existence. We must be very careful about claiming that they compose a theory, except in a loose and metaphorical sense. They cannot be either proved or disproved, anymore than the existence of an unconscious could be in psychoanalysis. But that does not imply that we cannot use these concepts fruitfully. Indeed we do so everyday in our teaching and in informing our work with patients. When we say awareness or contact, we might think of these as interpretations of human experience in the sense of what Wittgenstein means by a "language game." In that respect, they do something extremely useful, pointing to concrete identifiable human experiences, directing our attention to certain possibilities and framing them. For instance, no one worked with these concepts more exactingly than Isadore From. But how did he use them? Let me give you an example: Isadore would ask a training group, Who do you trust more — someone saying "I love you" or someone saying "I really love you?" The answer is generally clear enough — the one who says, "I love you." But why? Isadore would explain it this way: "I love you" might be a simple expression of a conviction, direct, authentic, and thus making contact in the sense of touching or moving you. Then, of course, you can reply "good" or "too bad" or perhaps a great deal more. But the "really" protests too much. It is superfluous language, a sign of retroflection, which is a disturbance of contact. The lack of conviction is conveyed because the retroflection frequently hides a projection, which is "you won't believe me, so I had better intensify it," meaning "I don't believe

163

myself." I have put this in terms of our so-called theory. But now tell me what theory could possibly predict Isadore's analysis? Perhaps the idea that superfluous language indicates retroflection and that retroflection may cover a projection might alert you about where to concentrate and explore. But beyond this formulation Isadore was delivering some provocative and ingenious literary or drama criticism here. It is the kind of acute if small insight that can make something new happen in the therapy session and move things forward.

The point is that this is an instance of Isadore's *practice*, grounded in the intersection of his personal style with a great deal of experience. I can't bring out enough the idea of a practice and of practicing, in all senses of the words. You can see from this example that you cannot get from theory to what it is Gestalt therapists do, except after the fact, although learning the concepts thoroughly before the fact — which is part of training — directs your sensibility and alertness. Our theory ought to be thought of more like theories of harmony and counterpoint in music. They are codifications abstracted from the practice of great composers, and they help inform and guide you. But you can't get directly from reading books on harmony and counterpoint to composing a string quartet. A lot of disciplined experience has to go on in between.

Finally, let me return for a moment to my psychotherapy theater. Transference is certainly a theatrical or even cinematic concept, invented by psychoanalysis to show how the creation of meaning and thus feelings in a present relationship was profoundly influenced by the past. Gestalt therapy, through Paul Goodman — I have written about this in an introduction to a collection of Goodman's essays — borrowed it rather directly without naming it as such and made it even more actively focused in the present situation. Goodman shows us not only how the patient is still constructing the present relationship to reflect what failed in the past one but also how the therapy session offers a chance to try out discovering a new solution with this new person, the therapist. However, I am less interested in the theater of transference these days than I am in what I will call the theater of transport, which not only suggests moving freely from one place to another, let's say, among multiple realities, but also implies absorption, accompanied by strong and often intensely pleasurable emotion, as the dictionary defines absorption. I don't know that transference is usually all that much fun, but I think transport is. The arts have often been thought of as entertainment that instructs. That would not be such a bad program for the future of psychotherapy. I'd like to think that psychotherapy in the 21st century could be less like taking your medicine and more like going to the movies.

∫ The Myth of We

Originally delivered as a Keynote Address at the 2nd World Congress for Psychotherapy, sponsored by The World Council for Psychotherapy, in Vienna, July 4-8, 1999.

I don't know whether it's more accurate to say that we invent stories or that they invent us. Probably both are true. Call them myths, call them dreams, call them realities, we need stories to live our lives. For one thing, they remind us that we are subjects, by and large shaping our own characters in a plot at least partly of our own devising. This is especially important in an era when so many forces encourage us to treat ourselves like biological objects. Stories reflect how it feels, what it is like, to be fully human. And they inform us that being human subjects means that we live in a world in which we are deeply embedded. They show us that our world is always in front of us, with us and behind us. We have to live in what you might call the between. Whatever the self might

*From *The Gestalt Journal*, Vol. XXIII, No. 1. (Spring, 2000). Reprinted with permission.

167

be, there is always otherness, and we continually meet it at every turn. Like the stories themselves, it is a world that we make, but it also makes us. We need the stories to live our lives because as humans we seem to need meaning to be able to live coherently. The collapse or loss of meaning tends to make us crazy, drives us to disintegration and destruction.

The good stories, the most valuable ones, also tell us that we can never know as much as we want to know. Not only is there little certitude about what is, so to speak, "out there," but we don't know with anything approaching causal predictability who we are and what we will do next. That life deals us continual surprises is what Heraclitus, the pre-Socratic Greek philosopher, meant when he said you can't bathe in the same river twice. You can't step into the same world or even the same self twice. Granted that we frequently behave as if we can, but making this a habit leads to repression, illusions of control, and neurotic fixations. Such is the human condition as reflected in stories.

What we know, perhaps all we can know, is our actual experience. Not what underlies it or what causes it. The best stories begin with our profound longings, but leave us with wonder and mystery. They insist that we live in a difficult world, one that is fraught with obstacles to our desires and our wills. They make it clear that we live in time, that there are disappointments, mistakes, and failures along the way, that we decay and die. Yet they still point the direction to a fulfilling life despite the drawbacks. The less valuable stories, or, worst of all, the dangerous ones, begin with our profound longings and then end up lying to us in order to soothe us. They tempt us to believe that love is eternal; that we can be heroes of efficient action or glamorous style; that we can be the fastest gun in the west or the lover every man or woman dreams of without even having to work very hard at it. They promise that we can get to the bottom of human motives; that we can conquer evil; or that we will achieve salvation from all pain and limitation and, at some point, probably after we die, return to paradise.

From its beginnings psychotherapy has been about stories. Nowadays there are schools of so-called narrative therapy, but they are hardly the only ones that tell stories. In *The Interpretation of Dreams*, Freud said that our dreams reveal underlying processes and forces, which reflected the scientific attitude of his time. But the stories he made up to explain dreams were Greek tragedies and Gothic horror tales of incest and patricide and castration. Today they seem more satisfying to us as dramas than scientific explanations. Already in Freud's time, both Jung and Rank tended to let the science go and allowed their fascination with stories to permeate their theories.

That we invent stories and that they invent us, that we make the world and it makes us, and that all we can know is our experience, which we participate in creating — these ideas are close in spirit to the philosophy called phenomenology. I say close to it because I'm not concerned with trying to be precise about the term at the moment. I simply want to point out that it's a view of the human condition at the heart of the psychotherapy that I practice and teach, Gestalt therapy. It is from this point of view that I want to deal with a particular story or myth about love, a mixed blessing of a story that I call "The Myth of We."

This myth of intimate togetherness contains at once the best and the worst of our enduring stories. Though it exists in many variations, they all address the same fundamental human need for love. It captures one of our most elemental aspirations — the desire for union with another — but also fools us into expecting certitude in love. Why would we want certitude? Because love, among our most basic needs, has a special characteristic: we want it desperately and we fear it at the same time. When you are hungry, you go to the world to get food, when you are thirsty you search for something to drink. Obviously there are situations where the coming together of hunger or thirst and the source of meeting those needs fails because the need is blocked or the supplies are scarce. But, as a rule, things go fairly smoothly. When we need love, however, we reach out to the world to get it — and everything all too often turns into a mess. Why? Why does it have to be so difficult?

Well, I think the reasons are inherent in an inescapable fact of human development. At the beginning of our lives, love and dependence are virtually indistinguishable from one another. For the infant or young child love, in a sense, is a matter of survival. This alone is surely enough to give love an uneasy edge. To make matters worse, we have the probably the longest dependence on adult caretakers of any animal. I once watched a documentary movie about sharks. Now, I don't know if I got it exactly right, but let me tell you what I thought I saw. There was a scene showing the birth of a baby shark. The baby shark was fighting its way out of a kind of egg or membrane. Some adult sharks, let's call them parent sharks, hovered nearby. When the baby shark got free of its egg, it sort of looked with a menacing grin (this is how I saw it) at the parent sharks, and it immediately shot out for the open sea. And I thought to myself, I bet there are no neurotic sharks.

For us the open sea is a long way off. We start out unable to distinguish love from dependence, and a great many people that I know are unable to distinguish love from dependence for the rest of their lives. I think the hardest thing in adult life is to separate love from dependence enough to find one's balance between them, since they are necessarily merged at the starting point. The striving for autonomy starts early, too, but how it goes depends on the family. Consider for instance, the stage of development that we call "the terrible twos" in the United States — I don't know what you call it in Austria, but I'm sure you go through it — first as children, then as parents. During the terrible twos a child begins to say no. Discovering the power of saying no (because up to this point the child pretty much says yes — although I have to admit that my son began protesting the minute he was born), the child begins saying no to absolutely everything in kind of ecstasy of negativity. So why does it later become the hardest word to learn to use comfortably or convincingly?

Some parents are made very anxious by their child's refusals, so they overwhelm the child's no-saying. But the child's no is crucially important because it is the beginning of his or her more fully separating out an identity from the first dependencies. There is, of course, some earlier separating as well. The first appearance of the individual's sense of "I," the psychological separateness from the mother or from adult caretakers, is accompanied by anxiety. This is probably our first knowledge of anxiety, though not necessarily our first experience of it. You could say that the sense of self and the knowledge of anxiety are born at the same moment. Classical psychoanalytic theory called it "primary separation anxiety." In my book, *Intimate Terrorism*, I speak of it as abandonment anxiety. But there is another important developmental anxiety as well. If parents, during the terrible twos, don't allow the child's no to evolve freely, if, for example, they are too anxious themselves and prevent the child's no, they fortify this other kind of anxiety which I call engulfment anxiety. (To be sure, there are some things you can't allow the child to say no to, but parents ought to be sensitive to which battles are worth fighting.) Engulfment anxiety is the fear of being devoured, controlled, colonized by the large, powerful caretakers upon whom one depends. We all grow up contending to some degree with both these existential anxieties — abandonment anxiety and engulfment anxiety.

Human development proceeds as an exchange, a continuous give-and-take, between two basic, somewhat opposed impulses — the need to belong and join intimately, which includes a measure of dependence; and the need to know and express one's solitary, idiosyncratic, willful identity. When you reach adolescence, the main developmental task is to reconcile and integrate these two sets of needs. Let me call them the claims of the "I" and the claims of the "we." The problems with this difficult integration come when there has already been an overdose of either abandonment anxiety or engulfment anxiety in the course of growing up. The work of integration requires the freedom to say no as well as yes. Woe is the child whose ability to freely say no has been tabooed or choked off. Then he or she goes into adult life doing battle with or clinging to an internalized parental "we," anchored in place by anxiety. And from then on intimate surrender to another feels either like a desperate necessity or a threatening loss of oneself.

During puberty and adolescence — a time of struggle with such delicate balances — western culture tends to hit us hardest with the Myth of We. In its most highly idealized and sought-after form it's known as romantic love. We learn that we are going to fall in love on some enchanted evening. Two strangers happen to look up from talking or eating or whatever activity at a social gathering and their eyes meet. The meaning of their lives up to this point suddenly falls into place. It's as if a bolt is released, and a door in the soul swings open. In a trance of destiny, this new budding "we" walks out of the party or dinner into the evening. There is a full moon, and the willow trees dangle their branches along the riverbank as "we" walk along it. Even the birds sing a different song that night just for "us." Romantic love is a marvelous experience, and I certainly wouldn't want to deprive anyone of experiencing it. I couldn't anyway.

The trouble in paradise comes when people cling to this beautiful, transient dream of love as an ideal or ideology on which to base every day ordinary intimacy, by which I mean making a life together over the course of years and maybe decades. Like benevolent parents who might block the child from saying no for the sake of family harmony (an early form of the Myth of We), the romantic ideal sweetly discourages disagreement, honest conflict, two people's capacities to openly say no to one another. Thus it leaves couples beached on the shoals of adolescence with the task of reconciling the claims of being oneself and being with another still unfinished.

What happens finally is that this dream of a perfect we, of two as one, like Adam and Eve in the garden before the apple, ends in a betrayal. It has to, because though it is wonderful for adolescent first love — and I hope that all of us, even at my age, can now and then experience renewals of adolescent first love — it provides no firm footing on which to build a life of intimacy. And with so little to support the formidable discipline of constructing an intimate relationship, people tend to fall into a profound disappointment. Whether it's an hour after making love the first time or whether it's the next morning or whether it's after the honeymoon or a year later in the marriage, whenever it happens, there comes a fall into disappointment. The disappointment may an inevitable stage of love — I tend to think it is — but heaven knows it is made worse, often fatal, when two people discover that they are not one unit but two solitudes struggling to choreograph differences that can generate innumerable possibilities of friction.

As a Gestalt therapist with a great deal of experience working with couples, I've spent a lot of time recently thinking about

Adam and Eve because I think they are an endlessly intriguing couple. Where else in history do you get a creation myth that is based not on magic animals, not on demigods, but on an ordinary middle-class couple who launch human history by doing what every married couple ever since has done? They set each other off on a contagious sequence of bad judgments; they blame each other when things go wrong. You notice, by the way, that Eve is the one who gives in to temptation. Throughout the ages Genesis has been used like a legal brief to suggest that women can't control their animal impulses, so men have to keep them in their place. That is the male myth of the fall. As a matter of fact, however, Eve is the member of the first pair who at least had a little initiative. Adam invented passive-aggressive masculinity. He believes in still another myth — that of the good boy. You can hold onto the Garden of Eden, which offers the best real estate on the planet and everything else you could want as long as you obey God the Father. In this version, Eve is a bad girl, but is she in fact governed by her wilder impulses? No, she is tempted by intellectual curiosity — she wants to know more. And why shouldn't she be interested in knowing more? But, to be sure, you are not supposed to be too curious — we are all punished for being too curious.

All Eve has to say to Adam is "try this, it's good," and he goes along with her and takes a bite of the apple. Whereupon God shows up. Adam and Eve go into hiding in the bushes because now they know they are naked, and they are embarrassed. God says, "Adam, where art thou?" You notice He doesn't even mention Eve. And Adam replies, "I'm here in the bushes, God. I'm naked." "Who told you that?" asks God. "It was the woman," Adam replies, "the woman made me eat the apple." And that's the beginning of marital scapegoating and power struggle that continues to this very day. It's still a usable parable, this story of Adam

174

and Eve. In the Garden of Eden they could have maintained a perfect union, a perfect we. Of course, they were naked there, too, and it didn't bother them in the least. Then they ate this apple, and what did they discover? The knowledge of good and evil, and the knowledge that they would die. This was the forbidden knowledge that would make them like God. Now Adam and Eve look at one another, and they "know" that they are naked. So they don the first fig leaves.

It has always been said that what they feel is shame. Their new self-consciousness about their nakedness is the beginning of sexual shame, and it is followed up by the Judeo-Christian war on sexual pleasure. Maybe so, but I'd like add something to this notion. I think it may have also been the first experience of intimate disappointment. Perhaps Adam and Eve looked at each other now with awareness of change and death and saw for the first time in each other's nakedness the signs of aging and decay. And they said to each other, "Oh, you are not really who I thought you were! Already your breasts are beginning to sag a little . . . Already you are getting a bit of a potbelly." There's still shame in this, but also disappointment. It's what happens in every relationship when two people leave the weeping willow-bird-song-moonlight stage — in other words, pass from the extraordinary state we call romantic love into ordinary love. This is a very difficult transition, and I believe that our culture needs rather desperately to support it by creating new stories that help us learn to live an ordinary love in the context of everyday life. This would be what it means to love in the here-and-now. One can see difficulties, of course: It's one thing to say to your partner, I love you passionately, I love you madly, but how do you tell someone, I love you ordinarily? Getting this across, after infatuation dies down, may be the more heroic work of art.

I am a Gestalt therapist who tends to avoid the specialized language of Gestalt therapy when I write, though I obviously have to refer to it when I teach. And I'm a psychologist who tends to stay away, whenever possible, from the technical language of psychology. I began my intellectual life writing poetry and studying literature, and I taught those subjects at two American universities. I have a strong distaste for the reified and abstract jargon with which psychology and the social sciences approach the human situation. Just as I would like to supplement the myth of extraordinary romantic love with a romance of the ordinary, I would like to restore ordinary language to the pursuit of psychology and psychotherapy. This gives me a kinship with a famous citizen of Vienna, Ludwig Wittgenstein, who insisted that philosophers use the language of our everyday conversation in order to bring philosophy home from its abstract flight into the metaphysical stratosphere.

But let me resort to a little Gestalt therapy jargon anyway for those of you who are familiar with its terms. Perhaps it is obvious that when I talk about the dream of a merged "we," created for the sake of certitude in love, I am talking about an important instance of what Gestalt therapy calls confluence. Gestalt therapy defines confluence as a mode of togetherness that lacks awareness of the boundary that separates beings or entities and enables them to preserve the differences that distinguish them in the act of meeting. And the idea of life in Eden, our most famous myth of the original "we," involves the absence of such a boundary. That Eden is a state of fixed confluence is made clear by the fact that it is utterly static and without conflict, a condition where all needs are met without effort. You could say that this archetypal garden represents the essential, perfectly healthy confluence between parent and infant that supports the first stage of human development. But after that, not much else goes on there. Thank God for the apple.

Given the fall into the unpleasant discovery that we are alone and that we live in time, such that nothing stays the same, perhaps we always need to remind ourselves that we also live our lives against a backdrop of confluence. This background is made up of our embeddedness in nature and our dependence on connection to others. If we are ultimately alone, we are also at home in the world by virtue of this confluent background. In moments of passionate or mystical absorption in otherness, the sense of connection becomes the foreground. Both aloneness and time seem to disappear. A nice place to visit, but you can't live there.

The problem with our traditional myth of romantic love is that it implies fixation of foreground confluence. The rest of life tends to be relegated to the background. You go to a party and see a couple you know holding hands. They go on holding hands for the remainder of the evening, and you may think to yourself, "Isn't it wonderful? They still love each other enough after twenty years of marriage to hold hands all night." But when you walk up and say to one of them, "How have you been?" the other answers, "She's fine." And from this new perspective you take a closer look at their hand-holding and notice that their knuckles are turning white. It's a death-grip, an immobile state that we call a fixed Gestalt. Such fixations are always the basis of pathology in Gestalt therapy. This couple's holding hands is like staring at a sunset. When you first look at it, it can be a stunning vision of vital beauty, but if you keep staring, the optic nerves and muscles grow fatigued, and the excitement drains out of your looking. What gives a sunset its vivid, particular grandeur vanishes from your looking, and you no longer really see it. The party turns into a funeral.

The occupational hazard of romantic love is that it is so exciting, like a gorgeous sunset between two people, that couples

177

are tempted to make a fixed Gestalt out of it. The result is a frozen "we," two people staring at one another until they no longer see each other. And then their life together feels boring and monotonous and deadly. At this point the anxiety-ridden power struggles between them may begin — if for no other reason, at least so they can prove that they are still alive. We could certainly use a myth of love based on a different set of images and possibilities. In Gestalt therapy we like to insist that contact between people needs to include respect for their differences, which emphasizes the separateness as well as the union in every meeting. Insisting on separateness in addition to the background and moments of confluent togetherness gives love breathing room, allows both the yes and the no that must always exist between two people, and thus resurrects the sense that love can be a continuing act of free choice.

But love based on the freedom to choose — the freedom to allow things to change, the freedom to be alone or together as one desires — feels risky and anxious-making, especially for those who rely heavily on the bond between love and dependence. The breaking of romantic confluence can even open the doors to violence. In my country, you read in the newspapers much too frequently that still another wife or girlfriend said, "I'm leaving you. I've had enough. I'm fed up, that's it." Subsequently she is found beaten to death or shot. Her husband or boyfriend has replied, in effect, "If I can't have you, nobody can." Maybe this tells us, among other things, that the traditional claim that women are the dependent sex is a convenient cultural lie, propagated by men and, until recent times, subscribed to by most women. It seems to me that only dependence on a relationship could lead a man to resort to such desperate, violent measures. These are hardly acts of love.

What is involved when a man demands that a woman stay no matter what is only too obvious. It suggests that men might be the more dependent sex after all, dependent on women to serve as mothers. Just as women need to continue coming more fully into their own power, which they have been doing as an organized movement over the past twenty-five years, men need a movement of their own to help them learn to separate psychologically from their desperate love-hate hunger for mothers. Then we might at last be able as a culture to imagine stories of love based on a better balance between surrender to the collective spirit and deciding not to go along, between self-expression and teamwork, between honoring one's own needs and honoring those of the other. I ask you, what is love worth if does not include these freedoms?

∫ The Speaking Body
(Or Why did Wilhelm Reich Go Crazy?)

This essay is adapted from a talk given in Montreal at The Gestalt Journal's International conference to honor Erving and Miriam Polster, August 2000.

Part 1: Historical and Philosophical Background

What can we say at this point in our history about the role of the human body in Gestalt therapy? How one treats the body in psychotherapy raises all the traditional philosophical questions about the nature of bodily existence. What is a human body anyway? Is it, as in some idealistic philosophies, merely congealed mind? Is it a complex organization of matter shaped by evolutionary adaptation, as in biological theory? Is the body the shabby outer garment of the soul, as some religions would have it? Is it a shell of nerve endings around a vacancy, as the work of certain

---

*From The Gestalt Journal, Vol. XXIV, No. 2 (Fall, 2001). Reprinted with permission.

behaviorists implies? Is it an elaborate plumbing system for transporting desire, which is pretty much how early psychoanalysis thought about it?

There are schools of psychotherapy aligned with just about every one of these views. At the extremes, some therapies have treated people as though they are at bottom nothing but bodies; others as though they are finally nothing but mind. Strangely enough, this sort of polarization is turning up more these days than it did in the past. But the tendency toward a split has always been around. Freud had hoped, when he first began working at unlocking the secrets of human behavior, to dissolve all mental life into the body, that is, into biology and neurology. He gave up on this first "scientific" project rather quickly, however. His subsequent invention of the "talking cure" concerned itself mainly with exposing and then interpreting the hidden twists and turns of the mind. A multilayered view of mental life has been the dominant legacy of psychoanalysis ever since. I remember a science fiction story I read when I was around twelve, in which the inhabitants of a future society had developed to the point that they were spheres filled with brain or mind. Legs, arms, torsos had evolved out of existence because they had become unnecessary appendages. I wonder now if they had all been through too much traditional psychoanalysis. Maybe not only id, but everything else as well, had been turned into ego.

With the discovery of powerful pharmacological medications, much of modern psychiatry seems to have found its way back to Freud's abandoned project. It reduces not only psychosis but also depression and anxiety to abnormalities in the central nervous system. In the current situation, psychoanalysts and psychopharma-cologists have each tended to choose one side of the Cartesian mind-body dualism. Thus drawing the line and arraying themselves on either side of it, they now fight over market share.

The actual history is not quite so simple as the above discussion suggests. The tendency in psychodynamic therapies, in general, has not been to eliminate the body, but to treat it as a collection of symptoms deposited by the unconscious. The psychoanalytic body tends to be a site of inhibition and suffering when it's not flowing with desire. Freud remarked that a neurotic feels his body, a healthy person his feelings. Wilhelm Reich took up this idea and expanded it. He passed it through the ego psychology of Anna Freud in order to elaborate it into a view of the body as a patchwork of resistances and mechanisms of defense. If the body had become a rather abstract mosaic made up of excitable neighborhoods — oral, anal, phallic — in Freud, Reich made it physically concrete again. Reich's revision directly influenced the beginnings of Gestalt therapy. He had been one of Frederick Perls's therapists, and Paul Goodman was much enamored of his work. In practice, the Reichian influence led to a new emphasis: When the patient produced stories and dreams, complaints and associations, the Gestalt therapist not only listened and reacted, but also paid the closest attention to the patient's bodily presence.

This method became a valuable and familiar part of Gestalt therapy. It involved shifting the foreground frequently from the patient's discourse to a clenched fist, a fixed smile or grimace, a lack of breathing, and other indications of the fixed gestalts we call retroflections. Some Gestalt therapists became so captivated with this change of figure that they subordinated the "talking cure" and focused on something that became widely known as "body work." When Gestalt therapy positioned itself among the so-called humanistic therapies during the 1960s and 70s, its receptiveness to Reich also opened it to influences from bioenergetics, Rolfing, the

Alexander method, Feldenkrais, as well as approaches to the body derived from eastern spiritual practices, such as yoga and Sufi, along with many other methods that were in the air.

So where does this history leave the already poor battered human body in Gestalt therapy? From its beginnings, Gestalt therapy has always repudiated the Cartesian mind-body dualism in favor of a holistic approach. In theory, at least, Gestalt therapists ought to be able to move smoothly without disjunction from mind to body and back again. Nevertheless in actual practice the question of how to introduce the body into therapy has spawned a good deal of confusion, becoming a pole around which controversy has swirled and "truths" have become fixated. The Reichian emphasis, along with other residues of ego psychology in Gestalt therapy, has made it difficult to maintain a consistent psychosomatic unity. As a result, new splits have penetrated Gestalt therapy itself.

For all the holistic thinking that Frederick Perls introduced into Gestalt therapy from his work with Goldstein and his reading of Smuts, his own reworking of Reich did not altogether fit well with holism. Perhaps unwittingly, Perls's approach helped foster a new mind-body split. This tendency became clear in the 1960s *Verbatim* period. Sounding like the Beatles or Timothy Leary, Perls came up with one of his numerous slogans: "Lose your mind and come to your senses!" (as though the senses were not already saturated with mind). Still, one can interpret this notion in Perls's late work as a way to change figure/ground in the hope of restoring more balanced functioning among the people he was teaching. His trainees were primarily over-socialized middle-class professionals (called psychiatrists, psychologists, and the like) who tended to be alienated from their bodies and their feelings. They were likely to respond to their abstract concepts and stereotypes with

more enthusiasm than to their clients or their lovers. A dose of
1960s Reichianism might have seemed like the ideal prescription
for them.

The trouble was that Perls, for all the startling brilliance of
his demonstrations, settled too readily for transcripts of the demonstrations peppered with diagnostic or prescriptive slogans in
place of comprehensive theory in those warm touchy-feely
bell-bottomed California days. Many of his followers treated his
catchy aphorisms and dramatic techniques as though they, in fact,
comprised the theory of Gestalt therapy. One result was an
anti-intellectualism that reintroduced the Cartesian split by coming in through the back door, or perhaps I should say, through the
rear end. Words were denigrated as though they were dead abstractions that served to evade authentic feelings. The body was
more palpably present and therefore more likely to reveal the
truth, although as Reich had made clear, the body could lie, too.
Indeed, much of so-called body work could be described as techniques to transform a body in hiding or playing possum — evident, for example, in the mask-like poker face that betrays no
shred of emotion, the polite shrug and upright posture of the good
student (or good patient), the slump-shouldered shuffle of the passive-aggressive character — into a more authentic instrument for
expression of feelings.

One can view a body as recalcitrant material, like a statue,
or as a vibrating instrument for emotional expression, like a guitar.
On the one hand, the body performs as an obstinate limit, restricting a self that strains against it to reach the world. On the other,
the body is a malleable instrument for transmission and reception
that partially takes its form from changing circumstances. It is like
the difference between the Newtonian particle and the quantum
wave in physics. From a Reichian perspective, the fixed particle is

185

the neurotic body; the wavelike experience the healthy body. This has been a rich vision for psychotherapy in many respects. But does it go far enough? There are many other ways of thinking about the body that psychological theory needs to take into account. We can consider the body as an object, as an organism, as a metaphor, as a construction, as a fiction or narrative, as a locus in the field of experience. Which of these various points of view are therapeutically useful? All of them? What does it mean to do "body work," if there are so many different keyholes through which to peer at the human body, which only yields up portions of its mysteries to the assorted peepers?

Such questions remind us that there is another conception of the body that entered Gestalt therapy during its early formulation. This alternative view derives from existential phenomenology, and it gives rises to a quite different idea of the body's place in therapy. From combining such thinkers as Husserl, Tillich, and Buber with the principles of Gestalt formation, Gestalt therapy developed a method of concentrating on how experience, including experience of one's bodily existence, is continually shaped and reshaped through one's present meetings with nature and a world of others. As Merleau-Ponty summarized the phenomenological outlook with its emphasis on the creative contribution the perceiver makes to all lived experience, "perception is already expression" (Merleau-Ponty, 1970, p. 6). The phenomenological body, sometimes called the "lived body," is more like a process or flux than a thing, a fluctuating subjective landscape, like a painting that the artist keeps revising from one moment to the next. To focus on a subject engaged in creating experience sits uneasily with the Reichian approach, with its focus on animal energies and muscular tensions. It sits uneasily, but that does not mean that these are mutually exclusive outlooks. The contraction and loosening of muscles, as well as the spread or containment of sensations, are among the raw materials that go into the conversion of the human body from animal organism into the lived (and partially constructed), experiential body. One encounters this phenomenological view immediately in the opening pages of Perls, Hefferline, and Goodman, where Goodman describes seeing, not in terms of retinas and optic nerves, but as the "oval of vision" close up against one's eyes. The point is that these two divergent formulations of the therapeutic body, both of which wend their way through Gestalt therapy theory, have never been sufficiently reconciled with one another.

The question of reconciling them bears importantly on how one might answer another important question: Is there really a difference, from the standpoint of Gestalt therapy, between the "talking cure" and "body work"? In my opinion, there is ultimately no difference in principle, even though the particular style and preferences of a given therapist may look very different in practice. The body, as a foundation in the construction of human experience, is never reducible only to the animal organism. It is eloquent with expressive languages and signifiers — gestures that reach or demonstrate, telling postures, idiosyncratic movements and positions that reveal meanings and values. And language, considered not just as formal structure (grammar, syntax, semantics) but as the expressive and receptive activities of speaking and listening (phonology and intentionality), belongs to the body as much as to the mind. French psychoanalysis, especially in the form it took under the baton of Jacques Lacan, considers the distinction between langue, which is the abstract structure of language, and parole, which is the actual spoken word (a distinction Lacan borrowed from the linguist Ferdinand Saussure) to be of central theoretical importance. There is no language without a body. The issue is whether the language is dead and desensitized just as the body can be dead and desensitized.

In the Cartesian view the mind is a mysterious spiritual substance, an invisible vapor that reasons, feels, and wills. It has the body at its disposal, so that it can drive it the way a pilot flies a plane. If I decide to pick up a glass on the table, I begin transmitting thought-like impulses, as if I had pressed the correct combination of buttons on a mental keyboard. These willful mental activities are received by my hand and arm which then get busy making the correct maneuvers to achieve the goal. Can you imagine Michael Jordan heading for the basket and sinking a shot in a series of steps like this? If this is how humans function, then the body exists pretty much in the same sense that a table or an automobile can be said to exist. The body is an elaborate external machine, and my consciousness sits at the controls. The Cartesian picture of human nature has often been aptly described as "the ghost in the machine."

The Cartesian division, which locates bodily existence in one realm of being and mental reality in another, led to all sorts of philosophical conundrums and contradictions. Philosophers tried every contortion, but there was no satisfactory way to bridge the two realms by logically connecting them to each other. Husserl came at it from a completely different angle: His phenomenology made the logical bridge unnecessary through eliminating the gap that required bridging in the first place. By bracketing off everything except the experiencing subject, he was able to join thinking and sensing together as aspects of one another in the same realm — namely, the realm of "experience." It follows that all of our sensations of our world are already permeated with mind, and vice versa. Separating mind and body then is a post-experiential act of abstraction.

From the phenomenological standpoint, it cannot be that my mind forms the idea of picking up the glass, and then sends a message to my arm and hand to carry out the order. A phenomenological account would proceed more like this: I become curious (Is this an antique glass?) or feel a need (I'm thirsty!) or encounter a problem (Does this glass go in the cabinet on the left or the right?). My reaching for the glass is from the start informed by and infused with my desire-filled attention. Such attention is not just sitting up here in my head and being directed from there. The attending is an essential part of the movement of reaching itself. Everything I do that involves the glass contains thoughts, sensations, feelings, interpretations and value judgments, as well as actions, in a simultaneous, closely knit web. I don't go through a linear sequence of steps to get from the idea to the activity. I simply pick up the glass in a single, unified sweep.

But even to point at unification or integration isn't quite accurate, because to say something is unified or integrated presupposes that there are separate parts that you are bringing together into an integration or a unity. This is not what is going on, except in the models we construct after the fact. To be sure, the models are useful for explaining things in retrospect, but they are only metaphorical ways of thinking about these matters late in the game. They are reflective afterthoughts. Phenomenology tries to get at something it calls pre-reflective experience.

I pick up the glass, and my mind is involved, my senses are involved, my will is involved, my interest is involved — activity and experience are taking shape at the same time. So what is a talking cure or what is body work in relation to this portrait of human conduct? When you use the phenomenological method, speaking is not just mind, and picking up a glass is not just body. They are both expressive, need-governed actions one can perform in responding to one's continually changing meetings with one's world. In other words, they are both what Gestalt therapy calls contact.

How do we know we have a body? If this seems obvious, it's not. Do we know it from more from the inside through sensations or the outside from our senses? I can't say whether animals "know" they have bodies — perhaps they just are bodies. We are different, because as humans, we rely so much on self-reflective knowledge. We require an epistemology in order to develop and get on. The other animals don't, so far as we know. What we can see of our bodies is distorted and limited. For instance, we can never directly see the back of our heads or our nostrils or teeth or our eyes themselves. Our visual knowledge of these parts of the body comes only through reflected images, such as through mirrors and photographs, reports from others, and inferences from touch. Such knowledge belongs to the register that Lacan calls "the imaginary," which is basic to his theory of how human identity develops. The ways in which we come to "see" ourselves, for instance with distorted body images, help make clear the extent to which knowledge of our bodies employs constructions that are not given by the animal organism. My sense of my body is "fleshed out" by impressions others have of me, so that my knowledge of my body always depends on the way it is embedded in the world and includes the world's responses to it (as though it were not only my body). In a somewhat analogous way, Winnicott said that the baby's first self is in the mother's eyes. But the world's involvement in our body knowledge extends beyond how others regard us; it is true also of our contact with inanimate objects. When I pick up the glass, I am touching it, but, in a sense, it touches me back as well, such that I feel this as a pressure that flows back through me and becomes part of the whole experience. One's body, as one comes to know it, is never an encapsulated entity but is always located in the field that it plays a crucial part in unfolding between oneself and one's world.

Emmanuel Levinas, the splendid French philosopher who died recently, takes the between-ness even further into the world than Winnicott or Lacan. He says that philosophy needs to begin, not with interrogating the composition of the world or the self, but with the face of the other. This seems plausible developmentally. When a baby opens it eyes and becomes conscious, one of its first experiences is the mother's face. This point of departure, it seems to me, leads Levinas to a richer understanding of the relationship between oneself and others than Martin Buber's analysis of it. Buber calls his beautiful conception of the I-Thou a "word," but Levinas begins with the wrinkled skin of the face of the other whose eyes are looking at you even as you look at them. You cannot look at the other's living face, he says, without it calling forth from you an awareness of ethical responsibility for the other. Only in what is evoked by such awareness does one discovers oneself, according to Levinas. And only in these moments of realization do both language and philosophy arise and take form. Therefore, Levinas claims, ethics precedes modes of philosophical thinking, such as metaphysics. For him, contact, human experience, and human relatedness all begin with expressive bodily presence, not of ourselves but of the other, and not in something so verbal as the I-Thou. The word is not first. The face and gaze of the other comes earlier. Such knowledge, for Levinas, is neither specifically scientific knowledge nor the kind of knowledge associated with the arts, though it may partake of both. It is, above all and first of all, ethical knowledge. Among the things Levinas has taught me is that the interminable debate about whether psychotherapy is a science or an art pales before the fact that it is an ethical position one takes in the presence of another human being.

So by now we can speak of the mind as existing throughout all experience with some depth of understanding about what this might imply for knowledge of the body. It's not just a question of whether the brain is the seat of the mind nor a question of the unity of mind and body. Maybe it would be most accurate to say that mind is to be found at work especially at the point where I touch and feel touched. When I speak to you, if I'm speaking without too much self-consciousness, you could say my mind is at my lips. (This would be the phenomenological description.) I am not thinking deliberately, which would be like talking to myself, but I am talking to you, just as I am looking at you and you at me. Yet certainly there is thought in my speaking to you. Again, this is exactly what Gestalt therapy means by contact. When the contact is talk, one's mind is not a separate executive dictating words to the mouth. If, on the other hand, we observe someone who is talking to us appearing to continually consult their brain as they speak (frowning, pausing, looking up), we might regard this as mildly obsessional retroflected activity, probably the consequence of having taken in too earnestly the command, "Think before you speak."

I once visited a master class given by an extraordinary piano teacher named Adele Marcus, who had been an associate of such pianists as Arthur Schnabel and Vladimir Horowitz. She had also been the mentor to some of the best concert artists currently performing. At the beginning of the class, she made a few brief but extremely telling comments. She said that when you play the piano, you will experience the feeling that you want to express in your abdomen. The only other thing that you should be aware of is the sensation of your fingertips touching the keys. Anything that enters your awareness in between these two points, she continued, is a resistance. Obviously this includes the head. You could say that when a pianist has something to express, the mind and the heart join together, and in the actual expression the mind is not lurking in the head; it resides at the fingertips.

Part 2. Clinical Issues

To what extent are Reich's concepts still useful in Gestalt therapy? The answer is that within limits they continue to inspire important work in Gestalt theory and practice. Reich's early thought contained valuable new insights into how the developing child's responses to anxiety and trauma can harden over time into character. His most significant discovery was that these lasting formations, which he called "character armor," appear not only in the patient's reports but in the speaking voice, not only in dreams, memories, and associations, but in physical inhibitions, tensed or flaccid muscles, anaesthetized portions of skin, incoherent actions, or inappropriate gestures of expression. Gestalt therapy calls these retroflections. Isadore From made their value for clinical practice particularly clear. He consistently taught that psychotherapy usually needs to start out with attention to the retroflections, precisely because they show up in the body (which includes the voice), so that we can see and hear them. Gestalt therapy also developed (partly from Reich's influence, partly on its own) techniques or experiments for undoing retroflections. But since retroflections bind the anxiety of blocked feelings which a person cannot yet, as a rule, support sufficiently to experience other than as anxiety, one needs to go about undoing retroflections with great delicacy and sensitivity to what the undoing may produce.

Which brings me to the limitations in the Reichian approach. I want to suggest to you that these are related to another issue, which is, "Why did Wilhelm Reich's theories go crazy?" It is likely that Reich himself went crazy while he was evolving his late cosmic theories. However it is also true that he was horribly and scandalously persecuted by the U.S. government, although that ugly episode in the long history of American witch hunts is not what I intend to discuss in detail here. Instead, I'm going to speculate about why Wilhelm Reich's theories eventually skidded out of control and finally off the track of usefulness. I hope that this will shed some light on why the Reichian perspective is finally inadequate and needs to be integrated with a phenomenological view of the body.

In teaching how to diagnose and work with the body, Reich's early work enabled Gestalt therapy to understand concretely how people's physical tensions and numbed-out body parts cripple their capacities for meeting needs, doing satisfying work, and forming successful relationships. His emphasis on paying attention to the body also brought an observable immediacy to psychotherapy, and thus taught Gestalt therapists a good deal about making use of the present situation in the therapy session. But what comes next? For Reich, the next step was strenuous intervention to release the pent-up energy that now remained frozen in characterological body configurations.

His approach led directly to bioenergetics and influenced the other kinds of body work which many Gestalt therapists have added to their repertoires. Almost all body work centers around undoing of retroflections in order to release blocked energy and feeling. There is no question that working on retroflections in therapy can free storms of activity and emotion. But toward what end? What is to be made from the storms? In the case of Reich himself, the release and the goal eventually merged, because his aim was to restore something he called orgastic potency. Reich felt that the chief neurosis in the modern soul sprang from a physical deprivation, a congealing of life force such that people could no longer surrender fully to any experience, especially to the experience of orgasm.

Even if you read Reich's exaltation of surrender to orgasm as his stand-in for all spontaneous, full living — and I do think this is what Reich had in mind — his vision still leaves unanswered what is supposed to happen after the therapeutic liberation of energy. Something essential is left incomplete, which makes the experience at once not enough and too much to handle. It's a little like those people who after making love immediately leap out of bed, get dressed, and call a cab. Given the tenor of Reich's later work, I think that his theories, and maybe Reich himself, became overwhelmed with the flood of liberated impulses, desires, passions, and instincts. Humans, unlike other animals, cannot rely on instincts alone in riding the waves of energized sensations and impulses. That is never the whole story for the human. Paul Ricoeur puts it this way:

> Because we have no genetic system of information for human behavior, we need a cultural system. No culture exists without such a system. The hypothesis, therefore, is that where human beings exist, a non-symbolic mode of existence, and even less, a non-symbolic kind of action, can no longer obtain. Action is immediately ruled by cultural patterns which provide templates or blueprints for the organization of social and psychological processes, perhaps just as genetic codes — I am not certain — provide such templates for the organization of organic processes. In the same way that our experience of the natural world requires a mapping, a

mapping is also necessary for our experience of social reality. (Ricoeur, 1986, pp. 11-12)

What drove Reich's psychology, and perhaps Reich, into craziness is that he did not differentiate between the animal organism, which has certain built-in maps, and the human subject, which always needs to construct maps of the body beyond what is given by the organism.

Reich had no theory of the body as lived experience, the body as continually re-imagined or symbolically reconstructed through the human capacity to give form to experience. Perhaps the other animals can depend on the hardwired programming built into their instincts to limit, contain, and guide their energies toward completing their purposes. But the human cannot depend on animal instincts. We need to make and give form to experience. This is the basis of social order, culture, and art. Reich, however, envisioned the pure release of biological and instinctual energy, and then there was no place to go from there except directly to the universe.

Which is exactly where Reich went next. His early work on character armor was followed by writings in which he concluded that therapy reawakened the same energy in the individual that moves the stars and the planets. In honor of the organism, or perhaps the orgasm, he named this cosmic fluid or ether "orgone." He came to believe that it controlled not only all living activity but also the weather and the tides. Driven by this mystical vision and a sense of urgency about the doom mankind was fashioning for itself through repression of instinctual life, Reich turned increasingly messianic and megalomaniacal. Some would say he became psychotic. He preached that the salvation of mankind depended on tuning in to the cosmic currents of orgone. And he invented a new body therapy to outdo all body therapies. He oversaw the building of special orgone boxes, somewhat resembling outhouses, designed to collect cosmic ray-like currents of orgone. By sitting in them people could absorb these currents in order to restore their sex lives, increase their *élan vital*, prevent cancer, and so on. A puritanical and perhaps equally megalomaniacal United States government got after him and indicted him for transporting orgone boxes across state lines. Reich died in jail.

Whether our life force comes from the cosmos or human nature, our situation demands that we make something with meaningful structure and form from it. The mere release of urges, appetites, interests, and longings can become a boundless ocean that drowns one's sense of oneself. What is required is an aesthetic principle in psychotherapy that enables patients to become creative agents capable of traveling on their own beyond the Reichian manipulating and opening of sensation and feeling toward their own discoveries of how to shape their lives. Our theories and practices of psychotherapy must correspond to this need. I think that the phenomenological foundation in Gestalt therapy, especially as it underwrites the conceptions of the contact boundary and gestalt formation, provides such a theory and implies such a practice. The Reichian influence still has its place in this scheme of things; what phenomenology adds is an embracing concern with the form-making creation of experience. As in art, form matters in therapy as much as content, and good form provides fluent possibilities yet limits and restrains at the same time.

When a work of art moves us profoundly, it is not just because of orgasmic excitement, even in cases where that is what the work is about. There is always a restraining element that creates a boundary (which is an important part of what we mean by form in art). It is exactly the same thing with love. Love is not only surrender to orgasmic fusion, although, heaven knows, one wants to count this among the moments of love. But when you make the flood of sexual excitement into the goal, you get the crazed romantic myth of love as fusion, which has very little to do with relating to another person. There is no relationship in this kind of fusion. Love requires restraint in order to make a limiting resistance, such that one still finds one's edge. Without awareness of an edge, we can't meet. We simply end up awash in a big puddle or soup of energy.

Of course, in a society where there is so much chronic tension and emotional isolation, it is not surprising that a renegade like Reich landed on the side of letting go and giving in. You can't love if you can't let go and feel your feelings. But that's only one side of the story of love. The other is that love calls for cautious respect for the one's own separateness and that of the other. That is what I mean by restraint. Reich had a wonderful understanding of the animal body and the damage that repression could do to it. But he had no theory of Eros as form-giving imagination. There is plenty of sex and energy in Reich but very little love.

Wittgenstein says that the body is the best picture of the soul. That is not a definition of a body that is only an animal body. When you are doing body work, you're massaging the psyche and the soul as well as the body, and you had better be careful about the massage. Another important drawback handed down from Reich's legacy is that the liberation of energy tends to remain under the control of the therapist who makes strong, hands-on interventions, even though it is the patient who experiences it as liberating. The consequence is the exchange of an old dependence, the dependence of the child on parents, for a new dependency on the therapist. Granted that the tensions and other bodily mechanisms of defense that Reich pointed to were formed in the field of that old dependency. So it may seem like a good bargain to trade it in for a new dependency on the therapist as liberator, the therapist as cheerleader of emotional release. So long as even the most benevolent dependency remains, however, psychotherapy is essentially a sadomasochistic structure, no matter how mild in appearance. It's as if the patient says, "Do it to me!" and the therapist obliges. It may be nice to have a cheerleader on your side for a while, but then it is crucial that the cheerleader step out of the way so that the patient can take possession his or her own experience, including the aesthetic form he or she gives to both body and soul. Getting out of the way is not enough respected in much of body work that derives from Reich. It then brings about invasive colonization of the patient.

Obviously invasive practice is not only an issue for body work. The sado-masochistic colonization occurs as much in talk therapies, even if the massage is more subtle and internal. This is the case in those kinds of psychoanalytic therapy where the analyst makes it clear to the patient that the only growth comes through accepting the therapist's interpretations. From the therapist's position of authority it is not difficult to force ideas on a person through talk, just as it is possible to force the arousal of feelings in a person through manipulating the body. You simply use different orifices. But the outcome — an infantilized patient, whether happy about it or not — amounts to the same thing. Equally invasive, if not worse, is too much therapeutic empathy. An overdose of empathy too closely resembles fusion for my taste. I am not against empathy if it operates from a respectful distance, like Buddhist compassion, such that it leaves the patient's otherness intact even as it pays careful attention to it.

By way of concluding, let me illustrate how integrating the Reichian view and the phenomenological view of the body might be put to use diagnostically. Consider, for example, how psychosomatic unity, which is part animal, part imaginative construction, might become distorted in the perversions and the personality disorders. I submit that both kinds of disorders are made through using the capacity to create form for an attack on a central facet of the human condition — that bodily existence in relation to the world is risky and uncertain. For both perversions and personality disorders, the uncertainty is too much to bear. My point is that both do it through an imaginary constriction of physical existence — to put it this way borrows from both Reich and phenomenology — with the aim of establishing an illusion of certitude and control against the uncertainty of life and love. There is nothing perverse about the so-called perversions except insofar as a person gets stuck in being able to express his or her sexuality in only one way. Why should anything in the spectrum of sexual possibilities be denigrated unless it is harmful to oneself or others? But when the result is an unnecessarily severe restriction of being limited to traveling for pleasure down only one road, you could call it perverse if you want to.

In the case of the perversions, feeling desire for or making love to the entire being, including the whole body, of another person seems too hot to handle. Unable to support so much excitement (one's own or the other's) because it shakes the foundation of the lover's sense of control, he or she limits the movement or the expressiveness of the other's body or reduces it to a part. For instance, if looking intimately into the face of a beloved is too anxious-making, maybe the lover can look intimately at a foot. If one cannot make love to the body of the other, maybe one can still manage to get gratification by making love to a part. The foot contains something of the person — as Rilke says in a poem, even the feet can weep — but it's personal on a small enough scale so that one can still feel in control. If it turns out that a foot is still too much, since it is composed of the other's living flesh, then one can fasten on a symbolic representation, such as underpants or some other article of clothing, and allow desire to flow out to this thing that is close to the person but inanimate. The perversions attempt to reduce the being of the other to a silhouette or a fragment or a substitute. But these reductions are nevertheless achieved through acts of creativity, although what is made is less, whereas we usually think of creativity as making something that is more. The narrowing is in the name of security and certitude.

The personality disorders, to a large extent, work in the opposite way (I don't pretend to account here for all the personality disorders, anymore than the preceding accounts for every perversion). Whereas the imagination lessens the being of the other in perversions, in the personality disorders one turns this capacity to reduce experience toward oneself. The goal is similar — to diminish the anxiety of uncertainty by making one's response to life more manageable and predictable. The personality disorders attempt to maintain control and certitude in all contacting the world, in intimacy and social relations, by constricting the sense of self. Then the spreading physical sensation of excitement aroused in moving toward the world is channeled into a narrow pipe or a rigid structure. (There is another kind of personality disorder that has too little structure, but I am not going to deal with it here.) With such limited equipment, a person can neither tolerate his or her own excitement nor take in much of anything from another. It would be too overwhelming. In many types of personality disorders there is little evidence of anxiety because that is what has been eliminated by filtering out unpredictability. But if you dig deeper you will likely find anguish, that thin burning thread of sensation, when too much is compressed into too little.

The perversions and the personality disorders demonstrate in dramatic ways the need we all have to invent a stay against the flood tide of life's uncertainties. Robert Frost alluded to this when he defined poetry as "a momentary stay against confusion." Since we are constituted by both our animal nature and our symbol-making, form-giving imaginations, we try to invent ways of living with uncertainty. Why? Partly because we live in time, conscious of the continual change that carries us toward death. Perhaps it is our peculiar existence as the creature who is aware of dying that makes our living only as an animal organisms not only inadequate but intolerable. Writing poems, philosophizing, doing scientific research are among the ways in which we reach beyond the organism and perhaps accept our dying. This must be what Socrates meant in Plato's Apology when he rebuffed his friends who wanted to rescue him from execution by telling them that the purpose of philosophy is to teach us how to die.

We may or may not long for immortality, but we don't want to live surrounded by infinity, like little boats buffeted by an endless sea. I remember seeing on an antique shop wall an eighteenth-century Armenian cherub carved of bronze. Its chin was tucked into wings folded across its chest, its eyes were closed, and it looked a little sad. Even angels, the sculpture suggested, grow weary of infinity. Given such consciousness we need to make sense of life, and we get some help from our ability to create those patterned finite structures that we call gestalt formations.

References

Merleau-Ponty, Maurice. (1970). *Themes from the Lectures at the Collège de France 1952-1960*, trans. by John O'Neill. Evanston, Illinois: Northwestern Univ. Press.
Ricoeur, Paul. (1986). *Ideology and Utopia*. New York: Columbia Univ. Press.

∫ What Lies Beyond the Field?

By now, you have heard a great deal about the field, the self, the between, contact, and relationship from the previous speakers. Of course I will draw on those concepts, but since I am the last to address you, I am going to wander off the path a little in order to talk about a subject that has long been of interest to me. I intend to concentrate on the radical implications for theory and practice that follow from the substitution in Gestalt therapy of an aesthetic model of health and pathology for the scientific approach that has dominated most other therapies. My emphasis is going to be not only on contact but on the artfulness and creativity involved in making contact. All arts and crafts depend on the human urge to make something, which even so sex-struck a writer as D. H. Lawrence thought was more basic than our drive to couple with another person. We then judge what is made by criteria such as its gracefulness, its liveliness and inherent interest, its scope and fluidity, and its satisfying economy of form. That such qualities are the

---

*From *Contact and Relationship*. Edited by Jean-Marie Robine. (Bordeaux: Éxprimérie, 2003). Reprinted with permission.

measure of healthy functioning in Gestalt therapy may be the most distinctive thing about it.

The starting point in Gestalt therapy is experience. However, the definition of experience in Gestalt therapy is unique in two respects. In the first place, it is said to occur at the contact boundary between the individual and his or her world, so that what we usually consider the subjectivity of experience is not simply relegated to inner life. Secondly, it does not just happen; it has to be made — and made again and again at each moment. Thus experience is a human creation. If this sounds like a road to a philosophical idealism, in which nothing exists but mind, that is not at all the case. The meetings out of which experience is composed take place in a field, and the conception of the field in Gestalt therapy is precisely a reminder that you can't make something out of nothing. If experience is not given, something has to be, and we call this something the field, a set of conditions that precedes both individual and world. In what sense, then, can the field be said to exist?

For me, the most useful way to think about it is to say that the field hovers somewhere between nothing and something. This is not an easy topic to discuss, but I have found some help in the work of the French philosopher, Gilles Deleuze, who defines the field as a "structure of possibilities" out of which a world as other can emerge for each subject. In other words, the field in Gestalt therapy, as in physics, can be considered pure potentiality. It exists not as objects exist, but as the possibility of coming into being. If the field is conceived in this way, then one's experience of both self and other appears at first as little more than a dimly lit glimmer barely perceived in an indefinite landscape. Neither self nor other take on full existence until the creative, form-giving work has been done of making both actual.

Two comments, drawn not from Gestalt therapy theory but from two literary figures, will give more color to what I am saying. The nineteenth-century American philosopher and diarist Henry David Thoreau wrote, "Only that day dawns to which we are awake." And a modern French poet and painter Henri Michaux puts it even more strongly in his strange account of a trip to Ecuador: "The world is not round, not yet. We have to make it round."

It is exactly at the point of transforming possibility into actuality that aesthetic values become important for both theory and therapy. One can get a closely-knit description of how this comes about in the well-known opening passage of Paul Goodman's volume of *Gestalt Therapy: Excitement and Growth in the Human Personality.* Goodman has no difficulty here discovering aesthetic values emerging directly from a phenomenological description of everyday experience. For him the phenomenological and the aesthetic are essential aspects of each other. To illustrate this, he gives the example of seeing, which he characterizes as an oval field of vision that is "close up against your eyes." The experience of seeing is neither more nor less than this oval, and it has very specific properties: "Notice then, how in this oval field, the objects begin to have esthetic relations, of space and color value." Goodman's analysis of hearing is similar: "And so you may experience it with the sounds 'out there': their root of reality is at the boundary of contact, and at that boundary they are experienced in unified structures."

Already in the first few sentences setting forth the first theory of Gestalt therapy Goodman has made a radical shift in theory. He wastes no time leaving behind the explanatory method of natural science (which might propose that seeing is caused by external objects stimulating the optic nerves). His concentration on the oval of vision is a phenomenological reduction that does not concern itself with either an external world or with the rods and cones and optic nerves. Instead, he turns from questions of cause and effect to questions of artistic quality.

As you focus on this oval, Goodman says, the objects begin to take on aesthetic properties, which implies that they didn't have them initially. They begin to have these properties only insofar as you give your attention to your seeing or your hearing, such that your seeing and hearing become active awareness, not merely passive reception. In other words, in seeing you become all eyes, in hearing all ears. The self, you could say, is in the looking and listening. Indeed, at such moments of engagement the self is nothing but the looking and listening. Something not just given has been created in this process. What it is can best be understood neither as internal nor "out there" (which Goodman puts in quote marks, like a good phenomenologist), but in aesthetic terms of value, structure, color, and form.

Goodman equates experience such as seeing and hearing with a reality that consists of continual change, perceived as a flux of unified structures. We call those structures gestalts, of course, and that they have unity, value, and form is what Goodman means by aesthetic relations. The unique contribution of Gestalt therapy resides not only in its conception of the field, not only in its focus on the relational, but in its original idea that our sense of reality — what we call our experience — is given structure and form at the meeting place between the organism and the novelty of the world. Whatever else it might be, the activity of gestalt formation at the contact boundary is aesthetic, so that we can regard reality — which we call our experience — in the same way that we look at and evaluate a work of art.

All of this reminds us of how much complexity goes into the notion of the present moment. It is interesting to think about this, because Gestalt therapy bases its work on the present moment. Yet there are complicated questions about whether the present exists other than as a linguistic construction. William James, an American philosopher who influenced Paul Goodman, wrote, "The literally present moment is a purely verbal supposition, not a position. The only present even realized concretely being the passing moment in which the dying rearward of time and its dawning future forever mix their lights." This is from his book called *A Pluralistic Universe*. The present moment cannot be pinned down any more than a subatomic particle can — both leave behind a trail giving evidence that they were there. So what do we mean when we ask a client, "what is your present experience?" It's important to be sensitive to this issue because the present moment is elusive and mysterious at best.

Indeed, that Gestalt therapy concentrates on something called present experience represents a significant change, a relatively recent one, in how experience is understood. In ancient Greece, the concept of experience implied not passing sensations or perceptions, but an established body of knowledge made up of past cases, useful observations, life histories, arts and skills. Experience was almost equivalent to culture. An individual could draw on it, whether from individual or social sources, as a guide to making judgments and carrying out tasks. We still often employ the word with this meaning, as when we say, "I need a referral to an experienced therapist," which implies a mix of personal experience with training in a collective body of knowledge, or "Where can I find a carpenter with experience in making Victorian moldings?" which means one that knows past techniques as well as present ones. The word experience here conveys a sense of acquired and assimilated arts and skills, techniques and wisdom. In other words, it is something complete, a finished product, which can be made available, transmitted, and put to use. The primacy of completed experience still dominates in ordinary conversation. We might say, "I had an experience last week that I want to tell you about." Or, we might look forward to its completion in the future, in a comment such as "This will have been an important experience for me." But it would seem very odd to say, "Please don't bother me, I'm in the middle of an important experience."

Obviously we mean something different when we talk about present experience, which we do as a matter of course, in Gestalt therapy. Our new twist on an old traditional concept derives, I suspect, from those modern philosophical movements, such as existentialism and phenomenology, which have influenced Gestalt therapy. Existential phenomenology places the person inside his or her world as an experiencing subject and makes this the starting point of philosophical inquiry, just as we make it the starting point of clinical work. Before such developments, it would not have made much sense to ask someone, "What are you experiencing?" (as we tend to ask our clients every five minutes). I think, though, that we now take the meaningfulness of this question too much for granted. It is a question we often use when we run out of ideas in a therapy session, and often enough the client has no idea what it means. For this reason alone it is worthwhile to preserve, even in present-oriented Gestalt therapy, the ancient and traditional sense that experience is a creation that includes values, choice, and meaning. What we add is that it includes them in the very process of being created.

The very definition of the self in *Gestalt Therapy* is based on Goodman's joining of the phenomenological and the aesthetic. The relevant passage is another well-known one near the beginning of the book: "The self is the contact boundary at work. Its activity is forming of figures and grounds. The self is precisely the integrator; it is the artist of life." Clear the idea of the self as the artist of life is much more than a suggestive metaphor for Goodman. It is a description of the part that the self plays in giving form and value to experience, as though it plays an artistically creative part in each moment of lived experience. This is an extraordinary idea, and one might wonder how Gestalt therapy came by it during an era when psychoanalysis reigned supreme, giving rise to a view of art as a product of unconscious fantasies and wishes.

Part of the answer no doubt comes from the fact that the founders of Gestalt therapy were all involved in the arts to some degree one way or another. Before he went to medical school, Fritz Perls was trained by Max Reinhardt, one of the great directors of German theater. Laura Perls was thoroughly absorbed in music and dance, and she imported ideas from those pursuits into her work with the body. Paul Goodman was a novelist, a playwright, and a very good poet. His literary works were published throughout his career alongside his formidable books of social and cultural criticism. Isadore From was not directly involved in the arts, but neither did he have formal training as a psychologist or psychiatrist. In college he studied philosophy. He was also deeply interested in literature. He once told me that he had learned at least as much, if not more, about human conduct from reading Proust and Henry James as he did from reading Freud. Thus strong interest and involvement with various arts accompanied the founding of Gestalt therapy.

How does this innovative aesthetic perspective influence practical clinical work in Gestalt therapy? Since the aesthetic basis of Gestalt therapy arises directly from an understanding of contact as a meeting between self and other that have to be made anew each time, then the job of the therapist is to pay attention to how it is made in the therapy session itself. Isadore From, one of the founding teachers of Gestalt therapy and perhaps its most consistent theoretical voice, always insisted on this point. Contact, he would say, is not a state that you are either in or out of; it is an activity. It behaves more like a verb than a noun, so it would be more accurate to speak of contacting. For example, he emphasized that one must work in therapy not with memories, as though the past is carried into the present situation of the therapy session like a fixed mental object, but with remembering, a present activity, in which the past is remade once again. To remember suggests a work of reassembling the members or parts of an old experience into a new whole. This is a distinction that is absolutely crucial to Gestalt therapy, not only because it makes process rather than products the priority but because it brings out that remembering is not a repetition but the creation of something new. In a similar vein, From was less concerned with labeling projections or introjects than with attending to the process of projecting or introjecting as activities that are taking place now.

The troubled client is as much an artist as the healthy person. He or she just happens to be busy at work producing illness instead of health. The aesthetic perspective in Gestalt therapy has considerable diagnostic utility. One of the most telling things you can say about neurosis is that it is bad art. Like paintings that we want to walk away from, it is repetitious, stereotypical, badly designed, and inappropriate. Above all, it is monotonous and boring. The more serious the degree of disturbance, the more monotonous the creation. The obsessive-compulsive narrative never moves forward. It goes over the same ground or performs the same activity again and again. The paranoid turns every situation, even a love story, into an espionage film or film noir about menace and betrayal. For the hysteric personality, every situation is a continual climax — the most wonderful or most terrible thing that ever happened — until the exhausted audience begs for an intermission.

Let me illustrate this approach in more detail by using the paranoid personality as an example of how the principle that the self is the artist of life figures even in pathological character formation. What kind of artist is the paranoid? Actually, a highly imaginative one. The American sociologist and anthropologist Ernest Becker, in his book *Angel in Armor*, suggested that paranoia is the poetry of a person who is standing on a very narrow pillar feeling frighteningly small and insecure. From this precarious, inadequately supported position, the paranoid looks out on a world that seems overwhelmingly large and tries to make meaningful sense of his painful condition by applying the creative powers of the human imagination. Dramatic, often brilliantly constructed plots around themes of danger, threat, conspiracy, and betrayal are the result. In other words, paranoia is the poetry of impotence.

From another angle, paranoia is a possible outcome whenever one experiences a chasm or gulf between oneself and others. This is especially the case when the gulf persists despite a demand from the others or a longing in oneself to become part of a "we." Of course, the gulf is self-imposed: No matter how powerful the demand or longing, the paranoid person has to keep himself apart from the group because he feels too small and helpless to maintain his individuality if he joins it. There is an intriguing article on paranoia in W. D. Ellis' *Source Book of Gestalt Psychology*, the book which Goodman used for his borrowings from classic Gestalt psychology. This article ("An Approach to a Gestalt Theory of Paranoic Phenomena" by Heinrich Schulte) defines the anxiety that gives rise to paranoia as "we-crippledness." The we-crippled paranoid, unable to join yet longing to do so, feels at once beside the group and outside it, according to Schulte. To be at the same time beside (which is to say, near to) and outside (still far from) the group is not a place one can tolerate without justifying one's existence there. There seems to be a basic human need to justify one's situation to oneself, and this is where the imaginative artistry of the paranoid comes into the picture.

It is well-established that paranoids are experts at projecting, which involves treating fantasies as though they are realities coming from the environment. The gulf itself forms an empty space — a blank interval in the continuum of contact — that can be filled with projections. The paranoid person uses projecting to invent an alternative way of belonging to the group without joining it. In effect, he writes a novel or a play in which he is the main character, such that everything going on in the group refers to him. If he sees some members of the group talking privately, it means they are conspiring against him. If they invite him to a social function, it is because they are planning to use him. If they don't invite him, they are trying to get rid of him. The group in question might be as small as one other person. If his wife receives a letter with no return address, it must be from her lover.

Or the group might be as large as the whole of society. If there is a car with two men sitting inside it parked in front of his house, they must be waiting for him to leave so they can break in and burglarize it. Sometimes, of course, the paranoid is correct and has good reason to be paranoid. It's not that the projections are automatically false, it's that the paranoid feels and lives as though they are always true. He not only makes something of his perceptions, he makes too much of them. Everything the group does is a drama or a plot set in motion in order to victimize him. And this is how he comes to feel a sense of importance and belonging — he is connected, however, negatively, to everything that is going on. This may be a miserable state, but there is at least the illusion that the gulf has been bridged and that a terrible way of life can be explained.

It is often said that Gestalt therapy is a nonjudgmental therapy. I disagree. Every human encounter involves judgments about value and meaning, interest and boredom, satisfaction and dissatisfaction, and the like. The Gestalt therapist and the client are busy collaborating in making judgments all the time — judgments, for example, about what works and what doesn't in the client's life, especially insofar as the client's moment to moment stagings of his or her life can be brought to light, explored and experimented within the therapy session itself. The kind of judgments that Gestalt therapy opposes in traditional therapies are the ones that impose overly abstract and universal views of reality — especially with regard to right and wrong, health and sickness — on the client. The aesthetic orientation of Gestalt therapy is not against science but it turns away from those "scientific" (cause and effect) explanations or interpretations that try to fit human conduct into fixed categories, norms of health, models of predictability, and so forth.

Gestalt therapists work (or ought to) like good art or literary critics. A good critic does not attack a work of art with general prescriptions, as if to say, "my expert knowledge of you is better than your clouded knowledge of yourself." Good Gestalt therapists pay close attention to how a client is typically drawing on and building something from his or her resources and opportunities. Then they might offer possibilities (often through collaborative experiments) for the client to create something more fulfilling from those resources and opportunities. As Isadore From once put it, the aim is to help clients make poetry out of their talking, dancing out of their walking. The accent here is on the fact that the talking and walking and, therefore, the poetry and dancing belong to the clients. If it is merely a case of the therapist transmitting ideas about what makes good poetry and dance, then therapy is nothing more than another enforced introjection, another neurotic loss of contact. Our clients (and ourselves) already possess an ample supply of these taken in from parents, teachers, priests, and other authorities. From's remark brings out unmistakably the aesthetic emphasis in Gestalt therapy and in addition makes it clear that the client, not the therapist, is the artist who matters.

∫ The Aesthetics of Commitment:
    What Gestalt Therapists Can Learn
    from Cézanne and Miles Davis

This essay is adapted from a keynote address the author gave at a conference on Gestalt therapy at Southern Connecticut State University, November 2001.

This essay is a meditation on a common Gestalt idiom — the expression "staying with . . . ," in the sense of staying with the truth of one's present experience, whether it feels positive or negative. This is such a common intervention from Gestalt therapists that it is almost a cliché. If you are a Gestalt therapist, it is hard to imagine a day of private practice going by without your suggesting to this or that client, "Stay with this angry feeling or" ". . . with this fantasy of killing your mother" or ". . . with this sensation in your chest" or ". . . with the way you are perched on the edge of your chair." Like every idiomatic intervention in every school of psychotherapy, telling your client to stay with what is going on can hard-

*From *Creative License: The Art of Gestalt Therapy.* Edited by Margherita Spagnuolo Lobb and Nancy Amendt-Lyon. (Vienna : Springer-Verlag, September, 2004). Reprinted with permission.

en into an empty and stereotyped technique when you can't think of anything else to do. But it has its roots in an important, original principle of Gestalt therapy — the replacement of the therapist's control of the client's experience, through such methods as interpretation or conditioning programs, with a basic respect for the client's subjectivity as a touchstone of psychotherapy.

In the early days of Gestalt therapy, the complementary notion for maintaining this sort of respect was the idea that the therapist must "stay with" the client, rather than go off on his or her own therapeutic agenda for what the client should experience. Nowadays, Gestalt therapy theory has begun to emphasize its ground in a conception of the emerging field rather than starting out with two already well-defined figures or roles, called therapist and client, as though both already know what they are going to do. So we might speak of "staying with" the unfolding process, as it surfaces, differentiates, melts, gives rise to differences again, and so on. We try to begin now more innocently and indefinitely, letting events assume their own proportions, even as we contribute to giving them form.

Such an outlook is more related to wave theory in modern physics than to the older particle theory. Gestalt therapy has always assumed the therapeutic primacy of collaborative attention between therapist and client at the contact boundary, rather than within the psyche of either the client or the therapist. However, the newer perspective goes beyond the classical formulation of two well-differentiated beings meeting at the contact boundary; for there is a more complex shape-shifting and shape-giving going on than that. But discussing this further would take me too far afield.

Notice that this emphasis on staying with something that is unfolding brings in the dimension of time and therefore of change and development. "Staying with . . ." begins in the present moment, but it is not about the moment. It is about the passing moment, which instantly turns into something else the minute you enter it. After all, we live in time, not in some timeless present moment, which doesn't exist anyway. To stay with a moment would be a neurotic fixation. Erving Polster introduces the temporal dimension of Gestalt therapy in the most direct manner by emphasizing how sequences, whether behavioral or narrative, are composed from the simple principle that "one thing leads to another" (Polster, personal communication).

When you stay with and ride such sequences, which sometimes can be like riding a bucking bronco, sometimes like driving a sports car on an open highway, you will find that all roads lead to Rome. In other words, you can begin any place in therapy, and if you follow the process, you get to the heart of the matter. But the question remains: What is "Rome?" I would argue that Rome is neither the core of the personality nor the authentic self nor even the important past traumas, though such issues might arise and become important on the way to Rome. What I would say is that Rome doesn't yet exist; it has to be made. The process of staying with the experience plays a central part in what one makes.

Staying With . . .

My intention here is to enlarge this question of "staying with" beyond a technical principle for psychotherapy. For me it has become both an aesthetic principle of transformation and an ethical position. I am going to call this a Gestalt therapy view of commitment. We talk a lot about commitment these days, but in a way that is deadening, as in "You should be more committed to this relationship," or ". . . to this career." A common contemporary formula for the failure of relationships is that "Men can't commit themselves to love." Would anyone want to commit himself or herself to love or a career dictated externally in this way? It turns commitment into a prison sentence, all too close to the word's meaning when psychiatrists "commit" someone to the locked ward of the asylum.

But there is a more organic and immediate sense of commitment, which goes something like this: If it feels good or important or useful today, you will probably stay tomorrow. I believe it was the 19th century American writer Ralph Waldo Emerson who said that a good life is an accumulation of good days. "Good" here does not mean necessarily happy or pleasurable but worthwhile, namely worthwhile to you. Neither Emerson's view nor mine is about what is often called the pursuit of happiness. You can't really pursue happiness or a good life, which can only be a projection because it is an ideal of something complete, so either you can never catch up with it, or it has already passed you by. But if you stay with the vital actuality of this moment and the next one, you might look back one day and realize that you have had a good life — or at least a full one. As a matter of fact, nothing that is complete inspires commitment. It is done, so you want to leave it behind before you get bored to death. When you have a great conversation with a friend, one way you know it is that when you say goodbye, you still feel you have a lot more to say. All the topics are still open and running. Healthy commitment is like this; you stay because what you are committed to still feels interestingly incomplete and thus alive.

In the case of these two artists I am going to discuss — Cézanne and Miles Davis — their art was always incomplete, so they kept searching. What I hope to show is that such a view leads to an aesthetics of commitment, not a tyranny of commitment. It may even give rise to a vision of commitment as a kind of cure for

220

ills such as anxiety and depression, in place of Prozac and Zoloft and their relatives.

Whatever else commitment is, it involves a kind of discipline. The founders of Gestalt therapy were by no means indifferent to either commitment or discipline. For instance, Frederick "Fritz" Perls wasn't much given to social or cultural criticism, as Paul Goodman was, though both were anarchists. He was interested mainly in the quality of individual life. But now and then he would launch an attack on some aspect of American society that he felt was playing an important part in killing off people's lives. His most telling critique was aimed at the American pursuit of happiness, which Perls called "hedonism." "We have made a 180-degree turn from puritanism and moralism to hedonism," he wrote in the opening pages of *Gestalt Therapy Verbatim*. "Suddenly everything has to be fun, pleasure, and any sincere involvement, any really *being here*, is discouraged" (1988, p. 1f.).

Perls was not attacking hedonism in the usual sense, which suggests a life dedicated to voluptuous sensual pleasure. That might have been OK with Perls. But he regarded American hedonism as a shallow, plastic conception of a good time, which mostly amounted to avoiding pain. The only way to accomplish this was to desensitize oneself. As a result, there was a profound loss of awareness because one gave up the capacity to feel anything, including love or joy or pleasure. The pursuit of happiness led to the loss of the capacity to experience life fully. You can imagine what Perls would have thought of instant cures like giving medication to everyone who goes through a period of anxiety or depression. He went on to say in *Verbatim*, "there is only one way to regain our soul, or in American terms, to revive the American corpse and bring him back to life. The paradox is that in order to get this spontaneity we need, like in Zen, an utmost discipline" (1988, p. 51).

Whereas for Fritz Perls, commitment and discipline meant staying with the moment-to-moment awareness of whatever was going on in one's actual situation, for Laura Perls, commitment and discipline meant staying with and accepting the limitations of one's actual circumstances and making the most creative use of what was available. In her beautiful little talk on a Japanese movie, *The Woman in the Dunes*, she says:

> As long as our man in the story cannot accept the limitations of the situation, he feels trapped. When he accepts his confinement, possibilities within its boundaries become realities: the desert becomes fertile, the woman a mother. This opens the trap, the boundaries widen. By committing himself anew to the somewhat changed but still limited and difficult situation, the man takes responsibility for the consequences of his own creative activities. . . . By accepting and coping with 'what is,' he transforms and transcends the situation and achieves true freedom. (1986, p. 13)

Laura Perls's statement seems to me particularly important. Like Hegel, she is saying that there is no freedom without necessity. In other words, true freedom comes after commitment and discipline — in both the arts and in love. Most people seem to think it goes the other way around.

Which brings me to my two central characters or "case histories" in this narrative. Why Cézanne and Miles Davis? Largely because they are two of my great favorites. But there is a theme that I think they both exemplify (and it will be obvious I could have chosen any number of other artists). Both were frequently troubled and at times just plain miserable, in their personal lives — Cézanne full of anxiety and self-doubt; Miles Davis full of dark rage and melancholy. What is important is that no matter how difficult things became neither of them ever wandered far from their commitment to the continual practice of their art and to the deepest search for personal truth within the framework of artistic expression.

Paul Cézanne

Cézanne's quest to give form to the subjective immediate truth of his perceptions never wavered once he left law school. He had gone to law school out of obedience to the wishes of his bourgeois father, who was a hat-maker and later became a banker. Leaving law school to paint was an act of rebellion against his family's way of life. It was not easy for him to do. It left him anxious, self-doubting, and angry for much of his life. He also remained terrified of his father. When he fell in love with a woman and moved in with her, he didn't have the nerve to tell his father, even after they had a child.

He was a difficult man. This is how John Rewald, his chief biographer and editor of his letters, describes him: "Lighthearted and carefree in his youth, he later becomes suspicious and withdrawn. His expressions vary between tenderness, even humility, and arrogance; his self-reliance sometimes changes to bitterness and disappointment; his forgiveness and politeness can rapidly turn into rudeness" (1986, p. 6). He was never satisfied. But he never stopped painting with the greatest intensity of focus. His suffering — his anxiety and anger — surely increased when the critics denounced his early paintings as trash and claimed that he had no talent. He suffered from this, but it never stopped him.

In 1874 when Cézanne exhibited his paintings at the first Impressionist exhibition, he was derided by the critics, as were most of the other Impressionists. But Cézanne got the worst of it. One critic described him as "a sort of madman who paints in delirium tremens" (Wechsler, 1975, p. 3). After three more years of this kind of reception, Cézanne withdrew from the public eye until 1889. In a state of relative isolation he kept on painting. If anything, he became more intensely committed to rendering the originality of his own vision, the truth of his perceptions.

By 1895 his reputation had changed: He had become known as a painter's painter — Pissarro, Renoir, Degas, and Monet were among those deeply impressed with his work — and by 1904, it was said that his influence was to be seen everywhere in the world of art (Wechsler, 1975, p. 5). By now, there has hardly been a modern intellectual movement that hasn't taken Cézanne to its bosom as a key figure and offered its own interpretation of his work. One art historian gives the following list: Naturalist, Symbolist, Neoclassical, perceptual, formalist, didactic, Marxist, psychoanalytic (both Freudian and Jungian), phenomenological and existentialist (Wechsler, 1975, p. 2). The English novelist D. H. Lawrence, the German poet Rilke, and the French philosopher Maurice Merleau-Ponty all wrote major commentaries on Cézanne.

Cézanne painted out of a loyalty to his subjectivity so pure that his paintings themselves became a way of seeing, rather than a way of adding feelings or symbols or meanings to what he saw. He single-handedly evolved a new language for painting, which influenced every painter in western civilization who came after him. His withdrawal from society and public view may have been inspired partly by anxiety or depression or whatever, but he transformed his aloneness into a kind of epistemological research into the perceiving subject through the medium of painting. This was a profound act of commitment. A recent critic, Kurt Badt has written:

> The mere fact that he took his own person and destiny as subject-matter for his art marked Cézanne out as a modern painter; his modernity was further demonstrated by the fact (not unconnected) that loneliness played a great and significant role in his art. By dedicating himself wholly to his art, he now accepted [around 1870] the fate of loneliness as an essential prerequisite of his work, surrendered to it, and thereby gained that new view of the world, which was expressed in all his work from now on. (in: Wechsler, 1975, p. 142)

Badt regards this as something approaching a conversion of a religious nature. He contrasts it with the Impressionists who saw nature as lovely and consoling:

> Whereas other artists worked in an atmosphere of self-enjoyment, in a subjective and intimate relationship with the subjects which they were painting . . . Cézanne on the other hand painted in a state of self-oblivion, dedicating himself wholly to the objects in whose essential nature he sought to penetrate. (in: Wechsler, 1975, p. 143)

Meyer Schapiro, one of the great art historians and critics of our time, said of Cézanne, that "his work is a living proof that a painter can achieve a profound expression by giving form to his perceptions of the world around him without recourse to a guiding religion or myth or any explicit social aims" (Schapiro, 1988, p. 29). D. H. Lawrence wrote that "the most interesting figure in modern art, and the only really interesting figure, is Cézanne: and that, not so much because of his achievement as because of his struggle" (Lawrence, 1980, p. 571). Cézanne's aloneness, his struggle, and his devotion to his own perceptions are all facets of his commitment.

Miles Davis

Miles Davis was also an angry and distressed man. He was raised in a well-to-do African-American family in St. Louis (his father was a dentist), a background that made him all the more sensitive to and enraged by the racism he encountered everywhere outside the family. His life was often a hell, first because of addiction to heroin and alcohol, both of which he kicked, later because of renewed drug use and serious illness. But nothing swayed him from playing the trumpet from the time he was ten, and during his extraordinary jazz career, he never stopped searching for new ways to give musical expression to his vision of life.

He was not exactly an easy man to get along with, especially where race was concerned. He was known for turning his back on his audience in jazz clubs and playing his horn to the other members of his band. When his mind was scrambled by drugs or alcohol, he was given to staging outrageous scenes in public. Here is a not untypical anecdote from the poet Quincy Troupe's biography of Davis:

. . . there was the time when Miles abandoned his Ferrari in the middle of West End Avenue after spotting a policeman he thought was following him. He was so paranoid and high on cocaine that he ran into an apartment building and jumped into an elevator. A startled white woman was already inside the elevator, when he saw her, he slapped her face and asked her what she was doing in his car. She ran screaming out of the elevator and Miles took it up to the top floor, where he stayed, hiding in the garbage disposal room until late in the evening. (Troupe, 2000, p. 22)

But then, contrast this with Troupe's description of Miles' playing:

Miles Davis was a great poet on his instrument. His horn could blow warm, round notes that spoke to the deepest human emotions . . . Miles' sound always made us sit up and take notice. It was burnished, brooding, unforgettable . . . When you heard Miles on the radio, you knew right away that it was him. You knew it by the sound because no one else ever sounded like that. Like Louis Armstrong's, Duke Ellington's, Thelonious Monk's, John Coltrane's, his voice was unmistakably unique. (2000, p. 1)

How does one get from the mess of Miles Davis' life to the poetry of his jazz? The answer is the unshakeable disciplined commitment to the mastery of his art. The need to play his horn enabled him to overcome his addictions because they interfered too much. He took a lesson in the need for discipline from his lifelong love of boxing. As he explains in his autobiography, his model was the great prizefighter, Sugar Ray Robinson:

> Anyway, I really kicked my habit because of the example of Sugar Ray Robinson; I figured if he could, as disciplined as he was, then I could do it, too . . . When he in the ring, he was serious, all business. I decided that that was the way I was going to be, serious about taking care of my business and disciplined. (Davis, 1989, p. 174)

Davis was by no means unusual among jazz musicians in his involvement with drugs, his moodiness, even his frequent bizarre behavior in public or on the stage, although few performers have produced displays as dramatic as his. The habits or behavior of jazz musicians, combined with the fact that their performances are based on spontaneous improvisation, may lead one to imagine that they are undisciplined about their art. But this is a thoroughly mistaken idea. In his book surveying the impact of Miles Davis on American culture, Gerald Early quotes the novelist Ralph Ellison, who knew jazz very well on this topic. Ellison makes it clear that he learned a good deal from jazz musicians about the commitment a writer needs:

> Now, I had learned from jazz musicians I had known as a boy in Oklahoma City something of the discipline and devotion to his art required of the artist. . . . These jazzmen, many of them now world-famous, lived for and with their music in-

tensely. Their driving motivation was neither money nor fame, but the will to achieve the most eloquent expression of idea-emotions through the technical mastery of their instruments . . . I had learned too that the end of all this discipline and technical mastery was the desire to express an affirmative way of life . . . Life could be harsh, loud and wrong if it wished, but they lived it fully, and when they expressed their attitude toward the world it was with a fluid style that reduced the chaos of living to form. (Early, 2001, p. 13)

Expression of Subjectivity

Perhaps neither Cézanne nor Miles Davis led lives that we are likely to envy. Some of us may think there is nothing we would rather be than a great painter or jazz musician. But it wasn't easy to be Paul Cézanne or Miles Davis. Both their lives were filled with trouble. Out of their turmoil, both withdrew from public view for many years. In the practice of their art, however, they were both committed to an extraordinary degree to their search for the fullest expression of their unique subjectivity. Miles Davis listened to the world and listened to himself. He listened to the voices of black people expressing anguish, lamentation, and joy. He listened to the whole history of the music they made, and to every other kind of music, and he listened to the branches swept by wind, the ocean's monologue, and the sounds of the city. And he strove to shape all of it into music that gave expression to what he heard as it made its way through his own existence. Cézanne looked at his world with an absolute absorption and then worked and worked at painting the experience of what he saw without resorting to ideology, convention, symbolism or any external props. Neither of them ever rested on their accomplishments because they never felt that the task was complete.

By virtue of their disciplined, undivided attention to and absorption in the subjective truth of their experience, each of these artists created new forms that changed the course of everything that followed. Neither painting nor jazz was ever again the same after them. Cézanne, leaving impressionism behind, almost single-handedly created modern art. Miles Davis, who came of age during the bebop era, invented almost single-handedly "cool jazz" and then went on to create most of the new possibilities that have shaped jazz to this day.

How would one apply this ideal of disciplined commitment to an intimate relationship, for example? As far as I'm concerned, no one gives us a better sense of this than D. H. Lawrence, whom I still regard as a wise authority on love. In a fine essay called *We Need One Another*, Lawrence writes the following about the relationship between commitment and sexual desire:

> And what is sex, after all, but the symbol of the relation of man to woman, woman to man? And the relation of man to woman is wide as all life. It consists in infinite different flows between the two beings, different, even apparently contrary. Chastity is part of the flow between man and woman, as to physical passion. And beyond these, an infinite range of subtle communication, which we know nothing about. I should say that the relation between any two decently married people changes profoundly every few years, often without their knowing anything about it; though every change

causes pain, even if it brings a certain joy. The long course of marriage is a long event of perpetual change, in which a man and a woman mutually build up their souls and make themselves whole. It is like rivers flowing on through new country, always unknown.

But we are so foolish, and fixed by our limited ideas. A man says: "I don't love my wife any more, I no longer want to sleep with her." But why should he always want to sleep with her? How does he know what other subtle and vital interchange is going on between him and her, making them both whole, in this period when he doesn't want to sleep with her? And she, instead of jibbing and saying that all is over and she must find another man and get a divorce — why doesn't she pause, and listen for a new rhythm in her soul, and look for the new movement in the man? With every change, a new being emerges, a new rhythm establishes itself; we renew our life as we grow older, and there is real peace. Why, oh, why do we want one another to be always the same, fixed, like a menu card that is never changed?

If only we had more sense. But we are held by a few fixed ideas, like sex, money, what a person 'ought' to be, and so forth, and we miss the whole of life. Sex is a changing thing, now alive, now quiescent, now fiery, now apparently quite gone, quite gone. But the ordinary man and woman haven't the gumption to take it in all its changes. They demand crass, crude sex-desire, they demand it always, and

when it isn't forthcoming, then — smash-bash!
smash up the whole show. Divorce! Divorce! (Lawrence, 1933, p. 36ff.)

I have been reflecting on these themes for a long time —
beginning with an old article called "Notes Toward Art and
Symptoms" (Miller, 1980). There I spoke about the aesthetic
transformation of mental suffering in psychotherapy, taking the
model from what artists do. This has led me to an idea not only of
transformation as the outcome but commitment as the process
that does not deny one's pain or difficulty in life, but achieves a
kind of "cure" by making productive use of it.

To my thinking, this sort of commitment is love in the
broadest sense, whether in an intimate relationship or in pursuit of
one's calling. It's a way of staying connected to life in a difficult and
imperfect world, rather than withdrawing into depression, which
often is just the other side of a demand that one's life be paradise
and a refusal to settle for anything less ("Paradise or nothing," goes
the depressive's cry).

As I have already pointed out in agreement with Perls and
Lawrence, such commitments oppose the shallow "pursuit of happiness," in which one throws out a relationship and seeks another
as soon as there are problems, or takes a pill in the hope of abolish-
ing anxiety and depression without any effort at self-exploration or
any taking of responsibility.

I'm not one who likes to mix psychotherapy and spiritual
questions. But I have to confess that an aesthetic understanding of
commitment, rooted in the quest to give form to the truth of one's
experience, sometimes makes me wonder if their relationship can
be ignored. The aesthetics of commitment is as close as I can come
to an ideal of faith or spiritual devotion that might direct one to-

ward a higher freedom. For me, artists like Cézanne and Davis exemplify the idea expressed in Kierkegaard's title *Purity of Heart is to Will One Thing* (Kierkegaard, 1956).

This doesn't mean being a monomaniac or an obsessive; it means giving your full attention to what you are doing at the moment and bestowing the fullest true form on the moment that you can give it. Kierkegaard contrasts this with what he calls "doublemindedness" (see Kierkegaard, 1956), by which he means denial, self-deception, evasion or anaesthetization of anxiety and depression. To give your wholehearted attention and creativity to the truth, even to the truth of suffering, leads to transcendence and transformation of it, as Laura Perls points out. Kierkegaard (1956) calls this willing the Good.

True enough, artists have often led questionable or terrible lives, but in their work they seem to discover how to will the Good. As models of how to live from day to day, their lives tend to be of little use, but their ways of working can teach us a great deal about the paths to a better life.

References

Cézanne, P. (1976). *Letters* (J. Rewald, Ed.). New York, NY: Hacker Art Books.

Davis, M., with Quincy Troupe (1989). *Miles: The autobiography.* New York: Simon & Schuster.

Early, G. (Ed.) (2001). *Miles Davis and American culture.* Saint Louis, MO: Missouri Historical Society Press.

Kierkegaard, S. (1956). *Purity of heart is to will one thing* (D. V. Steere, Trans.). New York: Harper Torchbooks.

Lawrence, D. H. (1980). Phoenix: *The posthumous papers*, 1936 (E. McDonald, Trans.). New York: Penguin.

Lawrence, D. H. (1933). *We need one another*. New York: Equinox.

Miller, M. V. (1980). 'Notes on art and symptoms.' *The Gestalt Journal* 3/1, 86-98.

Perls, F. S. (1988). *Gestalt therapy verbatim — With a new introduction by Michael V. Miller*. Gouldsboro, ME: Gestalt Journal Press.

Perls, L. (1986). 'Commitment — Opening Address, 8th Annual Conference on the Theory and Practice of Gestalt Therapy, May 17,1985.' *The Gestalt Journal* 9/1, 12-15.

Perls, L. (1992). *Living at the boundary* (J. Wysong, Ed.). Gouldsboro, ME: Gestalt Journal Press.

Rewald, J. (1986). *Cézanne: A biography*. New York: Abrams.

Schapiro, M. (1988). *Cézanne*. New York: Abrams.

Troupe, Q. (2000). *Miles and me*. Berkeley, CA: University of California Press.

Wechsler, J. (Ed.) (1975). *Cézanne in perspective*. Englewood Cliffs, NJ: Prentice-Hall.

∫ Ordinary Talk
— For Isadore

    Much of what I want to address here about the relation-ship between the ordinary and the extraordinary has to do with the nature of language and representation. This may sound more philosophical than clinical. Let me remind you, though, that Isadore From, before he became a Gestalt therapist, was trained as a philosopher. Throughout his life, he turned not only to Freud and Reich, Ferenczi and Rank but also Plato and Aristotle, Spinoza, Husserl, and Wittgenstein. The implications of how language represents states of mind and being were always impor-tant to him — not only with regard to psychological theory but also with regard to how patients expressed themselves. The same is pretty much true for me as well. I increasingly tend to think of psychotherapy as applied philosophy.

---

*This was a talk given at *The Gestalt Journal's* International Conference Honoring Isadore From which met in Boston, Massachusetts April 26 to April 30, 1995. It is somewhat revised here to make it more readable. I have tried to preserve its character as a talk rather than convert it into a fully developed essay.

Questions of language and representation came up for me sharply at a recent symposium conducted at the Harvard Medical School's Department of Psychiatry in which I took part. The symposium was designed around the question how different schools of psychotherapy might treat similar clinical issues. I was to appear as the representative Gestalt therapist on a panel alongside a Jungian, a psychoanalyst, a cognitive-behavioral therapist. Our assigned task was to read the same case history of a young man, a very distressed young man, and then each of us was to comment on how we would approach him from each of our particular disciplines.

I had the feeling, as I listened to the various presentations, that all four of us were touched by the account of this self-defeating, sad, and damaged young man and his story of having grown up with cold, neglectful parents.

Now, in his late 20s, he is still unable to detach himself from these parents and live his own life. It was apparent that he is filled with a great deal of pent-up anger that left him psychologically crippled in many important respects. As I said we were all touched by his story, even though we had his presence only in the third-person singular written down on paper.

As the presentations went on, however, although in a climate of empathy for this man's suffering, the man himself began to disappear. He began to dissolve into our diverse conceptual abstractions.

In the Jungian's presentation, the man took on more and more universal characteristics and seemed to become larger than life. He began to swell up with self-archetypes, mother archetypes, and parent complexes until, like a balloon, the poor guy rose up into the sky, as though his fate were similar to those old Greek tales about how heroes and heroines became constellations in the heavens. It was if he had entered a mythic realm. This was fascinating, but his individuality and particularity seemed to have become lost.

In the case of the psychoanalyst, whose orientation was object relations theory, it was as though the man had turned into a cubist painting. As in the works of George Braque or Picasso, the young man broke up into fragments and pieces — self-objects and parts objects, introjected good and bad breasts, and split egos— that were layered or mirrored or reattached where you wouldn't expect them to be at odd angles.

With the cognitive-behaviorist person, we entered the more austere but equally abstract atmosphere of evidence-based treatment and two factor models, of modeling, extinction, and response prevention, collaborative hypothesis testing, and schedules of protocols.

In each of these talks, the patient seemed to grow in size yet fade into something at once more conceptually spectacular but more limited in humanity than the rather simple, straightforward narrative account of him we had all read, the one that had originally moved us. In that narrative he was an ordinary suffering human being. But in our diagnostic treatments of him, he expanded into something extraordinary.

I'd love to tell you that I alone stayed down-to-earth and avoided climbing into the tower of abstractions that was being erected, like a specialist's version of the proverbial tower of Babel. But I'm sure I didn't, because the language of Gestalt therapy, too, with its contact boundaries, retroflections, confluence, and so on, can just as easily become reified as the language of all psychological theory tends to do once it is treated as more than a collection of flexible and mutable metaphors. Reification replaces the concrete thing itself with abstract, fixed descriptions of it and then treats these thing-like linguistic descriptions as though they are the actual reality.

Despite what I felt had been lost, it did seem to me that our common ability to feel for and engage with this young man and his suffering was still present. I believe that we were a group of committed therapists doing good work. But our ways of talking about our work seemed to leave the planet, as though the bulk of how we all live carrying out and experiencing our simple, mundane, everyday activities, feelings, and thoughts was not worth our exploring.

Each of us seemed torn between empathy and authority, between ordinary humanity and mystification, between openness to the contingent and the longing for certitude, between being curious, interested, and fascinated and presenting ourselves as knowledgeable experts.

Keep in mind that this, of course, was Harvard. One had to appear as though one knew something. So perhaps we all tended to put forward our most authoritative foot forward. I suspect, as I have said, that we were all better therapists than our presentations might have made us out to be.

I think that what was operating here was a tension that has characterized the whole history of psychotherapy, the tension between remaining an ordinary human being, with some special trained skills, to be sure, speaking to and engaging other ordinary human beings, and wanting to appear as a shaman or oracle or member of an arcane priesthood with the alluring promise of higher wisdom to bestow on our followers and patients.

It's a tension that besets many service professions and much academic work in our specialized and technological world. I think that the four of us may have felt at once connected and divided. What divided us was our insistence on each of us impressing the Harvard audience with our specialized bodies of knowledge, expressed in the language of our diverse theories. What join-ed us was an atmosphere of concern for the suffering of another, which existed between the lines of what we were saying. There was a generosity of spirit present, but it was encumbered by the ab-stract metaphysical and scientific language.

A week or so before the Harvard symposium, I spent most of a Saturday not as a presenter but as an audience. In the after-noon, I went to see a performance of Tony Kushner's hugely suc-cessful play *Angels in America*. This was "Part One." I couldn't even get tickets for "Part Two."

It was indeed a spectacular production, and at times, or so I thought, brilliant theater. And it was concerned with grand themes: The decline of our politics into McCarthyism. The de-cline of our personal integrity. The nature of manhood. (There was not really much on the nature of womanhood, because, for the most part, the women in the play seemed to be either harpies or dolls.)

The play raised powerful issues about sexuality, in and out of the closet, expressed partly with allusion to an Old Testament prophetic declaration about the possibilities of redemption in time of plague, brought up to date because the plague in the play was AIDS.

It's somewhat Brechtian style was hardly what you could call ordinary. There were intimations, in fact, of extraordinary events rumbling behind the scenes throughout, even extraterres-trial ones.

What emerged at the end was extraterrestrial indeed, since the play, at least "Part One," climaxes with an angel, in full heav-enly regalia, wings outspread, surrounded by celestial sound and light, crashes through the ceiling of a hospital room in which one of the protagonists is dying of AIDS. And she pronounces him a sort of leader, or progenitor, of the millennium to come.

I found "Angels" a powerful and thought-provoking play, stirring, but only intermittently moving. When the angel landed, I couldn't help thinking of the full-scale helicopter than lands on the stage in *Miss Saigon* and the massive chandelier that comes crashing down from the high ceiling in *Phantom of the Opera*. Effective theater, to be sure, but do such devices take you deeper into the subject matter?

Almost everywhere in our entertainment culture these days, there seems to be pressure to produce more and more extraordinary spectacles. Hollywood movies now rarely are about only two cowboys on either side of the law drawing six guns to shoot it out. Instead entire skyscrapers or bridges collapse in massive explosions as the hero and his partner or girlfriend barely escape by driving a car off the edge of a sixth-story parking garage or an elevated highway and somehow survive a fall from incredible heights.

By way of contrast, I went that same Saturday evening to see Louis Malle's film *Vanya on 42nd Street*. This beautiful film begins with an ingenious frame, in which a bunch of actors on their way to a rehearsal wander into a Broadway theater in their street clothes, begin chatting with one another and the director, and without any noticeable transition to cue you, you suddenly realize that you are watching a very intense and intimate production of Chekhov's play *Uncle Vanya* as translated by David Mamet.

Nothing spectacular happens in Chekhov's play. In fact, in one sense, almost nothing eventful happens at all: people come and go and they talk. It's just ordinary life.

There are no Schwarzeneggers or Stallones or Steven Seagals in this film. No Kim Basingers or Michelle Pfeiffers. There are no amazing displays of martial arts or to-die-for sweaty orgasms. There is just the coming and going of ordinary people telling stories of their sufferings and longings, failures and hopes to one another.

If you recall Freud's famous remark that all we can do is deliver our patients from their hysteric miseries back to the common, ordinary unhappiness, you could say that Chekhov is a master at portraying the hysterical miseries that we add on top of our inevitable ordinary suffering.

In *Angels in America*, the polemical message and prophetic intent almost wash away the individuality of the characters, such that they tend to become archetypes (despite some remarkable individual acting). But in *Uncle Vanya* there's neither polemic nor prophesy. Nothing is justified or explained. Yet every individual character is treated with kindness even, at times, if it's an ironical, chiding kindness. And they are all treated with the respect that comes of having Chekhov's full attention.

I found *Vanya on 42nd Street* intimately absorbing and deeply moving in a way that was missing for me in the brilliance and flash of *Angels in America*. The difference between these two experiences was a little like going on a date to an expensive restaurant with a glamorous sought-after man or woman for whom you feel admiration and awe contrasted with hanging out at home with a man or woman that you know and love deeply.

For me there was also another, more subtle effect of the difference between these two theatrical experiences. Both plays deal with human suffering. But *Angels in America* had the effect on me of inflating my sense of self. It seemed to call forth in me a particular kind of self-importance. I became concerned with forming my opinion and interpretation of the play's implications. I asked myself what is my reaction to and how do I understand my place among the big issues of our times? Will the dark fate of our corrupt and terrible politics overtake me?

Watching *Vanya on 42nd Street*, on the other hand, my sense of myself tended to disappear into the background, because I became so utterly absorbed in the reality of the characters. I think this comment somewhat oversimplifies the situation, but one could say that *Angels* generated, in me at least, paranoid projections and *Vanya* empathic ones.

In these two examples, I've established a kind of opposition between the ordinary and the extraordinary. Are they really in opposition? If they are both allowed to exist and become integrated with one another, particularly if the extraordinary has its roots in and grows out of ordinary experience, as is often the case, for example, in the best works of art, then there is an important sense in which they can be deeply connected. But how do these issues bear on the work we do with our patients?

I can best answer this, perhaps, by telling you a little about how I first became interested in this whole question of the extraordinary and the ordinary — not as an issue of psychological theory, but through thinking about certain cultural values as guides for human development, predominantly of men but increasingly of women, that came up frequently in my practice.

People come into therapy and tell you stories. And when it comes to stories, one of the important things you deal with inevitably is the issue of how selective memory can be. What I found with a number of my male patients, especially older ones, is that in telling stories of their childhood and growing up, what they remembered mainly were the extraordinary events that occurred in their pasts.

They would remember when they were on the high school football team and caught the touchdown pass that won the game. They would remember the awards and trophies they won in school and the graduation ceremony in which they got their diploma. They would remember that golden moment when the glamorous head cheerleader that all the guys were after spent a long night entangled with them in the back seat of a car. Moments of accomplishment or conquest, sexually, athletically, scholastically, stood out in their minds. So did in some cases moments of traumatic or tragic setbacks.

What was missing from their accounts, for the most part, were those ordinary moments of life — the everyday experiences of one thing leading to another that exists in the passages in between or on the way to the accomplishments: They remembered very little of what it was like to walk home every afternoon or play with other kids after school. What were the dominant topics of conversation in the family. What is was like doing homework, feeding the dog, and the rest of the ordinary domestic stuff. When I inquired further about the spaces in between the big events I found that they were pretty blank. It was not a question of repression exactly. You don't remember what you don't pay attention to. And for these men, so driven toward achievement, success, and conquest, the ordinary moments were not the ones worth attending to as boys or remembering as adults.

I think that the dismissal of the passages of ordinary life to focus on extraordinary events says a great deal about our culture and its values and how it tends to make us addicted to trying to become extraordinary or to seeking extraordinary experiences. But this emphasis suggests some interesting possibilities for how we might think about certain kinds of neurotic suffering and its formation. Let me describe what I mean through the example of a man I saw as a patient.

Now in his sixties, he had become a leading cardiologist. He grew up in a Jewish family in Detroit with a mother who held forth the promise that being able someday to say "my son, the doctor" would bring her great happiness. I wouldn't say that was the only reason he went to medical school, but his mother's wishes influenced his decision.

He had always been very successful in school and even more so professionally. When I asked him about his childhood, he described the grades he got, the teams he was on, having been a pretty good athlete, his honors at graduation and other awards. He had always been an "A" student. Over the course of his career he had been appointed head of several hospital departments; he was a partner in founding and directing one of the most powerful physician groups in his region; and he had a long waiting list of patients.

But when he came to me for therapy, it was with the complaint of a rather low-key but nevertheless chronic depression, a kind of general sense of malaise. He had paid off the mortgage on his house in one of the most expensive suburbs. His grown children had gone to Ivy League colleges, and at present were well-situated in successful careers. His second marriage seemed reasonably happy, although he lamented the diminishing of romantic thrill, felt increasingly uninterested in sex with his wife, and sometimes found himself unable to sustain an erection.

From our usual cultural perspective, his is a portrait of a pretty successful life, based on hard-won achievement. But in the midst of his depression, he found himself asking at this late mortgage-paid-off, kids-gone-through-the-best-colleges stage of his life, "Is that all there is?"

It was the existential poignancy of this question, which I heard from a number of older, professionally and domestically successful men, that got me interested in exploring our cultural-driven need to pursue extraordinary experience in order to feel worthwhile in contrast to what it might mean to live in harmony with the passing moments of ordinary life.

Applied to our children, our abiding individualism demands that we work very hard to stand out if we want to feel worth loving. In many families children come to feel that the only way to feel worthwhile and win love is to stand out by becoming a special — and especially successful — person.

Consider, for example, the cardiologist's loss of libido and at times his potency. When you think about the demand that the need to be extraordinary places on sex — that you have to be a sexual athlete in bed and every performance better be a touch down pass — for how long under such pressure can one still experience spontaneous sexual excitement?

Gestalt therapy is closer than most psychotherapies to eastern spiritual traditions, such as Buddhism, that proclaim that the most fulfilling human existence is to be found not just through the achievement of goals but through being fully alive to the present moment. But the fact is that most present moments of one's life are quite ordinary. If ordinary experience seems not worth paying attention to, living for the present moment holds little promise. Instead, one lives in the recollection of past glories and even more for future attainments. What do you do later in life, when the future begins to run out?

Is that all there is? So ask many successful people, like my cardiologist patient, when they look up from having achieved the goals they set for themselves. From their perspective, where nothing much seems important between goals, victories, and their pursuit, the only answer is yes. But yes leads to disappointment or depression only if one cannot imagine that the broad span of ordinary days in which we spend most of our lives could in itself also be a rich source of gratification — perhaps not the gratification of attainments that make one special in the eyes of the world (and thereby in one's own self-regard), but the kind that comes from giving one's full attention to the present moment.

∫ Drawing the Line

In essence, the theory of Gestalt therapy is an aesthetic vision of human nature and human functioning. Three major themes distinguish the way in which Gestalt therapy is inspired by the arts. The first, at least chronologically, was Perls's radical vision of aggression as a self-expressive creative force rather than a destructive derivative of the death instinct.

The second, although perhaps left mostly implicit in the book by Perls, Hefferline, and Goodman, presents diagnosis in terms of aesthetic qualities instead of ones resembling the natural sciences. This idea, combining Otto Rank's psychology of the artist with the concept of gestalt formation, suggests that health is like a well-made work of art, in which experience takes graceful, coherent, and economical forms, whereas pathology resembles bad art, full of repetitions, stereotypes, and monotony.

---

* From the *International Gestalt Journal*, Vol. 30, No. 1, (Spring, 2007). Reprinted with permission.

The third brings out an emphasis on temporality in Gestalt therapy. This does not amount to the past creating present consequences nor even being in the "here-and-now." Temporality in Gestalt therapy conceives all experience, including the experience of the self, as gestalt formation and creative adjustment produced by an incessant collaboration between the organism and the environment unfolding and changing through time.

In my notion of "drawing the line," I am attempting to integrate these three themes by introducing a unifying metaphor that expands the concept of the contact boundary. I hope that it may bring a new and valuable perspective to the theory of Gestalt therapy.

———

The idea of a boundary by itself seems to me too limiting for Gestalt therapy which is so rich in aesthetic possibilities. A boundary is just one kind of line. It is a spatial concept which suggests a border where two regions can meet, touch, and influence one another without losing their respective identities. It is evident that this describes an important phenomenon, but the concept of boundary describes it without expressiveness, form or temporality. Even if one speaks of a continuously changing boundary, it is still useful to enlarge this metaphor by introducing the idea of temporality and form through the more far-reaching possibilities that lines can convey. But psychological theory has little to tell us about the complex language of lines. We must therefore turn to the poets, painters, musicians, and philosophers.

A boundary is a border, and a line can also be a border. One meaning of the expression "drawing the line" is putting a definitive limit upon the desires and actions of others or even upon one's own. But a line is also a passage. That takes it far beyond the idea of a boundary. Above all, it implies that although a line can exist in space, it is also temporal. It can represent movement and development. As Manlio Brusatin, a historian of art and architecture, puts it in his excellent book, *Histoire de la ligne*: "Life is a line, thought is a line, action is a line. Everything is a line. The line connects two points. The point is an instant and there are two instants that define the beginning and the end of a line" (2002, p. 19). [*translation mine*]

Moreover, the line is the beginning of form. It can curve back on itself, make knots, outline the contours of almost any form; it can be continuous or discontinuous. Lines can cross one another and become braided, like the intertwining chiasm of experience that Merleau-Ponty thinks is at the core of human perception in his great work, *The Visible and the Invisible*. Think of the melody line, the line of poetry, and the artist's line. Many of the most exquisite and perfect expressions of our humanity are experienced through lines, whether ink or paint on an empty canvas, words on a blank page, the notes of a melody upon the silence, or even the line that a fly fisherman traces on the water when the elegant movement of the cast becomes more meaningful than catching a fish.

If we follow the thought of Gilles Deleuze in his book, *The Fold: Leibnitz and the Baroque*, one could say that Descartes is the philosopher of the boundary, which divides, contains, and thus imposes a separation that he does not manage to unify fully, ultimately leaving mind and body split off from one another. Leibniz, however, is the philosopher of the complex line, who emphasizes the continuity of experience with infinite possibilities of curves, evoking an existence which incessantly folds and refolds upon itself.

When I am sitting face to face with a patient, I don't look only at a boundary which might exist between us in order to make a diagnosis of disturbances. This seems to me too abstract an outlook for full exploration of the therapeutic landscape. What interests me also is knowing the expressive qualities of this person, if she holds my interest, if she moves me emotionally, how her presence otherwise affects me. In other terms, I pay attention to a patient's "line" (some examples in common use are "What's your line?" or "He's got a good line."), as well as how my own line intersects with that of the patient: Is it wide or narrow, does it have regular or irregular rhythms of shape and movement, does it travel in a straight line or makes detours, is it rigid or fluid, does it fold in upon itself or spirals outward, does it tend to be general and abstract or particular and detailed, what kind of form is this line on the way to creating between us?

These are questions which arise from the fact that we are in each other's presence, a proximity that can be partially described by a boundary. But it is also an experience which unfolds in time, in successive waves, in intervals which have a rhythm, a form, a tone and accent, all of which can be better characterized through lines. I am also mindful of the play between my lines and those of the patient — are they diverging, parallel, in counterpoint like a fugue, are they becoming interwoven, etc? Imagine a globe of the world floating along a river, turning on its axis on the surface of the water. Moment by moment different continents and countries appear above the surface while others disappear. But as it spins, it leaves behind for a few seconds its trail in the river. Such is the temporal aesthetic of psychotherapy and the changing lines it draws. We need to pay attention in therapy to the shifting forms on the revolving sphere but also to the trail it makes.

In making a diagnosis one certainly gets to an important part of the story by discerning how a patient makes disturbances at the contact boundary. This is without doubt a highly valuable tool. It can be richly elaborated, however, by paying attention to the spectrum of the patient's expressive responses — the direction and force of his or her aggression, which forms the line with an arrowhead that mathematicians and physicists call a "vector."

Psychotherapy is interested in the trajectories of curiosity, the expressive lineaments of desire and the absence of desire, the rising and falling lines of disappointment and fulfillment, the diagrammatic outlines, like a sketch by Matisse, of the body moving toward or away.

Then there are the complex blueprints of lines — lines of the body, of facial expression, of language — that are engaged in building a mausoleum to the past, and thus manifest themselves as depression. Or the jagged, unstable, and dispersed lines in the agitated expressiveness of a person who awaits a disaster. The latter might be called the lines of anxiety.

Therapy is concerned with freedom and seeks to release patients from the weight of repetition, so that they will be able to experience each new moment as new. "Unless there is a new mind, there cannot be a new line," proclaimed the poet William Carlos Willams. Another poet, George Oppen wrote: "The process by which sometimes a line appears, I cannot trace. It happens. Given a line, one has a place to stand, and goes further."

These ideas bring to mind again the thought of Deleuze, whose writings are full of fascinating ideas about lines. In *A Thousand Plateaus*, one of the books he wrote with Felix Guattari, he speaks of the relation between points and lines in a highly original way which can be stimulating for the psychotherapist.

Deleuze and Guattari set forth what they call the "punctual system," created by a horizontal line and a vertical one which serve, as in mathematics, to serve as coordinates for the placement of points. Other lines can then be drawn to connect the points and form a grid. Everything is thus determined by the fixed points. According to Deleuze and Guattari, systems of this type encode memory and history and keep them in place. But then, the authors go on,

> *Opposed to the punctual system are linear, or rather multilinear, systems. Free the line, free the diagonal: every musician or painter has this intention . . . A punctual system is most interesting when there is a musician, painter, writer, philosopher to oppose it . . . History is made only by those who oppose history . . . free the line and the diagonal, draw the line instead of plotting a point.* (Deleuze and Guattari, p. 295-6)

Such free diagonal lines pass between points and are therefore not imprisoned in the past. "There is no act of creation that is not transhistorical and does not come up from behind or proceed by way of a liberated line." claim Deleuze and Guattari (p. 296).

The portrait by Deleuze and Guattari of creativity as an interaction between the system of fixed points and the fluid system of liberated lines can be usefully applied to psychotherapy. One could consider such systems of fixed points and lines which can only be drawn through points in order to connect them as the stasis or fixation, the repetition compulsion, that characterizes neurosis. By contrast, the liberated lines which can take off on their own represent the freedom to create something new that we call health.

One can even apply this distinction to the therapy session itself. Psychotherapy resembles jazz more than it does classical music. The theory that guides the psychotherapist is more akin to a punctual system, like the chord progressions and the melody line that anchors a jazz group in a common enterprise. Yet the therapy sessions themselves, like each musician's solos in jazz, are improvised lines, liberated lines of creativity, which in the language of Deleuze and Guattari, "deterritorialize" the points and sweep them away.

There is a story in Zen Buddhist literature which demonstrates the kind of sensitivity one needs to cultivate in order to fathom the mysterious personal character of lines. A woman goes to a master Zen artist to learn how to paint with a brush and ink. When she arrives for the first lesson, the master asks her to sit next to him and observe as he draws a straight line with a brush and blue ink from top to bottom on a blank canvas. Once the line is drawn, the master takes the canvas into an adjoining room. For the next several weeks the lessons continue exactly in this manner.

Then one day the master has his student sit directly in front of the canvas and makes a sign that she should begin to paint. The student picks up a brush and proceeds to do exactly the same thing as her master, drawing a straight line from top to bottom in blue ink. The master then picks up the canvas and carries it into the other room. For many weeks that follow the lessons now continue in this fashion. One day when the student arrives, the master takes her directly into the next room. The student is startled to see hundreds of canvases on the walls displaying the same straight blue line. Among them she is unable to recognize the ones she had painted. The master, seeing her state of confusion, tells her that it is clear that she has not yet created her own line.

How does the line appear in human experience and toward what end? Let me give you some different points of view which taken together display the rich diversity of possible thinking about lines. For the Italian art and architectural historian Brusatin, the line is first discovered in the natural poetry evoked by a meeting between nature and human perception. For him, the original line is that of the horizon:

> *In the beginning there is the line of the horizon, where before there was almost nothing. And this line gave rise to high and low, to right and left, to outer and inner, to towards and away, comprising our vision.*

> *A line unites even as it divides. And it becomes an orienting arrow, ungraspable and violent, which burns the heart.* (Brusatin, 2002, p. 7) [translation mine]

One could connect the idea of horizon as Brusatin expresses it to the phenomenological horizon as Husserl conceives it, where each moment of being includes a beyond that distinguishes the known from the unknown, the present from a potential future, or, in the language of Gestalt therapy, support from contact. Brusatin also makes it clear that the line also can express the aggressive character of contact by becoming an arrow or vector that possesses direction and force.

Another aesthetic theory that seeks to explain how lines originate in human experience, is set forth by Henri Michaux, a great poet and equally great painter, in a poem entitled "Children's Ventures, Children's Drawings" from one of his last books, *Déplacements Dégagements* (1985) (which appeared in English in 1992 as *Spaced, Displaced*). Michaux describes how children are inevitably and hypnotically attracted to drawing and so soon go about teaching themselves to draw. What he proposes in this poem is nothing less than a vision of human development in terms of lines which has not only an aesthetic basis but also seems informed by sound psychology:

> *A child given paper and a piece of crayon will begin chaotically*
> *drawing lines—lines that make circles, almost on top of each other.*
> *Off he goes, he draws circles and more circles, on and on.*

Lines turning and turning in wide clumsy circles, Entangled,
Beginning again and again
and again
like spinning a top

Circles. The wish for circularity. Make way for whirling.
In the beginning is

REPETITION

Circling lines of the urge to include
(comprehend ? hold ? keep ?)

The risk and the joy of departure. The need to come back again.

At the start there may also be a phase of drawing lines —
lines all over the place — of gestures made for the love of it, wildly.

The child begins with circle, which reaches out and comes back, thus creating a world within the world, linking outside and inside, thought and imagination, containment and order. But then,

One day, one day after many days, a curving line will es-
cape from the bacchic round and fail to complete the circuit ex-
pected of it: a particular line, surprising the child, it slows and
halts, it says something to him, keeps him in suspense, makes him
hold back and begin to think . . .

What the child discovers is that this new curved, fleeting line reminds him in some odd way of his mother or his father, and thus of the human form in himself. At this moment, the child begins to draw one body after another because he or she . . . . *has seen the correspondence . . . . and realizes the human condition more fully by doing so than his ancestors did in inventing the wheel or in making fire by rubbing two sticks together.*

Acts of bringing close, of bringing into relationship . . . This
ability will always be there now. (Michaux, 1992, pp. 101-109)

In this manner Michaux show us how children absorb and transform their environment, giving it their own expressive form in order to discover correspondences between their creative inner experience and their given world — thanks to lines.

Here is another kind of vision, a cultural one, in which lines are given the widest possible importance: One is immediately struck in looking at the sculptured heads made by Yoruban artists in Africa by the way in which they are intensely grooved with lines. So, in fact, are the faces and bodies of the Yoruban people themselves thoroughly scarred with a multiplicity of lines. For the Yoruban people drawing lines on the human body and also on their land is the fundamental act of creating a civilization; lines represent what the hand of man imposes on nature. Drawing lines is how the Yoruba create their social and cultural world. According to the ethnologist Robert Ferris Thompson, "This land has lines on its face," means literally in Yoruba, "This country has become civilized" (cited in Ingraham, 1998, p. 2).

In the thought of the architect Le Corbusier one can find a dialectic of urbanization as well as a conception of the city based on lines. Catherine Ingraham, an architectural theorist, explains Le Corbusieis theory of the origins of urban landscapes as give-and-take between lines made by humans and lines made by donkeys (Ingraham, 1998, pp. 66-72). On the one hand, donkeys bearing loads of goods for commerce beat wandering paths through the jungle or forest, and the first cities grew up along these paths. But humans are able to oppose this with straight lines in accord with the ideals of Euclidean geometry. Le Corbusier contrasts the natural instinct of animals with human reason which idealizes control over its environment. He then claims that cities can spring from two kinds of lines. According to Le Corbusier, ancient cities, such as Paris, were constructed starting from the lines left by donkeys (In the Marais district of Paris, one finds a street named "la rue du pas de la mule," the street of the steps of the mule). Such cities are chaotic, he points out. He prefers the modern rational sensibility, which should construct cities based on the efficiency of straight lines.

What these different points of view — Bursatin, Michaux, the Yoruba, Le Corbusier — have in common is the belief that drawing lines constitutes the civilizing act that one discovers in the development of the infant, the founding of civilizations and cultures, and the history of art and architecture. How can one best incorporate this notion in a psychotherapy based on an aesthetic vision of the human condition?

Since a line is a passage, traveling from one place to another while it changes form, it can represent what happens between people. The work of the artist and cartoonist Saul Steinberg ingeniously evokes this aspect of the line. His complex lines, sometimes flowing out of the mouths of his characters, sometimes shown on their own, fold on themselves, make angles, break apart, curl up, make spirals that evolve into every imaginable form.

Whereas Freudians probe the hidden depths beneath all everyday experience, and mystics and Platonists seek to know transcendent universals beyond daily experience, those who pay attention to lines make phenomenological observations of the visible world in which we live day to day. Those who tend to occupy themselves with the essential or the extraordinary are liable to miss the lines that inscribe themselves on the surface of the ordinary daily world, where we attempt to reach one another by speaking, loving, hating etc. The Freudian unconscious and the Platonic essences are unchanging and atemporal, but conversing, making love, writing novels, and listening to music unfold in time. Lines trace the contours of experience which express this temporality in ordinary life.

Like Michauis artist-children, adults love to draw lines, bringing them meet one another in many forms — lines of poetry, melody lines, the lines of drawings or paintings. We love the tools that permit us to make lines — pens, brushes, musical instruments. (One can recall here Heidegger's sense of the intimate relationship which exists between tools and being.) The body itself can become such an instrument. In effect, the line can be perceived as the presence of the soul in the body. It is not easy to describe, but lines are at once profoundly recognizable and full of mystery. They seem to display a need close to the heart of our way of existing — the need to create something expressive, which Otto Rank and D. H. Lawrence considered our most primary instinct, more fundamental than the sexual instinct. Perhaps this is why one's signature can seem so important, sealing the contracts between oneself and others, as if it were a miniature personal landscape of the self. Perhaps it is also why poets like Michaux and Ezra Pound, as well as painters such as Robert Motherwell and Franz Kline, were fascinated by the calligraphic representations of the Chinese language, a language that wonderfully fuses image and meaning.

One of the last poems of Michaux, published in 1984, the year of his death, is titled, "Par des traits," roughly translated, "Through Lines" (in the sense of by means of lines). In this poem Michaux enumerates the possibilities of what lines can create and perform. I think that he is one of the great phenomenologists of the world of lines. I would like to end by simply quoting a few stanzas of this poem, which says just about everything I have said

259

and would want to say about lines (Michaux, 1984, n.p., translation mine):

> Gestures rather than signs
> take leave
>
> Awakenings
> Other awakenings

THROUGH LINES

> Approach, explore through lines
> Make a landing through lines
>
> Disclose
> debase through lines
>
> Provoke exalt
> Isolate through lines
>
> Disassemble
> divert
>
> withdraw to oneself
> reject what is close by
> offend
> make insignificant through lines
>
> Penetrate

DRAWING THE LINE

push
searching
searching always for

THE EXIT FROM THE BURROW

For withdrawing
For unclenching
for drying out
for unblocking
for exploding

always at the frontier
sniffing the evil which hides
the sickness which begins
the assassins who are ready

In order to start piercing the invisible wall
which always surrounds one there

BUTTRESS YOURSELF UPON LINES

Against the enemy disguised in the everyday

against that which "cuts short our days"
On the borders of the wells of the Incomprehensible

Cure through lines

unclutchings, exhaustions through lines
Lines : our therapy, our hygiene
Our perimeter of defense.

References

Brusatin, Manlio. (2002). *Histoire de la ligne.* Paris: Flammarion.

Deleuze, Gilles et Guattari, Felix. (1987). *A Thousand Plateaus: Capitalism and Schizophrenia.* Minneapolis : U. of Minnesota Press.

Ingraham, Catherine. (1998). *Architecture and the Burdens of Linearity.* New Haven : Yale University Press.

Michaux, Henri. (1992). Spaced Displaced [*Déplacements Dégagements.* 1985] Oxford : Bloodaxe Books.

Michaux, Henri. (1984). *Par des traits.* Montpellier: Fata Morgana.

∫ A Phenomenology of Time in Gestalt Therapy

I.

Kafka wrote that the "Positive is given. It remains for us to create the negative." We didn't waste any time creating it either. The first No was put into motion by the first woman, Eve, through disobeying God's commandment not to eat the fruit from the Tree of Knowledge. At least she did an active, direct No; Adam, the good boy, did the first male passive-aggressive one: "The woman made me do it," he told God when they were caught.

But God had already set the stage for our ancestors to exercise this human talent for creating the negative. He issued His commandment in the form of a "thou shalt not," a kind of pre-no or proto-no that made negation possible. Until then Adam and Eve, you could say, lived in the eternal Yes of Paradise. But once God forbade something, the endless abundance of Eden where

---

*This article appeared in slightly different form in French under the title "L'esthétique du temps en Gestalt-thérapie" in the *Revue québécoise de Gestalt*, volume 11, 2008.

every need was met immediately became uninteresting. Now only what Adam and Eve could *not* have captured their attention. This is a different kind of negation than a refusal — it is a lack, an interval in which one becomes aware of time. Thus, the first pangs of desire and first curiosity were aroused, and they were aroused by a gap between having and not having. Time began to flow to fill the gap. Feelings like longing and grieving, wanting, anticipating, and delighting all unfold in the currents of time. They are unimaginable without the passing of time.

The myth of Genesis implies that our capacity to negate, to speak or carry out a No is how we remove ourselves from our original confluent embeddedness in nature. The positive is given, says Kafka, but the special human talent or vice, depending on your point of view, is to create the negative, which separates human consciousness from nature. The other animals, so far as we know, go through their entire lives embedded in nature. Animals can refuse in a limited way — but not nature nor their own nature. With our separation that mixed blessing, the human condition begins, which is to say that temporality, and thus human history begins. The experience of negation and the ensuing separation is how we create temporality and from then on live in the dimension of time.

Eve's act has throughout the ages of Judeo-Christian been interpreted as her inability to control her impulses, rendering her vulnerable to temptation. But it seems to me that it was intellectual curiosity that moved her. Eve's thirst for knowledge, her inquisitiveness, led her to disobey. Desire, whether sexual and otherwise, and curiosity or wonder only come into being alongside our knowledge, terrible and fascinating, that we live in time, terrible because it means that we know that we die. The knowledge of death is the knowledge that Eden hid from us. But also without temporality, without the sense of time passing, there is neither desire nor curiosity, there is no wonder. Adam and Eve felt neither desire nor pain until God forbade something and they disobeyed. Even Eden, the best piece of real estate on the planet didn't excite them. In other words Paradise wasn't fit for human habitation. Yet we still long for it. What a predicament!

Immediately after the Fall, we are told, Adam and Eve look at each other and realize that they are naked, so they cover themselves with leaves. This has always been understood as the origin of sexual shame, accounting for why in civilized society ever after we hide our bodies from one another. But I regard it differently. I think it was the beginning of disappointment. Maybe now, under the rule of time, they see the beginnings of a sagging breast here, a pot belly there. They have a new awareness of their bodies as that which ages and dies, the symptoms of mortality. You could say that disappointment is the central measure of time through the lens of the human condition. Disappointment is a special kind of awareness of time passing through the affective experience of what is now less than it formerly was, until it finally diminishes, decays, and becomes nothing. Disappointment is about loss, and the ultimate disappointment of human existence is that we die.

It thus becomes evident how important a very serious consideration of time is for psychology and psychotherapy, which are certainly much concerned, at least since Freud, with desire, curiosity, disappointment, and the fear of death. Yet our psychologies and psychotherapies have, for the most part, been emphatically spatial. Even theoretical formations that have no actual spatial existence, such as the unconscious, the ego, id, and superego, or, for that matter, the self, tend to be represented as spatial in character or by spatial metaphors. The phrase "object relations" is telling in this regard. Psychological entities are represented and treated like objects. Thus the structures of mental life are easily reified, that is, treated as being like things — and things, of course, exist in space.

Why is this the case? I think it has to do with the attempt of psychology since the Enlightenment to imitate the natural sciences, like physics, chemistry, and astronomy. Objects in space are what can be precisely measured, and causal relationships established among them. Of course, physics itself, at least since quantum mechanics and Heisenberg's Principle of Uncertainty, has long since forsaken simple notions of precise measurement and causality. In this sense it has gone much further than psychology into the unpredictable mysteries of both space and time. The further that physicists have extended their reach out into the cosmos and the deeper they have penetrated into the subatomic world, the more they have been compelled to make use of probability, paradox, contradiction, multiple realities, as well as theories based on rather unpredictable waves and fields whose behavior defies common sense.

Yet psychology, it seems to me, is still pretty much lodged in Newtonian reality, a world of particles bumping into each other, flying apart, effecting each other, and otherwise behaving in concert or conflict against a background of a surrounding emptiness. What do most of our theories tell us about the nature of time in human functioning? Very little. Classical psychoanalytic theory has a weak and inadequate theory of time: It does not say much beyond insisting that our childhood past dictates the shape of our adult present. Psychoanalytic theories concerning the place of time in mental life have mostly to do with memory — that is, with both conscious and unconscious memories which are intended to account for the connection in emotional life and conduct between past and present. For example, analytic theory tells us that early past traumas take up residence like a cancer cell in the psyche where they spread a contaminating influence on our later feelings and conduct. This notion of repetition, so important to psychoanalysis, is extremely valuable, of course, but I think that it still needs to be located in a much richer context of thinking about the nature of time. Behavioral, cognitive, and neurological theories of human functioning have also emphasized memory, but go further in treating memory as a kind of thing. Neurology gives it a place in the brain. (Gestalt therapy, as Isadore From used to tell us, emphasizes not memories, which are thing-like, but the process of remembering.) It is true that certain recent trends in psychological research and in the practice of psychotherapy imply more complex theories of time. I am thinking of therapy that emphasizes how we construct narratives, and of the new research, such as Damasio's, on the role of affect in cognition and reasoning. But I say "implies" because as far as I know the implications of these new ideas for a psychology of time have not been carried out very far.

In order to move closer to material of immediate relevance to psychotherapy, let me now recast the mythic material from Genesis in developmental terms. Of course all theories of the first stages of development are essentially myths anyway, adult projections backward, since babies can't tell us what they are experiencing, and by the time they acquire language, the pre-linguistic past is already forgotten or changed. So I'll offer you my own developmental myth. In the unconditional positive, the yes of the womb, no time passed for the embryo, although it grew. This was even better than Eden. When the baby's life was carried on inside the being of another, even its breathing was done for it. But in its first moments in the world, the newly born infant suddenly realizes that it must breathe for itself. What an ordeal! — this is certainly a Fall. Now it has to seek its own oxygen. It is often maintained that this first cry is an attempt to get air. No doubt, but we usually imagine that we also hear a note of protest or longing, a refusal or a lack. I like to imagine that the baby's first cry is a cry of disappointment. With it begins in some rudimentary fashion the awareness of time passing. We breathe in time. Each inhalation and exhalation is like a clock now ticking off the seconds of human time.

For good reason Gestalt therapy has stressed the importance of breathing as the elemental model of contact and support, such that the therapist always pays attention to the quality of a patient's breathing in assessing his or her ability to feel and express emotions and to tolerate the excitement of a present situation without too much anxiety. I like to take this an additional step and say that breathing — expanding to take in something from the world, contracting to let go of it — is the elemental basis of Gestalt therapy's way of thinking about the rhythm of contact and withdrawal necessary to all living creatures. Of course, the moment we say "rhythm" we have entered the dimension of temporality.

I think that Gestalt therapy, with its emphasis on the self as a changing process, on contact as a kind of flux, on unfolding action rather than stationery entities, verbs rather than nouns, can provide the basis for a full and satisfying theory and therapy grounded in the temporal dimension. This is largely due to the fact that Gestalt therapy has gone down a path laid by modern philosophy. The great philosophers who placed time at the center of their thought were Kant and Bergson. Phenomenology and existentialism, both of which deeply influenced Gestalt therapy at its origins, have taken time rather than space to constitute the very nature of human existence. One of Husserl's key works was "The Phenomenology of Internal Time Consciousness." Heidegger called his masterwork "Being and Time." There is a crucial chapter in Merleau-Ponty's "Phenomenology of Perception" on the nature of temporality. And Emmanuel Levinas's second book was titled "Time and the Other."

A rich kind of temporal understanding is available in Gestalt therapy, but thus far mostly implicitly in flashes and hints. Gestalt therapy has been built from the eclectic crisscrossing of various schools of thought. There are many currents in Perls, Hefferline, and Goodman that collide with one another, even contradict one another. First of all, psychologies mix with philosophies: psychoanalytic ego psychology, Reich, Gestalt psychology, Dewey's social thought, Hegelian dialectic, Husserl's phenomenology, and Lewin's field theory influenced the beginnings of Gestalt therapy, and they often get in each other's way. There is still work to do to prune the garden of Gestalt therapy, to get rid of some of the clutter. Secondly, in the practice of Gestalt therapy, particularly as it was shaped by Fritz Perls and some of his successors a very inadequate theory of temporality became dominant in many quarters.

What I have in mind was the Perlsian commandment to live in the present moment. An extremely important and valuable idea — but when taken too literally, it becomes as reductive and inadequate as cause and effect in psychoanalysis or behaviorism. To live in the present moment, the famous here and now, taken literally, would be a strangely impoverished existence, nearly psychotic in character. It would be as if life were a series of disconnected nows: now, now, now, now. This is similar to the situation of the borderline personality, whose splitting into all good or all bad derives from a temporal existence in which each foreground moment of a relationship is experienced as the whole of the relationship and the background history keeps disappearing. Obviously this was not what Perls or anyone else in Gestalt therapy meant, and I'm not attacking Perls for it, but there have been too many followers of Perls who treat therapy as though it's now, now, now, now. Now I'm aware, now I'm aware, now I'm aware. Now compared to what?

That's not psychotherapy. Even less is it a philosophy of living, which people have often presented it as being. There are other seriously inadequate temporal models in Gestalt therapy, such as the cycle of awareness or the contact cycle, which treats experience as though all of us live out our time, like the motor of a car, going through the same cycle again and again, and we all do it in a similar fashion. We become aware, we get excited, we become mobilized, we make contact, we subside, there's closure, a finished Gestalt, and we begin again. An interesting metaphor up to a point, but taken as a universal description of human temporal conduct, it becomes as mechanistic as Newton's clockmaker universe.

The fact of the matter is that in Gestalt therapy, just as in the other psychologies, some wonderful metaphorical insights eventually become treated as the reality. Every poet knows that once you use a metaphor a few times, throw it out before it becomes a corpse. Don't spend your time trying to fit dead categories to life, because the dynamic and vital nature of lived existence, will always outgrow all our metaphors.

II.

The human condition, life under the overriding arch of temporality, like a rainbow whose two ends fade off into a remote, unknowable future and a mostly forgotten ancient past, is an existence composed of wonder and suffering. The newborn's cry reflects at once the surprise and the pain of being born. We are aware of the baby's painful needs, but we also witness in the baby an endless curiosity, a fascination with every new thing, every new moment.

What is this entity or process that we call time? How does it come into being? Nearly all philosophers agree that it makes no sense to speak of it existing without us. Its invention or discovery might go something like this: I have spoken of the beleaguered rhythm of the child's first breathing. A more general factor developmentally is that the child finds that it has to wait. Every need before birth was met instantly so far as we know. The mother's nutrients circulated right through the infant. Immediately after birth needs are met almost instantly, the infant's need and the mother's need to meet the infant's need coming together like two parts of nature, at least when things are going well. And then, at some point, the infant discovers that it must wait. Maybe in this waiting, like a sudden cut or gap, the experience of time comes into being. The poet Anne Carson asks, "How does a child discover that there is an edge?" And she answers, "By passionately not wanting there to be one." I would say something similar about time. How does the infant discover that there is time? By passionately not wanting there to be a wait.

Into this sudden cut or gap in existence, in the vacancy between the need or desire and the object of need or desire falls the shadow of time. It makes life difficult. It also makes life challenging. Without difficulty there is no creativity, no reason to invent or grow. The British historian Arnold Toynbee said that human events were not about cause and effect but they were about challenge and response.

Wonder and suffering are the qualities that accompany our existence as it unfolds in time. We are bodies that age and decay, a piece of meat that has beautiful form and function yet hurts, as

271

well as spirits that suffer, desire, and are endlessly curious about the unknown. You can see this combination in great works of art. A poem by the French poet, Stephan Mallarme begins, "J'ai lu tous les livres, et le chair est triste" — I have read all the books, and the flesh is sad. The great painters of the human figure have always understood this twofold character of human existence as wonder and suffering — Velasquez and Goya, Max Beckman and Francis Bacon. Recently I was in Paris teaching, and I went to a retrospective exhibition of the paintings of the German expressionist Max Beckman, a marvelous painter. Never has an artist rendered the flesh more vulnerable. Living flesh already turning white with its dying. Veins and arteries standing out in a kind of decaying green color, like something overripe, with wounds and openings that are bleeding. It sounds terrible, and yet these paintings are very beautiful, because as in all great art, there is transfiguration in Beckman's work, something transcendent in these representations of human suffering. The suffering I'm talking about is not the suffering of neurotic fixation. The tragic is not depression. And that difference between tragedy and depression is important to our understanding of how we exist in time. Because tragedy accepts the suffering of our existence living in time and finally goes beyond the mere suffering by transforming it into a gain in wisdom. Depression, on the other hand, involves a refusal to live in time through sustaining an unchanging misery over loss. I'll return to that issue later.

To my mind, there is finally not a great difference between philosophy and psychotherapy. I think of psychotherapy as being less medical treatment than applied philosophy. But there is an important difference of emphasis. In a sense, philosophy and psychotherapy have divided up wonder and suffering between them. The original philosophical question is why is there something instead of nothing. Socrates said philosophy begins in wonder,

Aristotle said philosophy begins in wonder; Heidegger said philosophy begins in wonder. The beginnings of curiosity are about the very fact of being itself: How can what is exist? It means that the most ordinary experience is also the most profound mystery.

If philosophy begins with the question of how can there be something rather than nothing, psychotherapy takes up a different question about being, one expressive of the suffering inherent in everyday existence but also a temporal question: It is the question — How can I go on? — the question one asks when life seems too much of a burden to bear. At those times one is likely to say to oneself, I want to get off the train, I want it to stop. But you can not get off the train; it will not stop. Existing is a responsibility that you cannot give up, as much as you may want to, except by suicide or its approximations through drugs or other addictions that provide only a momentary illusion of stopping. In one of the most interesting developments in modern philosophy, particularly existentialism and phenomenology, a merging of philosophical concerns with those of psychotherapy has taken place.

In this respect, the writings of the philosopher Emmanuel Levinas, a student of Husserl and Heidegger, are of great interest to psychotherapists because he wrote beautifully and powerfully about the painfulness implicit in the mere fact of existing and the forms taken by our desire to escape. (A Lithuanian Jew, he happened to be in a concentration camp when he wrote about this topic.) He approaches the suffering of temporal existence and the consequent desire to stop by undertaking a phenomenological analysis of fatigue, indolence, and insomnia, hardly the usual concern of philosophers. In *Existence and Existents*, he writes:

> There exists a weariness which is a weariness of everything and everyone, and above all a weariness

of oneself . . . in weariness existence is like the reminder of a commitment to exist, with all the seriousness and harshness of an irrevocable contract.
One has to do something. One has to aspire after
and undertake. . . . Weariness is the impossible
refusal of this ultimate obligation.

And Levinas continues:

Indolence is essentially tied up with the beginning
of an action, the stirring, the getting up. Indolence
concerns beginning, as though existence were not
there right off, but preexisted the beginning in an
inhibition. There is *more here than a span of duration flowing imperceptibly between two moments. Or
perhaps the inhibition involved in indolence is also the
revealing of the beginning which each instant effects in
being an instant.* (Levinas, 1978)

The analysis Levinas makes of weariness and indolence
aims at an account of how our experience of an instant itself comes
into being. It is similar, though far more complex, to what I suggested above about the child's formative experience of time as having to wait. Weariness is the wish not to endure the burden of
existing when it feels at odds with the unstoppable commitment to
exist. In the case of indolence, one doesn't even want to begin, yet
is already pulled forward because there is no discontinuity, no
pause, in existing. Tensions such as these, Levinas argues, are what
constitutes our experience of the instant. In our very holding back
we uncover the nature of time. Imagine picking up a very heavy

rock that you are trying to lift in order to move it. As you lift it, it seems to become heavier and heavier. Both your muscles and your will grow tired. But you are underway, the rock is halfway up to its destination. You are committed, because if you stop now, you will soon drop the rock, and then you will have to begin all over again. Our existence in time, according to Levinas, is an unavoidable contract like lifting this stone, wanting to stop and not being able to.

That the human condition as temporality is a state of tension, a form of anxiety, is a conception that begins to appear in modern philosophy with Heidegger. He was one of the first philosophers to place anxiety at the heart of his metaphysics. Dasein, literally "being there," Heidegger's term for one's existence in the world, has an orientation toward the future. For him, living fully and authentically means always being a little ahead of oneself, living in a present moment turned toward the future as the possibility of the next unknown, which ultimately includes one's death. So this entails living in a state of perpetual tension, a kind of primal anxiety, because you live with uncertainty about what is next other than the absolute knowledge that you die. Merleau-Ponty's philosophy also points toward the inevitable tension in our experience of time, which he characterizes as a state of continual flux. You can never inhabit completely a present moment in Merleau-Ponty's temporal world because it is already changing as you enter it, flowing back to make the past longer and the future seem shorter.

What follows is an attempt to outline a temporal phenomenology of both depression and anxiety, bringing together psychological ideas with some philosophical ones.

III.

When weariness and indolence, as Levinas described them, become chronic conditions, then we have entered the realm of pathology. Chronic existential weariness is a sign of depression, the loss of desire. If one thinks of desire as the life force reaching out through time toward a fulfilling though yet unknown future, the depressed person's lack of desire involves a refusal to live in time. Depression creates an illusion of being off the train, but this ultimately the death drive. Chronic indolence is perhaps more closely related to an anxiety disorder. Unlike simple laziness, which overcomes everyone now and then, it is a response to fear of any exertion that would carry one forward, because one has lost faith in one's ability to cope with the unknown.

If wonder or curiosity and suffering arise from living in a temporal world, anxiety and depression both attempt to get rid of time. To some extent they are inevitable experiences because anxiety accompanies all excitement and depression accompanies all loss. But when they become more than passing states, both become efforts to control temporality. In different ways, both try to stand outside of past, present and future. Anxiety and depression as fixations literally want to kill time in order to create a certitude which replaces the mystery of time itself.

To be genuinely curious, to love deeply, to live life as an adventure inevitably mix excitement and anxiety because they all require surrender to the uncertainty of living in time, which means accepting the future as unknowable. Curiosity makes us anxious: Will I find out something good or bad? Love makes us anxious: Will he or she stop loving me, abandon me, or control me? Anxiety accompanies all risk: Will riding this motorcycle give me a thrill, break my bones, or both?

But an anxiety disorder creates an illusion of certitude by anticipating only bad news. Actually it goes well beyond mere anticipation: Anxiety brings the future closer and closer, virtually collapsing it into the present, as though the future is already here, utterly known, and must be dealt with immediately. Pathologically anxious people are always mobilized for emergencies that do not yet exist and may never exist, but they live as though sure that something terrible is already waiting just around the next turn in the road. The possible disaster is already shaping their lives into a masquerade of emergency. The muscles tense, adrenalin flows, and the anxious individual is already meeting a phantasm, a nonexistent emergency.

When you are feeling very anxious you cannot tolerate waiting. That is one reason chronically anxious people are always in a rush and generally late for appointments nevertheless (if you are early or on time, what if the other person is not there yet? Then you have to wait). They don't want to deal with time. They don't even want time to exist. Imagine how time passes if you were to suspect that your lover is with another man or woman, because he or she was supposed to be home two hours ago. Another hour goes by, and you still have no idea where he or she is. If you try to read a novel or listen to music under such circumstances, you can barely concentrate because you are filled up with a dreaded version of the unknown future. People with anxiety disorders are like this all the time. In fact, they are certain that the lover is with someone else, has already betrayed them, and they are already beginning to take steps guided by panic. The lover is guilty until proven innocent. Because if you really don't know what's going on, then why is your heart thumping, why is all your adrenaline going? The anxious person lives as though driving along a highway, and there is a huge truck, out of control, heading toward him.

These days many people often complain "I have no time." This is a response shaped by a culture driven by anxiety, yielding a lifestyle that constantly tries to reduce the waiting between the future and the present, the interval between the known and the unknown. Such people cannot stay with anything for very long and pay close attention to it. They have little time for curiosity because they are in a hurry. Curiosity requires patience, a willingness to wait in front of the unknown. The psychoanalyst Edward Shapiro describes a phenomenon in families that he calls "pathological certitude," which is specifically an absence of curiosity. When the baby cries in such families, the parents who are anxious, the parents with "no time," cannot wait patiently to find out what among any number of needs the baby is expressing with its cry. They say, "Oh, she's hungry," and stuff a bottle in her mouth. You can imagine the kinds of eating disorders that this baby is liable to develop.

If you make the future known, you don't have one. Since our best sciences, strategies, or intuitions can only predict the future in limited ways, we can only live it as a possibility. Another way to say this is that future is infinitely other to us at any point in time, beyond our appropriating or controlling it. It is typical of anxiety disorders, however, that they try to control what cannot be controlled, try to create certitude where certainty cannot be, as though to eliminate the central mystery of time.

Like anxiety, depression also establishes an illusion of control over an unknowable and indeterminate future. In terms of the contact boundary, understood as a meeting between the known and the unknown, both anxiety and depression treat the unknown as already known. In this sense both are out of contact. But if both anxiety and depression eliminate the unknown aspect of the future, depression does so differently—in temporal terms, by erasing the difference between the future and the past. This is why depression's outlook is connected to grief, withdrawal, nostalgia, regret, and loss. Both anxiety and depression pull one out of absorption in the present moment but in opposite directions. Anxiety collapses the future into the present; depression projects the past onto the future, so that the future is not only known, but known in the way that something that has already happened is known.

Ordinarily we think of actual loss as behind us, and we grieve it, which is a necessary and healthy response because the grieving helps us eventually move forward. But for the depressed person there is no forward worth moving to, and he or she is already mourning the future. Like the anxious person, the depressed person functions in a realm of certitude, knowing beyond a shadow of a doubt that things will not get better, that time heals nothing. In a broad sense anxiety is also about future loss, but the anxious person still has some hope of doing something to prevent it, whereas the depressed person has given up all hope.

In *Repetition*, a philosophical narrative written like a novel, Kierkegaard gives a perfect example of the peculiar temporality of depression. It is the confessions of a young man in a small Swedish town who falls madly in love with a beautiful girl of about sixteen. She knows nothing of his existence and cares nothing about him. Completely preoccupied with her, he courts her intensively, and his courtship is so beautiful executed that she indeed begins to fall in love with him. But the moment she returns his love, this avid suitor immediately sinks into a terrible depression, ignores the girl from then on, and stays home to write poetry (almost a sure sign of depression!).

When the girl responds favorably to Kierkegaard's young hero, it would seem natural for him to be quite beside himself with happiness, but the problem is that he cannot stay in the present moment. As soon as he realizes she wants him, he rushes to the end of their story together, where he can imagine nothing except the two of them, now very old, living together completely bored with each other, sitting in front of the fireplace, waiting to die. As soon as love becomes a real possibility for this young man, the story is already over. He responds as though everything has already turned into loss, emptiness, death.

The chronically depressed person, as spring arrives with flowers beginning to bud and leaves filling in the trees, does not experience the excitement of new birth. Depression looks at this world in bloom and already sees the leaves turning brown, withering, and falling to the ground. If something is born, it's as though its life is already over. Such is the temporal existence of pathological depression. For the depressed person, time is all used up, and there is nothing left. This is how the depressed person lives so close to death. The self-deception in depression takes the form, I don't have to worry about when I will die, because I am already nearly dead. What's the use of getting excited, why take a risk, why work for anything, it's not worth it. Life has nothing to offer.

Depression's refusal to inhabit the realm of time, which has the power to bring unpredictable changes from the future toward one, is perhaps even more profound than that of anxiety. The depressive is trying to create a world in which the passing of time has no effect, in which nothing changes. Jean Paul Sartre, in his little treatise on the emotions, describes depression as an incantation that casts a spell over the world turning it entirely gray, so that nothing is alive with color and distinctions disappear (Sartre, 1948). Depression makes an enchanted world that is completely uninteresting and thereby has justified its lack of desire to reach out and contact such a world.

I said earlier that time did not pass in the Garden of Eden. Our punishment for disobeying God and eating the apple was to be compelled to live in time, discovering as a consequence that we will suffer change and die. For the severely depressed individual the life outside Eden not worth living. What such a person is saying to us is, give me paradise me or give me nothing. Considering what I have been through, I am entitled to nothing less than paradise. Everything that the world offers, insofar as it is not paradise, will just increase my misery, and I'd rather kill myself. To be the parent or child, the husband or wife, or the therapist of such a person is to feel continually punished for not delivering paradise.

IV.

This is essay is only a beginning at sketching out a psychology that aims to locate its roots in our experience living in time. It does so as a corrective to our most established traditions in psychology. Obviously we live out our lives in both time and space. But as I suggested earlier most of our psychological theories have largely drawn upon and emphasized spatial and space-like concepts to describe human conduct and feeling. Spatial concepts lend themselves more readily quantitative measurement and causal propositions, from the old-fashioned ways of measuring galvanic skin response to determine levels of anxiety to the current MRI studies of how emotions light up various sectors of the brain. And even the major concepts of most psychodynamic and psychoanalytic theories have been built around spatial metaphors.

Beyond simply counting seconds and minutes in linear fashion, however, time is subjectivity. I assume that is the reason why the existential and phenomenological philosophers, who strove to understand the human condition as subjective experience, have so eagerly brought the temporal dimension into the foreground. I have turned to them in order to bring their work to bear on Gestalt therapy, including my own somewhat idiosyncratic revisions and extensions of Gestalt therapy, which I believe is still the psychology that best directs therapists toward the heart of what they must attend to — their patients' emotional life, which is above all subjectivity that unfolds in time.

References

Kierkegaard, Soren. (1964). *Repetition: An Essay in Experimental Psychology.* Trans. by Walter Lowrie. NY: Harper and Row.

Levinas, Emmanuel. (1978). *Existence and Existents.* Trans. by Alphonso Lingis. (pp. 24-26.) The Hague: Martinus Nijhoff.

Sartre, Jean-Paul. (1948). *The Emotions: Outline of a Theory.* Trans. by Bernard Frechtman. NY: The Philosophical Library.

Part Two:

Commentary

∫ Reflection on Cornell:
   The Aesthetics of Sexual Love

I find myself in deep accord with William Cornell's wish to restore sexual passion to its once venerable place in psychotherapy. And I am glad that he writes about it with considerable eloquent force. It is good to be passionate about passion. I like to imagine that psychotherapy is, among other things, about the restoration of the freedom to be passionate — and not only sexually passionate but also passionately curious, passionately spontaneous and playful, passionately interested in acquiring new skills, passionately absorbed in the task at hand, *etc.*

So I join Mr. Cornell in deploring the fact that much current psychotherapy has taken a turn toward restricting itself to mild, safe, and pious sentiments, such as mutuality, trust, empathy, caring, the relational, etc. These all too often seem in the service of proving that the therapist is a good soul, custodian of a

---

*From the *British Gestalt Journal*, Vol. 12, No. 2 (December, 2003). Reprinted with permission.

hygienic theory of human relationships, from whom one has nothing to fear. The sanctimonious view of love in the quotation Mr. Cornell chooses from Judith Jordan illustrates the point perfectly. I am not claiming that these are bad ideas in themselves; obviously they are all on the side of virtue. But in so benevolent a setting how does one's patient open up and explore the darker fears of childhood, the bottled up aggressive desires, the messy, effusive animal of the body?

Consider a patient who has struggled to survive the terrifying and often secret libidinous and violent impulses — from parents and siblings, as well as from himself or herself — threaded through family life. On the other hand, take a patient whose family tolerates only harmony and good feelings, so that there was no place to express suffering, grief, hate, lustful desires, and other so-called negative emotions. Neither of these patients is likely to be in very good shape to make his or her way through an adult world where, alongside opportunities for growth and fulfillment, lurk predatory love, aggressive willfulness, and sadistic authorities parading as experts who claim to know what is in your best interests. To introject therapeutic benevolence is not going to help patients in search of intimacy to learn to navigate the hidden shoals, hungry marine life, and treacherous undertows that make every deep erotic experience such difficult going.

What has happened to the Freud who was said to be seen leaving a therapy session barely able to disguise an erection? Or to the Ferenczi who wrote a brilliant article entitled "Nakedness as a Means of Inspiring Terror," as well as a book called *Thalassa* which portrays sex as paradise mixed with catastrophe, and who sometimes sat a patient on his lap? Or Jung, who had an affair with Frau Spielrein, his patient who began as a schizophrenic and ended up a psychoanalyst? Or Otto Rank, who engaged in a tumultuous and ambiguously close relationship with the novelist Anais Nin and helped free her to become a passionate writer? I am by no means advocating all these behaviors — some of them cross-ed borders that probably should not be crossed, although I do think that the whole question of borders needs to be reexamined rather than merely subjected to automatic assumptions of thera-peutic political correctness. For example, one might ask how far a therapist can go in responding to a patient's sexual desire yet keep his or her (the therapist's) needs from muddying the waters. At any rate, I am impressed with the early psychoanalysts' willingness to risk engaging the more volatile emotions inherent in intimate human encounters. It is not difficult to guess how a culture, in which sexual harassment and abuse by caretakers (including thera-pists) and bosses number among our prevalent crimes, would look upon the conduct of those early analysts.

No doubt fallout from this cultural atmosphere has helped make psychotherapy since Freud turn increasingly pale in response to anything to do with sex and just about everything else that might be charged with libido. Another factor is the extent to which psychology, in theory and practice, has either stripped the psyche from the body or made the human body itself an abstrac-tion, as if to eliminate its sloppy ambiguities in the name of squea-ky clean science. The body was strongly present in Freud's own theoretical musings, although its orifices and portals (oral, anal, phallic) lost a good deal of their physicality as they became psycho-logical categories in his developmental theory, and the vagina was not even there — it was just an absence left behind from a missing penis. The growing tendency to eliminate the body from psycho-analytic thought is by no means only a product of modern psycho-analysis. The body had already pretty much disappeared from the view of the Freudian revisionists, such as Eric Fromm and Karen

Horney, who tended to dissolve biology and instinctual life into sociology. For them, human nature was equivalent to social nature.

In Milton's *Paradise Lost*, the archangel Raphael is sent to Eden before the Fall to chat with Adam — it is a kind of top-down debriefing session on a variety of important topics — the creation, free will, the laws of heaven, the dangers of disobedience, and the war between good and evil. But after they discuss these and other weighty matters, Adam cannot resist a bit of sexual curiosity. In elaborately circumspect terms, he asks Raphael whether the angels engage in sexual intercourse. Raphael blushes (he is more or less incarnate for the purposes of the visit) and responds in the affirmative. But then he goes on to explain that in heaven the angels are pure spirit, unencumbered by bodies. When two angels are attracted to each other, they can simply mingle essences, totally and ecstatically.

So much for eighteenth-century celestial passion. I do not get very excited by this ideal of sex between Platonic essences. We cannot live by it anyway. Behind it lies the Puritan's distaste for the animal body, which gets lustful now and then and eventually rots. You could say that tame relational mutuality in therapy is our secular version of this distaste. In our times we have also invented another more general version of bodiless sex, which you might call digital passion. Sylvester Stallone and Sandra Bullock, in a sci-fi action film called *Demolition Man* (1993), give a neat illustration of it. Stallone is an old-fashioned (late 20th century) action hero who, for some reason or other (I cannot remember why) had been cryogenically frozen and is thawed out a century or two later to help a future society take on evildoers. When the Bullock character decides to have sex with him, she brings out two complicated-looking electronic helmets. They don these and sit across from each other, whereupon they both begin moaning with delight. But the aroused Stallone then wants to touch her. And she, repelled by such a crude idea, explains that the mixing of bodily fluids is a disgusting unsanitary habit from the past. It is no longer practiced because it led to lethal diseases like AIDS and a subsequent host of even worse diseases.

At least they sit across from each other. In actuality we have by now taken things further: with sex on the internet, all physical presence disappears from the proceedings. Or if you wish, identity itself can be dissolved in cyberspace, so that you can have anonymous passion made up of nothing but throbbing electronic bits that find their way to your screen. Diseases, computers, and religious beliefs aside, one reason we have so much difficulty with physical sexuality, either vastly overrating it as the road to paradise (as in advertising) or banishing it from sight (as in certain right-wing religions), arises from our denial of death (see Becker, 1997). Sexual love not only holds out the promise of blissful transcendence, but it also reminds us that we die. The other, whom we desire and often come to depend on, decays and dies, and so do we. This is why the whole enterprise of sexual love is fraught with anxiety and, at the extreme, can drive us mad.

Wilhelm Reich

An important exception to this whole cultural trend, including the trend in therapy from Horney and Fromm to object relations to relational psychoanalysis, was Wilhelm Reich. Whereas the revisionists elaborated one side of Freud — his view of conflict between the individual and society — Reich took Freud's theory of psychosexual drives and mechanisms of defense directly back to the living body and its vital energies. Years before his involvement with Frederick and Laura Perls, Paul Goodman, himself more than a little influenced by Reich, foresaw how the loss of the body from psychology implied a psychotherapy of social adjustment. If human nature is social to the core, as Horney and Fromm implied, then the individual is indefinitely receptive to being shaped by society. Such was the thrust of Goodman's penetrating critique of the Freudian revisionists in a debate with C. Wright Mills and Patricia Salter originally published in *Politics* in July 1945 (Goodman, 1991). Thus the Freudian revisionists helped set the stage for modern liberal social engineering.

It is a striking historical fact that both Horney and Reich were personally involved in Frederick Perls' development as a therapist. From Horney he learned much about the social behavior of neurotic personality — how, for example, it manipulates support from the environment by presenting others with a carefully maintained inauthentic facade. But he also (literally) fleshed out Gestalt therapy by converting Reich's theory of character armor into his own theory of retroflections, which is a valuable guide to understanding how the neurotic deforms and constricts his own body to prevent feeling or expressing powerful emotions. In this sense Perls brought back together the two streams into which Freud's thought had been split.

I consider Cornell on the right track in wanting what he calls the impassioned body back in therapy and in recruiting Reich to help get it there. I especially like his insistence, taking a cue from Muriel Dimen, that sex is a force not a relation. I hate the words "relations" and "relationship" applied to erotic intimacy — they are terms that properly belong to mathematics, although I confess that I cannot figure out how to avoid them altogether. But Cornell also makes it quite clear, though I wish he had gone into more specific detail, that he does not think that our contemporary bodywork therapies offer a satisfying vision of passionate love either. Again, I agree with him. The very name bodywork hints at something that sounds more like fitness training than preparation to grapple with Eros.

We need a more passionate view of the body not only in psychoanalytic and other psychodynamic therapies, not only in bodywork, but in Gestalt therapy as well. Gestalt therapy has its own revisionists who have seized on one rich central theme in the work of Perls and Goodman — the concept of the field — and have turned it into a rather sterile landscape without fully incarnate inhabitants, as though psychotherapy were akin to the study of electromagnetism. On the other side of the psyche/soma divide, Gestalt therapy also has its body therapists, who take their cue from the work of Reich.

But for all its value, I do not think that the Reichian body alone does a good enough job to serve as a basis for reintroducing sexual love into psychotherapy. It can lead us to better sex but by itself not necessarily to better love. The reason I think so is because Reich has a great deal to teach us about sexual release but very little about what it takes to give form (in the way that an artist gives form to expression) to this release. (I discussed this problem in Reich's work more fully in an essay a couple of years ago (Miller, 2001).) Along this line, let me say a few words in favor of restraint, an aspect of passion that Mr. Cornell does not address, because it plays an important role in shaping the forms of love.

Barriers and Restraint

In the first place, I do not believe that there is any meaningful passion without restraint, just as it makes no sense to speak of a brilliant summer day without the contrast of winter cold in the background. Love is a dialectic of release, which expresses the self, and restraint, which respects the mystery of the other. With no restraint, no limiting resistance, passion as mere release is a surrender to nothingness. This comes close to what the poet Robert Frost meant when he said that writing free verse is like playing tennis with the net down. It is why the passionate spontaneous improvisations of the jazz musician are anchored in a structure of chord progressions, which also enables communication with others in the band. The Gestalt psychologist Kurt Koffka gives a surprising example of what can go wrong when there is no limiting resistance. He writes about a first-rate German weight-lifting team that everyone was sure would win the world championship. But at the championship match, which took place in a brand-new sports arena in Switzerland, the German team utterly collapsed and lost by a wide margin. A Gestalt psychologist (of course!) was dispatched to research the disaster. What he discovered was that members of the team had been able to lift with such power because they had learned to take a fix on the opposite wall and then lift against it. But in the new arena the lighting was such that the glare made the opposite wall seem to disappear. The team had nothing to lift against except its own bootstraps. Herein lies a lesson that can be applied to sexual intimacy: that the recalcitrant differences of the other from oneself, no matter how far one might penetrate them, constitute a limiting resistance to self-expression. This is why it takes discipline and artfulness to create a form of love that satisfies both partners.

Every tale of romantic love contains forces that resist the possibility of coming together. Sometimes these are so overwhelming that they result in tragedy, such as the sea channel that divides Heloise from Abelard and the feud between families that violently opposes Romeo's and Juliet's longings to be with each other.

Sometimes they produce comedy, such as the misunderstandings and missed opportunities that keep Tom Hanks and Meg Ryan apart in *Sleepless in Seattle* (1993), along with the lovers in every other Hollywood (or Shakespearean) comedy. The interplay or counterpoint of barriers and unions is what holds our emotional interest in these stories, reminding us that love, however desirable, is also tense, uncertain, and threatens loss. The contact boundary in Gestalt therapy can be understood as a limiting resistance to our yearnings to merge with each other or with the universe. Every contactful meeting with otherness contains elements of both union and differentiation. From the point of view of Gestalt therapy, contact leads to moments of feeling merged, but these are preceded and followed by awareness of one's inevitable separateness.

So I want to supplement Mr. Cornell's argument for the impassioned body with my own plea for the aesthetic imagination in sexual love. At one point Elizabeth Costello, the title character in the South African Nobel Prizewinning novelist J.M. Coetzee's latest work, is standing at the railing of a cruise ship and ruminating about the mouths of underwater creatures. She thinks to herself, "Only by an ingenious economy, an accident of evolution, does the organ of ingestion sometimes get to be used for song" (Coetzee, 2003, p. 54). And, I would add, the organ of elimination for love. But neither song nor love is simply a matter of the body; they are also products of the creative imagination. The body is their instrument of expression.

References

Becker, E. (1997). *The Denial of Death*. Free Press, New York.
Coetzee, J.M. (2003). *Elizabeth Costello*. Viking, New York.

Goodman, P. (1991). "The Political Meaning of Some Recent Revisions of Freud." In: Stoehr, T. (Ed.), *Nature Heals: The Psychological Essays of Paul Goodman*, pp. 42-70. Gestalt Journal Press, Gouldsboro, ME.

Miller, M.V. (2001). "The Speaking Body (Or, Why Did Wilhelm Reich Go Crazy?)." *The Gestalt Journal*, XXIV, 2, pp. 11-29.

∫ Presenting the Present— A Book Review

Stern, D. (2004).
The Present Moment in Psychotherapy and Everyday Life.
New York: W.W. Norton & Company.

Our mainstream psychological tradition, as Daniel Stern points out in his latest book, has paid scant attention to the implications of the present moment for psychotherapy. Perhaps this is largely because classical psychoanalysis, during the era when it dominated psychotherapy, tended to reduce present experience to repetitions and variations of the past. An exception, of course, is Gestalt therapy, which has always put forward the present as the temporal site of maximum therapeutic effectiveness. For Gestalt therapy the present moment is also a basis for health: The methods of Gestalt therapy aim to help patients live more fully in the

---

*From the *International Gestalt Journal*, Vol. 29, No. 1, (Spring, 2006). Reprinted with permission.

present tense, making more possible spontaneous self-expression and meeting of needs in touch with an actual world.

But now Stern, a distinguished researcher and theorist of human development, has written an entire book on the present moment. What does this mean for Gestalt therapy? Lacking a thorough account of early human development in their own literature, many Gestalt therapists have drawn upon Stern's 1985 book, *The Interpersonal World of the Infant*, to fill the gap because Stern brought to developmental theory a new emphasis on the intersubjective give-and-take between infant and mother. Are Gestalt therapists likely to take to Stern's latest book with similar enthusiasm?

Although I have a number of reservations about this book, I think that Stern has nevertheless accomplished something important through subjecting the present moment to detailed scrutiny from many angles. For all its emphasis on the "here and now," Gestalt therapy has never thoroughly enough explored the form of the present moment.[*] Most Gestalt therapists pretty much take for granted that we can all know the here and now intimately through experiencing it. And in a way this is certainly true. But the minute that you begin to investigate the idea of the present theoretically, it becomes complex and elusive.

What is its character and structure? Is it a mere point or a slice in a continuum or is it a brief interval of awareness? Does it "exist" or is it nothing more than a linguistic device for pointing to something in our experience? How does consciousness access it or

---

[*] Among the few exceptions, an important one is Frank-M. Staemmler's article on the here and now in the *British Gestalt Journal* (2002)

vice versa? To what degree do we shape it and to what extent does it shape us? Questions like this have perplexed philosophers for centuries, because they give rise to puzzles about the whole nature of our relationship to time. One comes away from such questions with a sense that the present moment is at once absolutely ordinary and indescribably mysterious.

William James, for example, thought that the present moment is an artifact of our language without any demonstrable existence: "The literally present moment," he wrote, "is a purely verbal supposition, not a position, the only present ever realized concretely being, the 'passing moment,' in which the dying rearward of time and its dawning future forever mix their lights" (James, 1909/1977, p. 254). The late Gilles Deleuze, one of the most profound and intriguing modern philosophers, also felt that the present moment is beyond our grasp. In his book on Henri Bergson (who was one of the great students of temporality), Deleuze wrote that "of the present, we must say at every instant that it 'was,' and of the past, that it 'is,' that it is eternally, for all time" (1991, p. 55). What is suggested here is that the past can be said to exist because it is fixed in place, whereas the present moment, like an electron, has already disappeared the instant we reach for it, leaving behind only a trail hinting that it might have been there.

Daniel Stern, however, displays no qualms about insisting that the present moment exists as an almost palpable unit of time. He not only finds that he is able to describe its "temporal architecture," as he puts it in one chapter, but he believes that one can measure how long it lasts. Drawing on research data from neuroscience and experimental linguistics, as well as studies in the perception of musical phrases, the temporality of action, and parent-infant interactions, Stern claims that the typical present moment, an interval he considers extremely important for psychotherapy, ". . . lasts from between one and ten seconds, with an average duration of around three to four seconds" (p. 41). That Stern has written a book investigating the present moment in meticulous detail is very useful in many respects — especially since no Gestalt therapist thus far has bothered. That he affixes a range of numbers to its duration, however, ought to give Gestalt therapists serious and prolonged pause for thought (more than one to ten seconds, one hopes) about their own position on the nature of the present.

At the outset Stern is quite clear about the subjective character of the present moment. He writes,

> Given the unique and fundamental position of subjective 'nowness' in everyone's experience, we propose to begin an exploration of clinical theory and practice, as well as everyday subjective experience, by placing the phenomenal 'now' at the center — as our starting point. Existential and some Gestalt theories have certainly done just this, but with large brushstrokes. (p. 8)

Although he is certainly right about the large brushstrokes, one wonders what he means by "some Gestalt theories." His vague and indirect reference, by the way, is nearly the only credit he gives to the existence of Gestalt therapy, if that is even what he is alluding to here.

Given Stern's reading of the "now," it comes as no surprise that the four chapters that comprise Part I of the book largely reside in a neighborhood already settled by a small group of both historical and recent theorists who draw on phenomenological thinking, such as Binswanger, Minkowski, Boss, van den Berg, Ricoeur, the group around Stolorow and Atwood, Kimura Bin, and contemporary French philosophers who have been exploring psychopathology, including Henri Maldiney. This seems a promising direction for Stern's topic because phenomenology, following the lead of Husserl and Heidegger, gives subjectivity and temporality priority in its understanding of human nature. (And, of course, this is why phenomenology provides a philosophical basis for Gestalt therapy.)

In particular Stern borrows much from Husserl's *The Phenomenology of Internal Time Consciousness* (1964). Like Husserl, Stern maps out the trajectory of temporal experience with the help of a musical analogy. Stern points out,

> The challenge is to imagine the present moment in some kind of dialogic equilibrium with the past and the future. If the present moment is not well anchored in a past and future it would float off as a meaningless speck. If it is too well anchored it becomes diminished. (p. 28)

And he continues,

> In this sense, a musical phrase contains an immediate past and future. The form of the musical phrase is revealed and captured by the listener as the crest of the immediate present instant passes from the still resonating horizon of the past (of the same present moment) toward the anticipated horizon of the future . . . (p. 29)

These passages are not only quite lovely but also rich in implication for the therapist who focuses his or her attention on the present situation in the therapy session.

So far so good: Stern has situated us confidently in the realm of subjective life, and he returns us to it in his chapter on narrative construction of the present. But although he alludes to the tendency in our psychologies to conceive of mental life, including temporal experience, in spatial terms (which makes psychological concepts readily subject to reification), he fails to some extent to avoid this trap himself once he attempts to quantify the duration of the present moment.

For example, Stern points out that the present moment must have duration, because duration is necessary to experience. But although he offers an intriguing analysis, by way of his musical metaphor, of how duration is experienced as a lived continuous whole, he then goes on, without any transitional discussion, to explicate duration as a quantifiable measure of time. It seems that he has either ignored or misunderstood one of Bergson's central tenets, even though he includes one of Bergson's[*] works in his bibliography.

According to Bergson, you can only know duration, which is an organic, continuous lived experience that cannot be divided into parts, through a faculty that he calls "intuition." For Bergson, intuition gives you immediate knowledge of a whole, somewhat the way you grasp the form of a work of art. By contrast, the conceptual interpretation of psychological experiences, such as time, on the basis of scientific measurement — an approach that Bergson calls "reason" — necessarily breaks these experiences down into

---

[*] Bergson was the philosopher par excellence of duration.

discontinuous exterior facts (see Bergson, 1912). What one comes to know through reason are merely approximations of an experience from outside it and can never capture its essence.

I am bringing in Bergson to illustrate a serious theoretical difficulty in Stern's book. Whether one accepts Bergson's distinction or not, it is the kind of distinction that has to be grappled with in going back and forth, as Stern does, from subjective experience to the results of scientific experiments. It is true that Stern does find interesting correlations among quantitative measurements of brain activity, research into both memory and behavior, and the phenomenal experience of the present moment. But the manner in which he brings these matters to bear on one another gives rise to an important question, an old one: Can one use such correlations to build a bridge from the conclusions of empirical science to the subjectivity of personal experience without falling into one or another reductionism, such as biologism, behaviorism, reification, or other determinisms, on the one hand; idealism or postmodern con-structivism, on the other? This is not only a philosophical question about the nature of entities and methodologies in psychology; it also has immediate and crucial implications for how one conceives change in psychotherapy. And it is not a question that Stern attempts in any explicit way to answer.

In one kind of reductionism, "the world is too much with us, late and soon," as the poet Wordsworth put it, and the environment (the medication or the therapist's techniques or interpretations, for instance) gets too much of the credit for therapeutic change. In the other, the self, with its presumed inner depths, is given too much isolated responsibility for awakening repressed memories, releasing blocked feelings, or constructing a new life narrative.

I think that Stern himself does mostly get around falling into reification and reductionism (they are both occupational hazards of psychological theory) once he invokes intersubjectivity. Nevertheless he leaves behind a theoretical weakness, which does not surmount the dangers of either reification or reductionism. One way of saying what is missing in Stern's argument is that he has not dealt sufficiently with the difference between the "present" as a temporal conception, which might or might not be subject to empirical measurement depending on one's view of temporality, and "being present," which cannot be measured. (This difference was a major issue for Heidegger throughout his work.)

It seems to me not enough to portray the present moment as an experiential structure that lasts a certain number of seconds, and then claim, as Stern goes on to do, that for psychotherapy we are interested mainly in intersubjective present moments. These, he says, are possible because our central nervous systems are set up to empathetically vibrate to one another's experience, and thus we, in effect, know the mind of the other.

The final step in this argument is that therapeutic change takes place mainly as a meeting of the minds during such one-to-ten second periods. This is simply too much neurobiological assumption and too little phenomenological analysis. You cannot go from subjectivity to the brain and nervous system and from there leap to intersubjectivity, as Stern does, without encountering a great many problems. For instance, even if one agrees that the present moment is a brief length of measurable time, would one be satisfied to say that we are present to each other or experience each other's presence for a certain number of seconds?

Stern is staking out his position in very difficult territory. Bringing descriptions from within the experiential framework of the perceiving, feeling subject together with the conclusions of scientific studies that analyze it from outside poses one of the biggest challenges in current psychological thinking. It amounts to integrating a phenomenological perspective with the approach of natural science, and no one has yet done it with complete success. At least Stern gives credence to both sides, whereas much of modern psychiatry, satisfied with correlations between neurobiological evidence and behavioral observations or reports, tends to ignore the phenomenological.

In Part II of the book, consisting of the next four chapters, Stern devotes himself to the topic of intersubjectivity — a topic that has been a central concern for him throughout his career — refocused here through the lens of the present moment. Much of the material in these chapters is drawn from the valuable developmental research into interactions between infants and their mothers that Stern and his colleagues have pursued for years. They also draw on brain research and behavioral studies, sprinkling in a dose of phenomenology here and there. These chapters are filled with interesting evidence from various fields in support of moving away from individualistic psychologies and psychotherapies to intersubjective ones. But in some respects they compound the problem of reconciling subjectivity and empirical science because Stern continues to enter muddy theoretical waters and then swim too rapidly from one perspective to another without grappling with the troubling questions that surface along the way.

How does all this connect to the practice of psychotherapy? Bringing intersubjectivity to bear on the present moment, and the present moment to bear on intersubjectivity, allows Stern to go finally where he has been hinting that he will go throughout the book: to the clinical situation in order to demonstrate that the most important events in psychotherapy, the ones that actually bring about change in people's lives, are co-created present moments between patient and therapist. This is the main subject of the chapters that make up Part III, the last section of Stern's book. Do I need to point out that it is also what Gestalt therapy has been proclaiming, teaching, and practicing for over fifty years?

I will not take up these chapters in detail. Suffice it to say that judging by the many examples he provides, both in clinical circumstances and outside of them, Stern is an astute observer of inter-subjective exchanges and sequences and probably a good therapist. As a Gestalt therapist I can hardly disagree with the approach to psychotherapy he sets forth. I have no hesitation in saying that this book ought to be recommended reading for psychotherapists.

What disturbs me, however, is Stern's intimation throughout the book that he is the first to propose the revolutionary new idea that episodes of intersubjective contact in the present moment ought to be the basis for psychotherapy. If he does not make this claim explicitly, he gets it across clearly enough in two respects. First of all, this kind of statement is repeated more than once in the book:

> . . . I am suggesting that we look at psychotherapy differently, through the magnifying glass of the present moment and from a phenomenological perspective. This altered vision will lead to changes in how we think about our work and what we do from moment to moment. . . . One of the more far-reaching ideas proposed is that we view intimate human relations and psychotherapy at a micro level made up of moments that occupy a subjective now . . . (p. 135)

Stern's claim to a radically new outlook is bolstered by his complete lack of reference to the writings and teachings in Gestalt therapy that precede his book by a half-century. I do not know whether this stems more from arrogance, disingenuousness, or self-serving politics. It is certainly not from ignorance, since I do know, as do many people in the community of Gestalt therapists, that Stern has had direct personal contact with Gestalt therapy through a visiting alliance with an Italian Gestalt institute.

By emphasizing that the most valuable psychotherapy consists of contact episodes between therapist and patient that unfold in the present moment, Stern has in effect written a book that is a variant of the theory of Gestalt therapy. To be sure, Stern has brought forward fresh insights through his thoroughgoing analysis of the present moment. In this sense he has made a contribution to the theory of Gestalt therapy. But he has done so without appearing to notice that Gestalt therapy addressed in similar terms almost everything important that he has to say (and with more consistency than he manages) over half a century ago.

References

Bergson, H. (1912). *An introduction to metaphysics.* New York & London: G. P. Putnam's Sons.

Deleuze, G. (1991). *Bergsonism.* New York: Zone Books.

Husserl, E. (1964). *The phenomenology of internal time-consciousness.* Bloomington, IN: University Press.

James, W. (1909/1977). *A pluralistic universe.* Cambridge, MA: Harvard University Press.

Staemmler, F.-M. (2002). "The here and now: A critical analysis." *British Gestalt Journal* 11/1, 21-32.

Part Three:

Founders and Shapers

Introductions and Elegies

∫ Introduction to the Gestalt Journal Press Edition of *Gestalt Therapy*

Isadore From died on June 27, 1994 from complications during treatment for cancer. He was seventy-five years old. He had been through a period of increasingly serious illness and endured it with courage, ironical reserve, and a complete lack of self-pity. He had also remained in close touch with his numerous friends in the United States and Europe. For Isadore, friendship had always been the sine qua non of the good life.

As much as he loved literature and philosophy and paid careful attention to language in both his teaching and practice, Isadore refused to write. He profoundly influenced the theory and practice of Gestalt therapy through the medium of the spoken word — through teaching and supervision. His few published pieces are transcripts of talks or interviews. So it will come as no surprise that he left the actual writing of this introduction to me. We did have a chance, though, to get to-

---

* Introduction (with Isadore From) to *Gestalt Therapy: Excitement and Growth in the Human Personality.* By F. Perls, R. Hefferline, and P. Goodman. (1994). Gouldsboro, ME: The Gestalt Journal Press.

gether for some long conversations about an early draft before his illness and its treatment with chemotherapy fatigued him too much for further exchanges of that kind. I sent him the final version shortly before he died. I don't know whether he had an opportunity to read it all the way through.

So I am compelled to take full responsibility both for the quality of the writing and for any errors in what follows. However, Isadore so deeply shaped my own understanding of Gestalt therapy that what I have written is saturated with his thought. This introduction certainly belongs to him as much as it does to me. I also want to express my gratitude to Hunt Cole, Isadore From's companion for thirty-four years, for his skilled editorial scrutiny of the manuscript.

— M.V.M.

Cambridge, Massachusetts

I

If the reception of this book when it first appeared in 1951, published by the Julian Press, had been based on the whole of what is between its covers, its influence on the subsequent history of psychological theory and psychotherapeutic practice might have been momentous.

The new outlook that the book presented began from a radical though by no means disrespectful examination of the limitations of psychoanalysis, and it thus anticipated by decades criticisms that have only begun to emerge fully (and not so respectfully) during the last few years. But it also went a good deal further than diagnosis of difficulties in psychoanalytic theory: it set forth a comprehensive foundation for a profoundly new approach to psychotherapy, one that did not so much scrap what had been learned from psychoanalysis as weave it into an altogether different view of human nature and its foibles. In place of the psychoanalyst's concentration on excavating the patient's past and interpreting the unconscious as primary sources for therapeutic discovery, it shifted the center of gravity to the patient's present experience. And rather than leave the therapist half-hidden in the wings in order to encourage regression and transference in the patient, the heart of psychoanalytic method, it brought therapist and patient onto center stage together in order to illuminate their actual relationship as clearly as possible.

Yet, more than forty years after its debut, Gestalt therapy still wanders down the back roads of contemporary psychology and psychotherapy. Almost everybody has heard of it, but relatively few people have any idea what it is really about, not even in the professional communities where psychotherapy is taught and practiced. Many factors, institutional and cultural, may have been

311

involved in preventing Gestalt therapy, despite its original promise, from assuming a more significant place in the evolution of psycho-therapy. But it cannot be denied that, almost from the start, Gestalt therapy has colluded in weakening its own voice amid the growing number of contemporary therapies clamoring for both public and professional attention.

That the official debut of Gestalt therapy took the form of a book is not surprising. In a similar fashion, psychoanalysis first began to attract general notice in the late nineteenth century with the publication of *The Interpretation of Dreams*. The first edition of *Gestalt Therapy: Excitement and Growth in the Human Personality*, however, was a strange concoction, consisting of two wildly dis-similar volumes bound together, a format that gave the book a split personality. This bibliographical idiosyncrasy was no accident, for there were real conflicts underlying the book's peculiar doubleness.

The second volume (Volume I in this edition), a theoreti-cal work written in uncompromisingly difficult prose, set forth a highly original vision of human nature. It also reinterpreted the origin of neurotic troubles from a new perspective that took more account of the role of social and environmental forces than perhaps any preceding view. And it provided the foundation for an alterna-tive approach to psychotherapy that made a decisive break with the dominant psychoanalytic model without overthrowing, as did behaviorism, for example, what was valuable in psychoanalysis.

If Volume II is no easy read, it is not because its concepts are served up in a crust of obscure jargon, as is too often the case in our psychological and sociological literature. Although much of Volume II is based on the ideas of Frederick Perls, an expatriate German psychoanalyst, the actual expression, elaboration, and further development of them was left to Paul Goodman, one of the most important social critics and inventive psychological thinkers this country has produced, as well as a poet, novelist, and playwright. The difficulties have the feel of modern life itself, with its contradictoriness, its alienation and longings, its vacillation between inhibition and spontaneity. Goodman had no more wish to thin out human complexity in order to make his formulations easy to digest than did, say, T. S. Eliot or Henry James.

Volume I (Volume II in this edition), the product of collaboration between Perls and Ralph Hefferline, a professor of psychology at Columbia University, took the opposite tack: yielding to a trend in American publishing that was just beginning to gather momentum, it reduced difficult material to something approaching what we nowadays call pop psychology. It boiled down the theoretical conceptions of Gestalt therapy to a set of self-help exercises, derived from the sort of interventions Gestalt therapists sometimes make, and presented them accompanied by commentary in a style of exposition that fell somewhere between popularized versions of Zen Buddhism and *The Power of Positive Thinking* by Norman Vincent Peale, complete with testimonials — a staple of the self-help and human potential movements — from students who had tried them.

Although the contrast between the two volumes reflected differences in the intellectual disposition of their authors, it also exemplified a basic division in American culture. In his essay, "Paleface and Redskin," the literary critic Philip Rahv claims that American writers have always tended to choose sides in a contest between two camps — the result of "a dichotomy," as he put it, "between experience and consciousness . . . between energy and sensibility, between conduct and theories of conduct." Our best-selling novelists and our leaders of popular literary movements, from Walt Whitman to Hemingway to Jack Kerouac, number among the group Rahv called the redskins. They represent the restless frontier mentality, with its reverence for the sensual and intuitive over the intellect, its self-reliant individualism and enthusiasm for quick triumph over obstacles. The hero of a recent best seller, *The Bridges of Madison County*, with his pickup truck, his blue jeans and well-worn boots, his guitar lashed to a spare tire, could qualify as a card-carrying member of this camp. While the redskins took to the open road, jotting down their adventures along the way, the palefaces tended to congregate in the cities, where they drew heavily on European literary and intellectual traditions. They put at least as much stock in the value of artistic transformation and intellectual reflection as they did in capturing the raw data of the emotions and senses for their portrayals of human experience. James and Eliot would be leading figures among the palefaces. Both of them eventually left America, a society that they came to regard as crude, to spend the balance of their lives in England.

Rahv was addressing a lack of integration in American literature, but his analysis also helps to explain a bifurcation in our schools of psychology and psychotherapy. By now we have seen enough of both an aloof analytic priesthood at one extreme, delivering oracular, arcane interpretations, and a crowd of John Wayne-like psychotherapists at the other, all blood and guts, to be just about jaded with the whole enterprise.

Not that the founders of Gestalt therapy exactly conformed to these stereotypes. Perls arrived in New York from a bourgeois European upbringing and a classical training in psychoanalysis. Yet no one could have joined forces with the redskins — at least in their West Coast hippie version during the 1960s — more readily than he did. Goodman was hardly a genteel literary Anglophile; his thinking was rooted in colloquial, pragmatic, and democratic currents of the American mainstream, and he led his life on the streets of New York, as well as on campuses in the thick of student rebellions. But he was also every inch an intellectual, thoroughly versed in both classical and contemporary European thought.

Although the authors of *Gestalt Therapy* intended to begin with a presentation of theory and then follow it with an exposition of technique, the publisher felt that reversing the order might make the book more commercially successful. Obviously the authors must have agreed to this arrangement. Redskinism had prevailed, if not in the writing, at least in the publication of *Gestalt Therapy*, as it would prevail shortly thereafter in the teaching of Frederick Perls. The book's radical import, contained in Volume II, which might have significantly influenced the history of modern psychology and psychotherapy, was largely lost. How many committed practitioners of psychotherapy, steeped in the intricate tradition of psychoanalytic thinking about human development and character, could be expected to slog their way through to page 227 where Volume II began? [*]

Thus the stage was set for Gestalt therapy's checkered career. Not that there is anything inherently wrong with the exercises in what is now Volume II. Their aim is to illustrate methods of heightening an individual's awareness of deadened feelings and sensations, of reawakening the knowledge of a person's agency in shaping what he or she takes for granted as a fixed reality, of rediscovering the rules planted in the psyche during childhood by cus-

---

[*] We are grateful to Joe Wysong and the Gestalt Journal Press, not only for reviving *Gestalt Therapy* in a new edition after it has been out of print for nearly four years but also for reversing the two volumes once again in accord with the authors' original intent.

todial authorities and institutions that can perniciously inhibit adult behavior. The creation of experiments along these lines is an important activity in Gestalt therapy sessions; their purpose is to help the patient derive insights from immediate experience rather than the therapist's interpretations. Thus the patient is given a high degree of control over how and what he learns from psychotherapy (which by and large has been a rather authoritarian discipline).

Such experiments, properly understood, are part of the collaborative give-and-take between patient and therapist in a psychotherapy session. To use them oneself for self-improvement may be valuable, but that is almost beside the point with respect to their use in Gestalt therapy, where they are guided by the relationship between the patient and the therapist. One can also interpret one's own dreams in the psychoanalytic manner — Freud himself did it in the *Interpretation of Dreams*; what other choice did he have? — which is not the same thing as psychoanalytic psychotherapy, in which the transference plays such a key part. The loss of precisely this kind of distinction helped feed a reductive tendency, both in the world of mental health and in American life generally. What became known as Gestalt therapy was a version stripped of its theoretical context and readily debased into slogans for living. The use of the present moment for therapeutic leverage became an imperative to live in the "here and now." The attempt to discriminate between what one had learned that was crucial to one's growth and what one had simply absorbed by fiat became an inverted puritanism, a moral imperative to get rid of all "shoulds."

These tendencies were supported by Perls, whose clinical showmanship dominated the subsequent development of Gestalt therapy. Freud, who was no fan of America, worried about the fate of his discoveries in the hands of Americans, who were initially much more enthusiastic about psychoanalysis than his own countrymen. He feared that the voracious American appetite for novelty and progress, indeed for anything that promised a better life, would vulgarize the discoveries he so jealously (and sometimes tyrannically) guarded. Perls had no such misgivings. Through his peripatetic teaching and his career as a guru at the Esalen Institute in Big Sur, California, he liberally sprinkled his audiences and trainees with slogans and made up new techniques on the fly, presenting the latest ones as the essence of Gestalt therapy, even while he spoke out in almost the same breath against reliance on gimmicks and shortcuts in therapy.

By virtue of his influence, Gestalt therapy presented itself during the 1960s and 1970s as a set of techniques resembling psychodrama, overlaid with a thin patina of existentialist philosophy, to induce emotional release in the name of the freedom from restrictions. Many people, both with and without previous training and credentials in psychotherapy, thus felt encouraged to hang out their shingles as Gestalt therapists after taking a couple of weekend workshops at Esalen or at one of Perls's watering holes along the road. Or they bid for larger market share — and this practice still goes on — by offering the public a combination plate called "Gestalt and — —" (fill in the blank with any one of the countless therapies that have bloomed during the last few decades), whether the combination involved views of human functioning that were philosophically compatible or not. The best-known version of Gestalt therapy during this period was a way of life called simply "Gestalt." Pure redskinism. The paleface term "therapy" wound up in the wastebasket.

Perls's later books were for the most part directly transcribed from tapes of his lectures and demonstrations, which further supported the impression that there was little coherent theory behind Gestalt therapy. After he moved to Esalen, he rarely referred again to the book that resulted from his collaboration with Hefferline and Goodman. Nevertheless, the book stayed in print for many years, in two paperback editions that reproduced the Julian Press format. You could hardly peruse a hip person's bookshelves two or three decades ago without coming across a copy of the Delta Press edition of Perls, Hefferline, and Goodman buried between books by Herbert Marcuse and Baba Ram Das.

Whether the book was read or not, Gestalt therapy gained popularity in the countercultural climate of the times. The content of Volume II was still taught carefully in some quarters, notably in New York, where the training institute founded by the Perlses continued to flourish under the stewardship of Laura Perls, and to some extent at training centers in Cleveland, Los Angeles, San Diego, Boston, and elsewhere. But even this small legacy became increasingly hard to maintain once *Gestalt Therapy* by Perls, Hefferline, and Goodman had vanished from the bookstores, as the last residues of the countercultural mood that kept it in print dried up. Moreover, the quality of teaching and practice in many of these institutes had been contaminated by the mixed-grill approach that combines "Gestalt" and whatever else is *au courant*. Obviously one should learn as much as one can from many sources, but not at the expense of intellectual integrity about the materials one deploys when engaged in so sensitive and urgent an enterprise as intervening in other people's suffering.

II.

To raise questions about the impact of Perls's later career on the reception of Gestalt therapy is not to make light of the inventiveness or originality of his earlier achievements. Gestalt therapy had its first stirrings when Perls wrote a paper in the mid-1930s concluding that the so-called "resistances" — the psychological means of saying no to oneself or others — were oral in origin. The import of this consideration is not shatteringly revolutionary — it represented a small change in a traditional psychoanalytic emphasis — but its ramifications were subversive nevertheless. Apparently the analysts recognized this immediately: Perls mentions in his writings that the paper, which he presented at a Freudian congress in 1936, met with disapproval.

Classical analysis considered the source of resistance to be anal — the anus being the seat, if you will, of a dark, frequently hostile refusal, an early childhood form of which is captured in our phrase "the terrible twos," when children say no to everything they are asked or told to do. Some schools of psychoanalytic theory, following Klein, for instance, regard all this as among the evidence of the child's inherently barbaric nature, in need of taming in order to shape it into civilized behavior. Eric Erikson put the anal stage in a more benign light: he considered the child's development of willful control over the sphincter muscle to be important evidence of autonomy. Parents may also intuitively recognize the signs that their child is becoming more of an individual even in its irrational refusals, but they will usually see to it that for its own good — and often well beyond that — the child is compelled to obey their will.

The psychoanalytic term for the child's receptiveness to parental imperatives — a term which Gestalt therapy was to retain — is "introjection," which means learning by taking in values, rules, and modes of conduct from the environment, in this case the environment of parental authority, without questioning the information or its source. Psychoanalytic theory suggests that children must continue to learn chiefly through introjection at least until the Oedipal stage, around five or six years of age, if they are to be properly socialized.

The shift from anal to oral refusal implies a different possibility. It lifts the capacity to no as freely as yes, to rebel as well as to accommodate, from where it lies buried in a lower chamber to the mouth, the locale of eating, chewing, tasting, but also of language and sometimes of loving. In other words, to a more obvious meeting place between the individual and the world. Perls had not yet formulated a concept of the "contact boundary," so fundamental to Gestalt therapy; that remained to be done in his collaboration with Goodman. But the first seeds of the idea were already planted here.

Certain implications of orality were more fully elaborated in Perls's first book, *Ego, Hunger, and Aggression,* published in 1942. Here he made what was perhaps his most important contribution to an alternative view of human development: he used the emergence of teeth in an infant of eight or nine months as an encompassing metaphor for the steadily growing complexity and refinement of the motoric abilities, senses, and mental equipment in general. Perls proposed that just as the infant, now armed with teeth which enable it to chew food rather than merely swallow it, begins to develop its own sense of taste about what it likes or wants and doesn't like or want, it can also begin to discriminate and select from what it swallows psychologically from the environment. In becoming a critic of experience, the child forms an individual personality.

Thus the need to learn primarily through introjection — through identifying with and modeling oneself after the caretaking and disciplining adults — can start to be replaced by self-determination much sooner than the Freudians claimed. In Perls's view, to support a child's tendency to go beyond introjection early is not to consign the child to barbarism; it is to respect a natural, self-regulating process of healthy growth. If there is anything barbaric in the picture, it is the attempts of anxious or overbearing parents and educators to interfere unnecessarily with nature.

It follows from this line of thinking that Gestalt therapy came to regard the function of aggression in a very distinctive way. In *Ego, Hunger, and Aggression*, Perls described its origins in what he called "dental aggression," the biting off and chewing up of one's experience in order to absorb the parts of it one needs and get rid of what one doesn't. This emphasis puts aggression in a positive light, bringing out its role in both preserving a sense of oneself and reaching out to contact the environment. Aggression enables one to risk having impact on one's world, and it frees one to be creative or productive. This, of course, is virtually the opposite tack from that taken by Freud, who linked aggression to anal sadism and the death instinct. For Gestalt therapy, aggression is by nature healthy and in the service of life. The healthy personality is shaped by a child's own idiosyncratic sequences of yeses and noes; as Jakob Boehme, the German mystic who so influenced Hegel, put it, "In Yea and Nay all things consist." When people can't say no as readily as yes, they tend to accept uncritically a view of reality or a way of life dictated by others. Perls took the absence of no to be caused by repression of dental aggression, due to fear of conflict, which he regarded as a fundamental source of neurotic pathology. It's not aggression but the inhibition of it in the personality that produces impotence, explosions into violence, or desensitization and deadness.

Every method of psychotherapy presupposes, whether it makes it explicit or not, a view of human development. Whereas psychoanalysis encourages the patient to regress and reintroduces

321

introjection through interpretation, a very different approach springs from Perls's claim that the capacity for self-determination and self-support develops early. As it subsequently evolved, Gestalt therapy didn't so much throw out interpretation — all psycho-therapists make interpretations — as it offered in addition experiments that enable patients to discover for themselves. Included importantly among these experiments are those generated by the therapist's obligation to make sure that the patient retains or frees up the ability to resist and criticize the therapist's interpretations.

In other respects, *Ego, Hunger, and Aggression* did not stray very far from the psychoanalytic camp, particularly on one funda-mental point: Despite its critique of Freud's focus on the sexual instinct and its references to Hegelian dialectic, Marx, and a smat-tering of minor neo-Hegelians and Nietzscheans, semantic theo-rists, Gestalt psychologists (not Gestalt therapists), and other holistic thinkers, it put forward a view of human nature that still kept the encapsulated individual at its center. The full coming of age of Gestalt therapy had to wait for Paul Goodman's proclama-tion at the beginning of Volume II of Perls, Hefferline, and Good-man that "experience occurs at the boundary between the organ-ism and its environment . . . We speak of the organism contacting the environment, but it is the contact that is the simplest and first reality."

With that definition in place, Gestalt therapy was formally launched on waters remote from those where psychoanalysis, be-haviorism, and every other theory during that period fished for its truths. A radical shift in the observation post for psychological understanding is proposed in this passage. The looming, self-regarding self of psychoanalysis is no longer the sole object of psychotherapy; indeed, it often diminishes in size and nearly fades from view, becoming part of the background, from which it can be brought forward, however, when needed. The primary site of psychological experience, where psychotherapeutic theory and practice are to direct their attention, is the contact itself, the place where self and environment stage their meetings and become involved with each other.

By now the term "contact," having been filtered through the encounter groups and human potential movement therapies of twenty years ago, has made its way into the drawing rooms and bedrooms of middle-class culture. People in certain circles nowadays are likely to tell each other such things as "I want more contact with you," as though contact always had to do with furthering communication or intimacy, along with hugs and kisses. But whereas the popular expression means something akin to closeness or simply spending time together, that is hardly what the authors of *Gestalt Therapy* had in mind. They introduced the term "contact" as an abstract formal concept (in the sense that all theoretical concepts are abstract, though not mathematically rigorous, in psychological theory — i.e., at a similar level of abstraction as, say, "unconscious" or "libido" or, for that matter, "the self ") to order to distinguish their fundamental premises from those of virtually all the other clinical theories of their times. In their view, to the extent that psychology has limited its interest to the isolated individual, it distorts how life is lived.

Gestalt therapy, especially as it is spelled out by Goodman, takes for its starting point something so obvious that our human and social sciences usually seem to overlook it: the exchange that goes on unceasingly between the human organism and its surrounding environment in all areas of life ties person and world inextricably to one another. Breathing means absorbing oxygen and returning it in changed form, and this minimal give-and-take must continue even when one is asleep; eating entails seizing parts of nature and converting them — "destroying" them, Gestalt therapy would say, in order to bring out the aggressiveness required — into something digestible; laboring suggests usefully reshaping a portion of the environment, but also having one's activity in this regard organized by the resistance that the environment puts up or the limits it establishes; talking means talking to someone, who in general is likely to reply; making love means that two people have consented to the deepest use of each other's bodies. The world of Gestalt therapy is a busy world fairly humming with constant action and transaction, a place in continual flux. Within this flux, the experience of the "self" changes in size and scope depending on what's going on. It may be very small, almost negligible, when one is lost in contemplation of a work of art or absorbed in love; it can take over the entire foreground of awareness, however, when one is in pain, for example, during which time the self, in effect, becomes the pain.

Even cognition is not merely receptive: Gestalt therapy draws on classical Gestalt psychology's notion that the unending, inchoate mass of data presented to us by the environment is organized and shaped by the perceiver into "wholes," which typically have form and structure, and that it is these subjectively structured wholes, not the ultimately unknowable raw data, that compose a person's experience. The particular way in which the wholes of experience, called "Gestalts," are made is influenced by a person's needs, appetites, impulses, interests, and so forth. Thus Gestalt therapy reintroduced the nineteenth-century romantic poets' idea that we half-create what we perceive and gave it a new motivational impetus. And if one assumes that there is this subjective element in all human experience, it follows that no two people experience exactly the same reality.

All the activities of contacting the environment (or being contacted by it) occur across an experiential — and by no means necessarily physical — demarcation between what the organism takes to be itself, what it has already domesticated, so to speak, to its purposes, and the wilderness, as yet unknown, that is the inexhaustible otherness of the world. To this fluctuating edge where self and other meet and something happens, Gestalt therapy gives the name "contact boundary."

Thus in Gestalt therapy, the space between the self and the other is no vacuum, as it is in most other psychological theories. Experience unfolds in a field, rather like an electrical field, charged with urgency — will, needs, preferences, longings, wishes, judgments, and other expressions or manifestations of being. Contact between two persons, for example, is not a collision between two atomic particles each of which is filled up with interior neurobiological plumbing or conditioned habits and beliefs or an ego, id, and superego. Gestalt therapy neither has to assume nor to reject any of these constructions; it can even allow for all of them — because its concern is solely with the activity at the contact boundary, where what is going on can be observed.

If all this is not too far from common sense, and some of it even self-evident, it was nevertheless a highly innovative way of reformulating psychological theory in a manner that called for an entirely new way of practicing psychotherapy. Gestalt therapy argues that it is precisely at the contact boundary, the site of meetings between self and other and of withdrawals from them, that psychology can best explain, and psychotherapists best witness and reflect back to patients, the responsibility that people have in shaping their own experience. Moreover, the contact boundary is where growth occurs — which, after all, is what psychotherapy is about — because it is where a person's next need and what in the environment is available to satisfy it join up or cross swords, depending on whether the meeting is friendly or unfriendly. Growth comes from metabolizing the unknown, which is taken in from the environment, and making it known, which transforms it into an aspect of the self. For example, a child mounts a bicycle for the first time and goes wobbling off fearfully. She does not yet experience this activity as an integral expression of herself. By the tenth or twelfth ride, she may announce proudly that she is a bicycle-rider, an attribute that can now begin to number among those that make up her identity. One can spend a certain amount of time lording it over one's real estate: Up to a point, as the poet Wallace Stevens put it, "Everything comes to him/From the middle of his field." But on the whole, one grows by traveling out to the fences and perimeters where one's ownership dwindles and one begins to approach the wilds of human contact.

Because contact and withdrawal go on tirelessly as long as life does, changing from moment to moment as a need is met or an interest pursued and others allowed to arise, what follows in Gestalt therapy is a translation from interpretation of traumatic events in a patient's past to an intimate examination of how the patient goes about creating his or her experience (including replicating the responses to past trauma) in the present. Gestalt therapy is not so interested in questions of where development may have been arrested in a patient's childhood as in helping the patient identify and work through the present anxieties and blocks, perhaps better called disturbances of contact than resistances, that prevent the next imminent act of growth (for example, ending therapy) from taking place.

From this perspective comes the therapeutic value in Gestalt therapy of paying close attention to the present moment, which means that in a therapy session, observation of the changing contact boundary between the therapist and the patient becomes of paramount importance. Then both can learn exactly how and where the contact becomes disturbed. It is a crucial correction of the record to stress that the idea of the present moment — the famous "here and now" of Gestalt therapy — is a way of notifying the therapist and the patient where to concentrate their attention while doing Gestalt therapy. The present moment was introduced in Perls, Hefferline, and Goodman as the most effective therapeutic methodology, not as the best way of life. Gestalt therapists were not supposed to behave like Buddhistic spiritual masters, preaching the ethical value or the pleasures of living in the moment, even though it may have come to seem that way given the legacy derived from the later work of Perls and the mood of the 1960s. If a person decides to conduct himself or herself in accord with some notion of living in the moment, that's fine, but it has less to do with therapy than it does with one's personal conception of the good life. If, on the other hand, a person makes a free and considered choice to live a life of nostalgia, Gestalt therapy would have no objection. Would Proust have been better off living more Zennishly in the here and now?

III.

Perhaps the most important reason for resurrecting this book and urging that it be widely read is that it may help provide much of what is needed to rehabilitate the deeply troubled foundations of psychotherapy.

Freud's imposing edifice, which for so long dominated the landscape of psychotherapy, is foundering under heavy critical bombardment. No doubt this was bound to happen, given that our historical situation and cultural imperatives have undergone profound transformation since the late nineteenth century. Psychoanalysis rested its case on two fundamental assumptions: infantile sexuality and unconscious motivation. Both were radical inventions in their day that enabled us to make sense of behavior that had seemed incomprehensible. Both, however, require a leap of faith, a belief that the roots of all adult conduct are planted in vague or invisible primitive mental events during early childhood that give rise to irreconcilable conflicts in every individual's inner life. This conception has provided a rich tradition of outlooks and insights for all the humanistic disciplines, as well as for psychotherapy, but the widespread conviction from within the tradition that psychoanalysis constitutes a science has left it vulnerable to a great many questions. As a result, the entire psychoanalytic approach is currently being pulled apart from several directions at once.

For one thing, not only psychoanalysis, but all psychotherapy is being elbowed aside to some extent by a resurgence of an older biological determinism. The return to biology, of course, both leads and follows the widening acceptance of drugs in the psychiatric community as the best answer to depression, anxiety, obsessive-compulsive disorders, and psychosis. Meanwhile, Freud's metapsychology and interpretative method are taking a beating from philosophical critics who argue that claims of psychoanalysis to causal truth are unscientific because there is no means for subjecting them to empirical verification — for example, there is no way to prove that childhood repression produces adult symptoms.

Even Freud's character, alas, is being bludgeoned by lapsed analysts and disillusioned literary critics who consider his false starts, changes of mind, and tendency to belittle opposition as resistance to be ample justification for calling him a liar, coward, and opportunist. Such name-calling is in keeping with our current epidemic of biographical muckraking, a kind of renewed puritanism, seemingly dedicated to the proposition that exposing enough questionable conduct in the life of a revered innovator invalidates the art or achievement, or renders the theory and practice unworthy of serious regard. One can imagine that psychoanalysis may eventually wind up dismantled and tossed without so much as a departing wave of gratitude on the scrap heap of Eurocentric, male-chauvinistic history. This is a strategy of moving on by savaging where we came from that we euphemistically call "deconstruction."

If Gestalt therapy may still contain some promise of bringing fresh perspective to this increasingly raucous debate, it is because the theory of Gestalt therapy has given up altogether the model of natural science, and it has done so without turning to mysticism. The theoretical half of the book by Perls, Hefferline, and Goodman, instead of attempting to describe health and pathology in terms drawn from causal science, presents a phenomenonological understanding, based on observable and immediately reportable experience, of how a person goes about creating — and keeps on creating — a healthy or neurotic reality. This represents a fundamental switch of paradigms for psychotherapy, one that suggests that Gestalt therapy need not become mired in claims and counterclaims about whether psychology or neurophysiology represents the truer science of human suffering. In its quest for an objective empirical reality, a physical world that could be described by the laws of logic and mathematics, modern science, which originated in the late sixteenth century in the thought of Galileo, Descartes, and Francis Bacon, created a split between the subject, the knowing mind, and the object, that which is known. Virtually all subsequent western thought has maintained this dualism, which gives rise to all sorts of problems about the relation of mind to matter. The phenomenological movement in philosophy, initiated by Edmund Husserl in the early years of this century, can perhaps be best understood as an attempt to restore the unity of subject and object. Phenomenology is, above all, an alternative method to the dominant scientific method: It neither affirms nor rejects the existence of an "external" physical world; it simply insists that philosophical investigation begin with the world in the only terms we can know it — as it is presented to consciousness. Therefore, philosophy is to be the study of the structure of immediate subjective experience.

Gestalt therapy is applied phenomenology. As conceived by Gestalt therapy, the contact boundary is a phenomenological construct. So is the receding and advancing self, and so is the dawning and dying away of the present moment. None of these conceptions represents a fixed entity, one that pauses long enough to be reified or quantitatively measured. If we do in fact fix them briefly in time and space in order to discuss them or illustrate a point or make a diagnosis, that is simply another level of sometimes useful abstraction. Chronic and unaware fixation treated as reality is evidence of neurosis — in a theory as well as in a person.

Phenomenological philosophy, like the academic Gestalt psychology of Wertheimer, Köhler, and Koffka, to which it is closely related in certain respects, concerns itself mainly with problems of perception and cognition. As a theory for psychotherapy, Gestalt therapy takes on the willful, active, emotional, and anxiety-ridden features of human existence as well. One can capture the particular flavor of Gestalt therapy by borrowing a formulation of Arnold Toynbee's formulation. Toynbee claimed that history cannot be based on the model of natural science because human actions are not a cause but a challenge, and their consequences are not an effect but a response. The response to a challenge is not invariable, so history is inherently unpredictable.

In a similar way, Gestalt therapy views the course of human development — and, for that matter, the therapy session itself — as challenge and response, rather than cause and effect. Where there is challenge rather than mere causality, there is anxiety that cannot be eradicated. But it can be transformed into something more productive than symptoms or neurotic character. Gestalt therapy, taken seriously, offers no cure for all the problems that humans fall prey to by the simple fact of inheriting the human condition. It offers no passage back through the gates of Eden. But, as psychoanalysis had once promised, it can help one learn to live better in a fallen world.

— Isadore From
— Michael Vincent Miller

∫ Paul Goodman: The Poetics of Theory

Paul Goodman was unquestionably brilliant, prophetically ahead of his time, combined immense learning with a plain-spoken common sense rare among intellectuals. He was a social critic, poet. novelist and playwright, utopian city planner, educator, psychotherapist and psychological theorist, and he published books in all these areas. Yet he spent most of his days — till he was forty-eight years old, at any rate (he died at sixty) — living the life of a starving artist-scholar. He was persistently undervalued and misunderstood throughout his writing career of some thirty-odd years. There was a notable exception, of course: For a spell during the nineteen-sixties, he connected with a college generation that shared his alienation from the social mainstream and his hopes for social change. He had just published *Growing Up Absurd*, the book that brought him a kind of fame, and many in this new generation found in it a convincing analysis of their experience. By the end of the decade, however, both the student radicals, frustrated and

---

[*] Introduction to *Nature Heals: The Psychological Essays of Paul Goodman*. Edited by Taylor Stoehr. (1992. Gouldsboro, ME: The Gestalt Journal Press.)

badly divided among themselves, and the counterculture, increasingly wrapped in a cloud of drugs and mysticism, mostly lost interest in Goodman, So his influence was once again on the wane.

Why did he have such a difficult time? Was his career another instance of the modern artist's plight — a datum in the sociology of culture? Or was there something in Goodman's nature that was too jaggedly individual and thus succeeded in pushing people away? Was he too declamatory, too insistent in public about his anarchism and homosexuality, his feisty lack of reverence for authority and celebrity, even his tenderness and haunting sense of failure? Certainly his writing style is anything but distancing. God knows, he makes more lively reading than the ponderous abstractions of Herbert Marcuse or the arcane mythologizing of Norman O. Brown, contemporaries with whom he shared certain intellectual emphases. Goodman's writing, on the contrary, is highly self-revealing, which may be more than readers expect or tolerate from their prophets and radical theorists, even though we live in an age of confessional poetry, use histories by the patients themselves, novels that are barely disguised diaries of their authors' sexual problems in marriage. There is personal drama in Goodman's writing, as well as intellectual drama: one feels always that he was discovering himself along with a new way of characterizing neuroses or another facet of social oppression.

Many people may have been put off by Goodman's salty personal presence. though I, for one, can't see why. I spent some time with Goodman on two occasions — once in 1964, when we were both commissioned to write articles about the Berkeley Free Speech Movement for *Dissent*; and again in 1970, when he came to M.I.T., where I was teaching at the time, to give a poetry reading and address student radicals. I found him gentle and responsive, totally unpretentious, intellectually enthusiastic and open. It is true that some tones of bitterness entered his voice now and then at the later date. His son Mathew's death at twenty in a hiking accident three years earlier had left him deeply shaken. Moreover, the rift between Goodman and the students was widening, especially since Goodman deplored the recent drift toward violence of some factions in the student movement. At one talk I heard him give, militant student activists heckled him the whole way. I recall how patiently and thoroughly he dealt with their challenges. Anyhow, I felt an immediate affection for the man.

Indeed, I think that Goodman considered himself a kind of exile from every group, even at the height of his fame in the sixties. There is a very touching passage in an essay he wrote late in life, called "The Politics of Being Queer" (included in this collection of his psychological writings), that shows how penetratingly Goodman felt his isolation: "Frankly, my experience of radical community is that it does not tolerate my freedom. Nevertheless, I am all for community because it is a human thing, only I seem doomed to be left out." This from a social thinker who devoted himself to a utopian vision of free human beings living and working together in a fulfilling way!

It fits right into this pattern that Goodman is a relatively unsung founding father of Gestalt therapy, although he is still perhaps its most eloquent and important theoretical voice. Of course, everyone who had been in on mapping out the original terrain of Gestalt therapy — Laura Perls, Isadore From, and others including Goodman — tended to fade from public view in the shadow of Fritz Perls, who besides being a masterful, inventive clinician, was a shrewd publicist for his new therapy. Goodman's influence did not make its way far from New York among budding

Gestalt therapists.* They were too impressed with Perls' charismatic genius; besides, many got swept away on the tides of "human potential" movement religiosity — Goodman's old-fashioned humanism — his psychological writings are filled with references to Aristotle and Kant as well as Freud and Reich — and his insistence on the political implications of Gestalt therapy did not much appeal to the inward-gazing spiritualism at Esalen, for example.

Goodman's own cast of mind is probably responsible in part for his lack of recognition as an innovative psychological theorist. Nothing he wrote fits neatly into the conventional categories. He ranges over the humanities and social sciences in his own idiosyncratic fashion, and brings a great deal to bear on whatever subject he takes up. There is something a bit cranky and uncompromising, I suppose, about his citing everybody from Yeats to Federn to Gandhi in his treatise on Gestalt therapy, just as there was about his habit of invoking Socrates or Milton before an audience of student activists about to go get tear-gassed at the barricades (although Goodman also paid his dues at the barricades). Goodman makes a charming comment about this propensity of his in an essay concerning his own literary method. "I have found it delicious," he announced, "when I was being most outrageous, to be quoting Aristotle or Spinoza and feeling that I was most orthodoxly innocent." As usual, a serious principle lurks behind the casual tone. This was how he tried to get across to people his connection with the humanistic tradition that he always felt supported his radicalism.

---

* Except to Cleveland — the founders of the Gestalt Institute there were trained by the original New York group.

So I suspect that most psychotherapists don't know what to make of Goodman's manner of presentation when he writes about therapy. On the one hand, I can imagine that the bureaucratic professionals of mental health would consider his psychological writing more "literary" than "scientific" and thus would have trouble taking it seriously. It's bizarre that such an emotionally engaging profession should enunciate itself, with few exceptions (Freud being one of them — just read his case histories) in such cold, cumbersome terminology. For that matter, even in Gestalt therapy, the term "contact" is not exactly heart-warming. On the other hand, the high-voltage energy-releaser therapists often seem more interested in new techniques for cheerleading their patients on to victory than in enriching their theoretical knowledge. Goodman fits neither mold very well. More of his refusal to compromise.

Poetry is the mode of speech that fuses ideas with personal revelation of feeling, and Goodman's writing is never far from the act of making poems, even when he is grappling with an abstruse or subtle point about infantile character-formation. During his early Freudian phase, he wrote about the Oedipus complex in a manner more related to the parables of Kafka than to the usual eisegesis by psychoanalytic practitioners. (Cf. "The Golden Age" and "Eros, or the Drawing of the Bow" in *Nature Heals*. Conversely. Goodman published a book in 1947 called *Kafka's Prayer*, a brooding psychoanalytic exploration of Kafka's works.)

In fact, to my taste, Goodman's social criticism and psychological writings are more poetically satisfying than his poetry. His leaps are more inspired; he comes up with more far-reaching metaphors. As a social critic Goodman has had few peers in America. He stubbornly held forth a vision of individual self-realization through love and work against the dehumanizing pressures that bureaucracy and technology were producing. This was not a Darwinian vision of self-reliance or American rugged individualism, however, but of anarchist community. Goodman believed that groups of people, dealing directly with one another on a small scale, could begin to handcraft a new and humanly decent community out of the sprawling over-centralized mass of post-industrial society. He wrote about these matters — both the evils and the possibilities of changing them — with an intelligence that in its precision, common sense, and passionate conviction often rises to lyrical heights.

I do not mean to suggest in the least that Goodman was incapable of rigorous or systematic thought. Few could analyze the implications of Freud's model of the ego or Reich's "primary masochism" better than he could. His attack on the revisionist psychoanalysts — Horney and Fromm — is a stunningly sustained argument involving the relations among human instinctual life, psychotherapy, and the social order — and devastating to its targets. This essay was originally published in *Politics*, Dwight MacDonald's anarchist magazine of the nineteen-forties, and it prompted the new left sociologist C. Wright Mills and Patricia Salter to collaborate on an unusually nasty piece of invective against Goodman in the next issue. Goodman took them on and, as far as I'm concerned, made intellectual hash out of them. Luckily, Taylor Stoehr has reprinted the original essay, "The Political Meaning of Some Recent Revisions of Freud" and the subsequent debate in *Nature Heals*. I think it is one of important debates in recent American intellectual history.

However, Goodman's central theoretical achievement, indispensable reading for Gestalt therapists, is the second volume of *Gestalt Therapy Excitement and Growth in the Human Personal-*

338

ity, which Goodman wrote twenty-seven years ago. In it, he brought together his background in Freud, Reich, Rank, and the ego psychologists, his own innovations, and his collaborator Perls' new ideas and spun them into a dazzling original and comprehensive view of human nature and character development, healthy human functioning and psychopathology. This is still the definitive text to date on the theory of Gestalt therapy. Among other things, it carefully spells out the processes of growth and change, the resistances to them, and therefore makes clear what can be accomplished in therapy. These are pages that must be thoroughly digested by everyone who considers himself or herself a Gestalt therapist.

Nature Heals might be thought of as a diverse, highly readable supplement to the second volume of *Gestalt Therapy*. If *Gestalt Therapy* displays Goodman in the midst of system-building, Stoehr's collection of psychological writings represents him in his most lyrical, angry, sensitive, polemical, and autobiographical moods, in addition to his theoretical ones. Written over a quarter-century, from 1945 to 1969, these essays, reviews, speeches, etc., are rarely limited to strict clinical matters. There are pieces on war, social powerlessness, racism, making films, the oppression of homosexuals, and the literary process, as well as on guilt, aggression, grief, child-rearing, sex, Freud, Reich, and Gestalt therapy. At times, it may seem as if Stoehr made some rather arbitrary choices by put-ting certain pieces in this volume instead of in the literary or political volumes. But he thereby demonstrates the extent to which Goodman's thinking reached across disciplines.

I can think of three reasons immediately why every Gestalt therapist *should* (there, I said it!) read *Nature Heals*. First of all, the writings included in it give one a vivid feeling for the evolution of

339

Gestalt therapy from World War II to the present. Secondly, they are crammed with deep, directly applicable insights into character and psychopathology that sharpen one's clinical awareness. And thirdly, they stretch one's horizons about the social ramifications of psychotherapy, at the same time as they chasten one by making as clear as any literature I know the limitations of therapy, given an unsatisfactory social environment.

Stoehr's excellent introduction is particularly useful for tracing Goodman's development among the currents and trends in psychotherapy after World War II. Goodman's own theoretical shifts — from the Freudian unconscious to Reichian cha-racter-armor and sex-economy to the phenomenology of the con-tact-boundary — recapitulate the development of Gestalt therapy itself. His changes of mind were a movement of intellectual inte-gration, not the convert's jumping from doctrine to doctrine. He never dropped anything useful along the way, but added on, modi-fied, and synthesized.

This is an important point. Goodman was clearly an inno-vative psychological thinker, but he never became unhinged from his post in a tradition. One can see in his pages even more clearly than in Perls' the debt Gestalt therapy owes to Freud. Perls, though trained as an analyst and close to members of the early Freudian circles, had complicated feelings about Freud; and after his first book, *Ego, Hunger, and Aggression*, which is still strongly psychoanalytic in many respects, he often pushed differences into divisions and apparent breaks with the Freudian tradition. Like many other original and unorthodox therapists who grew up on a diet of psychoanalytic associations. Eventually, he chose to hook up Gestalt therapy with the encounter group movement at Esalen, where he was lionized.

340

But Goodman was free of Oedipal feelings about Freud, and thus having little need to reject him, tended to look for the best in him. Interestingly, he always insisted on the radical content of Freud's doctrines, though he maintained that Freud himself, beleaguered, protective of his young movement, growing weary and old, backed off from the revolutionary implications of his discoveries. In the first two essays in Stoehr's collection, Goodman treats this side of Freud with a lovely mixture of reverence and pathos. Goodman liked the fact that Freud had rooted psychology in biology, unlike behaviorists, psychoanalytic revisionism, most social psychologists, etc. As Goodman saw it, the implication was that humans come into the world bearing an innate set of dispositions — such as Freud's instincts of eros and aggression — and these dictate what people must get from the environment in order to survive and grow. Therefore human nature itself puts absolute constraints on the nature of community — a bad society is one that doesn't respond to or distorts the individual's natural animal rhythms and needs. This is a basic Goodmanian principle that appears over and over again in his writings. It is a source of his moral position about what the good society ought to be like and thus links his psychology to his politics. It is also an important value in the development of Gestalt therapy.

So Goodman went back to Freud to discover a theory of human nature compatible with his anarchism. In an ironic twist, Goodman was able in the essay on the revisionists to use Freud himself against those psychoanalysts, and against the liberal social engineers, certain sociological Marxists, and all those who maintained that human nature is indefinitely malleable and simply needs to be redesigned to fit a social order, itself assembled by experts in the masses' best interests (shades of the Grand Inquisitor).

341

Or take a point more immediately pertinent to the clinical practice of Gestalt therapy. Goodman was able to keep what's valuable in Freud's great discovery of the transference, that shadow that the unfinished past situation casts on the present. But Goodman extends the idea to indicate why interpreting the transference is not going far enough. Freud's notion implied, Goodman saw, that the lively present leverage for working in therapy is the compulsion to repeat. The trouble is that the patient keeps trying to finish up the old situation in the same ineffectual way, i.e., by having neurotic symptoms. Therein resides both the heart of the pathology and the innate surge toward health. The "cure," Goodman claimed, the true dissolving of the transference entailed "a new experimental try with a real person." Here in a nutshell is the shift from the psychoanalyst's explication of the past to the Gestalt therapist's emphasis on the here-and-now.

One more example of Goodman's reinterpretation of Freud. Goodman insisted against the customary view that Freud was a social psychologist, that all his basic concepts are drenched with social meaning. I think Goodman may have been stretching a little here — of course, Freud knew there was a family and a culture out there that had impact on the shape of the young psyche, but his psychology did not portray them in very full dimension. However, it is worthwhile to see what Goodman meant by "social psychology," for his understanding is quite different than the behavioristic and role-theory definitions current nowadays. For Goodman, all good psychology *must* be social in that it studies what happens *between* the organism and the environment. Symptoms, character-form-ation, growth all take place at the boundary between self and other. This was a crucial point for the development of Gestalt therapy's approach to working at the con-

resistance — love

away	towards
fixed	changing
closed	open
known	unknown

342

tact-boundary (a concept Goodman treats fully in his half of *Gestalt Therapy*).

If Goodman located the philosophical roots of both Gestalt therapy and his anarchist position in Freudian formulations, he turned to Reich for practical means to connect psychotherapy and social revolution. There was a contradiction, Goodman felt, between Freud's therapy, which tended toward liberation of the instincts, and his conservative politics, which proclaimed the need to keep them repressed, so that they only trickled out in sublimations. There wasn't time to encourage sublimation, thought Goodman; the society had gone too far wrong. Reich showed more plainly than Freud how the industrial social order got under people's skins and colonized their psyches, chiefly through the family and the schools. Upbringing and schooling lead children to turn against themselves and bury their spontaneous animal needs — thus far Freud and Reich were pretty much in agreement. This blocking process, Reich went on to indicate, has anatomical and physiological components: It is accomplished by holding the breath and tensing the muscles against the urge for instinctual expression. Once this becomes chronic, a rigid shell of personality forms, which Reich called the character-armor. The result was a passive, inhibited populace, its capacities to make contact through love and sex, anger and labor, left badly crippled. Such individuals were hardly in any shape to start building the new society Goodman dreamed of, much less realize themselves.

Here's where psychotherapy entered the picture. Goodman believed with Reich that good therapy could release people's creative energies from the bondage of wounding character-formation, and then these liberated individuals would spontaneously move toward social revolution. Effective psychotherapy can help one recover the lost aliveness, force, and spontaneity that characterize healthy human functioning — in other words, restore the power to make good contact. But contact with what? Certainly with other individuals and one's work. One could have real friendships, fulfilling sex, do battle when necessary, finish up conflicts and move on, be productive. However, the sea in which these renovated beings still have to swim, in Goodman's (and Reich's) view, is still polluted by institutions bored on sexual repression and distorted aggression, such as bureaucracy, advertising, and war. Obviously the quality of individual life cannot be isolated from what the surrounding culture makes available. Most people channel their loving and sexual feeling into marriage, but Goodman noted that monogamy under our social conditions more often becomes a mode of sexual oppression than a reflection of natural loving commitment. If one's choice is homosexual love, at least when Goodman was writing, one has to contend with the threat of jail, scandal, brutal attack, loss of employment. And as Goodman never tired of pointing out, one's livelihood, with few exceptions (the artist being Goodman's favorite) amounts to spending most of one's time at boring, empty, or immoral jobs.

In the face of this social situation, the path of individual therapeutic liberation is not easy, and Goodman commented on the dangers of undertaking it. He agreed with Reich that people who recovered anything approximating their full human powers would inevitably refuse to live in such a world. They would feel impelled to drop out and create alternatives or try to change the existing structure through social action. Since the social order has a stake in its own preservation, it could hardly be expected to respond amiably. "Aggressive psychotherapy is inevitably a social risk . . . ," Goodman warned, "society forbids what is destructive of society." It was the revolutionary message, if not the emphasis on therapy, contained in Goodman's analysis that made his thought so congenial to the sixties generation — to young people trying to shape new lifestyles, forms of neighborhood community, alternative schools, and involving themselves in nonviolent protest against war and racism.

Goodman regarded Reich's tendency to make the therapeutic liberation of full orgasm the whole story as "excessively simple and Rousseauian," reductive of Freud's rich complexity. He points out several times in his essays on Reich that Reich's theory is an interim measure; nevertheless, Goodman adds, at this moment in history, "it has enormous revolutionary dynamism."

From this discussion, it comes as no surprise that Goodman's ideal of therapy is never restricted to purely individual psychotherapy but always includes what might be called the therapy of society through analysis, criticism, action. In this sense, his psychological writings are inseparable from his social thought, politics, and to some extent even from his literary criticism, as Stoehr's selection amply demonstrates. The way in which Goodman takes up a question of human development or psychopathology always involves the "Thou" as well as the "I," the surrounding social environment as well as the individual organism. This approach is fully compatible with the fundamental tenets of Gestalt therapy, for instance its stress on the contact-boundary — that meeting place between self and other where they have impact on and change one another through collision, love, influence, struggle, reconciliation — or its concept of the self as the structuring of the organism/environment field. But though Gestalt therapists have always declared chose to be principles of contact and work with them in therapy, Goodman was one of the few who addressed their larger meaning with full seriousness.

∫ Introduction to the
Gestalt Journal Press Edition
of *Gestalt Therapy Verbatim*

I.

The first time I saw Frederick "Fritz" Perls demonstrate Gestalt therapy — this was in 1966, and he was already in his seventies — he was dressed in baggy colorless trousers and an embroidered African dashiki. He looked more like an old bohemian painter than a European psychiatrist. We sat around in a circle, and at intervals one of us would dart up to a pair of empty chairs next to Perls to "work" on a dream or submit some other bit of ourselves to his scrutiny for the benefit of the group. He chain-smoked through it all. In place of the psychoanalyst's interpretations, he barked commands like a ballet coach or theater director in a thick German accent spiced with west-coast hippy idiom. When someone responded by playing a "phony role" (one of his favorite pejorative terms), he acted bored or irritated, rolling

---

* From *Gestalt Therapy Verbatim*. By Frederick Perls (1990, Gouldsboro, ME: The Gestalt Journal Press)

his eyes in mock frustration or disbelief. He frequently made sarcastic jokes at the expense of the volunteer "patients," like one of those nightclub comics who strolls with his microphone from table to table provoking the customers, although there usually turned out to be shrewd therapeutic points embedded in Perls's jokes. Now and then he glowed with approval when someone came to life and expressed a convincing emotion. He was alternately mischievous, vulgar, intimate, bullying, brilliant, seductive, cantankerous, and tender. In every respect, his behavior was profoundly at odds with the poker-faced neutrality considered necessary for the practice of psychoanalysis, which in those days still ruled the clinical world.

I had been lured by a good friend, a social worker who was in training with Perls, to a weekend workshop for psychotherapists. Perls conducted these once a month in various Bay Area locales — this one took place in the living room of a rambling apartment overlooking the bay from one of San Francisco's oddly abrupt hills. Perched up there amid a crew of therapists, surrounded by the ocean, I felt somewhat giddy and disoriented, a common state of mind in San Francisco during the 1960's, as one stumbled from new experience to new experience on almost a daily basis. The mood in the room was one of intense absorption mixed with pent-up anxiety or excitement — it was hard to tell which was more present. Achieving "personal growth" had become one of the new heroisms of the 1960's. There was even a kind of sexual hum in the air, as though the promise of so much self-disclosure might be an orgiastic rite. I recall a girl in sandals with black hair down to her waist, a kind of Perls camp-follower, who flirted with me tenaciously until I did my turn in the empty chair. It might have been her way of taking part in the therapeutic process. I must have said something foolish or maybe I just failed to dramatize my personality sufficiently, because she lost interest at once. I felt like a rookie halfback who had fumbled the ball and lost my chances with the cheerleader. We imagined we were witnessing the birth of a new therapy, a notion that Perls cultivated, although Gestalt therapy by then was already about twenty years old. But it was still not widely known, and he was bristling with energy and impatience, like a man in a rush to impart his message before it's too late. Indeed, he had only four more years to live.

I also remember my surprise as I watched a vastly overweight mental health worker burst into sobs of deep grief within moments after Perls asked her to imagine that she were a beached whale. The whale had appeared in a dream about marine life that she had just recounted. With prompting from Perls, she seemed to melt before our eyes into a neglected child alone in her room, bitterly lamenting the emptiness of her existence. Usually this sort of epiphany occurred, if at all, only after a long spell in therapy. When Perls told her, as her tears dried, to become the sea in her dream, her huge shape seemed for a moment not just the visible burden of her self-hatred but an indication that she could be teeming with life.

Upon leaving the chair — Perls called it the "hot seat," and indeed it appeared to be one — she was quickly replaced by a psychiatrist whose disdainful manner made it clear that he already knew everything he wanted to know about himself. He presented Perls with a dream in which he was driving down a long stretch of highway through desolate farmland. After making a few wisecracks about his pomposity and rigid self-control, perhaps to soften him up, Perls removed him from the driver's seat, told him to switch chairs and speak as the highway. The psychiatrist's arrogance collapsed, and in the angry whine of a small boy, he said "everyone rides over me." Again I was struck by the mysterious speed with which this method plunged people into long-buried areas of childhood or dramatically brought out hidden contradictions in their personalities. There were no detours by way of the unconscious. The childhood experience was suddenly and simply available and the person absorbed in it.

Perls was particularly intent on discovering and evoking oppositions. Often he would create a kind of dialogue between polarities — adult and child, or contrasting images in a dream, or incongruent aspects of a person's presence — by using the two chairs. Once these different sides of a person had it out through airing their disagreements, he explained, a reunion could take place. Then the "inauthentic" (another of his favorite diagnoses) adult, occupied with covering up or getting rid of vulnerabilities, might take a step toward a more genuine adulthood.

The people in this group — highly qualified mental health professionals from local hospitals, clinics, and private practices — by turns wept, raged, and giggled as they boarded the so-called hot seat. My astonishment turned into consternation, when a slim, elegantly dressed woman, a psychologist, went up and confessed her urge to fart. Perls said "Go ahead," whereupon she did. Here was an opposition that may have been therapeutic, but it went beyond the usual diagnostic categories. Perhaps the goal was to put the self back in touch with its original animal nature or to deliver a message to the group that even well-groomed Ph.D.'s pass gas. But one thing seemed clear to me: Important psychological material, repressed or sloughed off or otherwise denied, was being brought into the open almost instantaneously, such as the thin, sad deprived little girl that emerged from the obese mental health worker's beached whale or the submissive, resentful third-grader that peeped out from under the aloof superiority of the psychiatrist. It was not until sometime later that I came to realize that these startling metamorphoses might open the door to further therapeutic exploration, but they were not the therapy itself. Self-discovery can rarely be assimilated in so apocalyptic a form.

These were the sixties, and this was the version of Gestalt therapy (he had passed through several) that Perls had developed to fit the times. It was an era of anarchist utopian dreams, botanical and chemical experiments with reality, antic attacks on bureaucracy, and angry marches against war and oppression of minorities. The young were carrying democratic ideals to their limits by insisting on everyone's freedom to expand the horizons of experience and to practice full self-expression sexually and emotionally as well as politically. Perls, decked out in his baggy trousers and rumpled dashiki, poking fun at the pretense to authority among the mental health professionals in his groups, blowing smoke contemptuously at the ceiling or looking absently out the window when people confessed their misery in tones of self-pity or hid their hostility behind deference and politeness, seemed very much at home amid a rebellious generation. The weekend itself was filled with perplexing events. Personalities seemed to be transformed on the spot, symptoms to vanish into thin air — whether for the moment or forever, I had no idea at the time — under the direction of Perls's baton. I was a graduate student of literature at the University of California in those days, and I thought to myself, as Perls persuaded eminent-looking psychiatrists to talk and behave like circus animals, elevators, fountains, and umbrellas, mostly images derived from their dreams, "Can metaphor really go this far?" His effect on me was long-lasting in any event: It launched my eventual move from offering students exeges of "The Rape of the Lock" and Moby Dick to contending with people's psychological problems.

II.

Gestalt Therapy Verbatim is pure Perls, a series of live performances in the late 1960's at the Esalen Institute, that West Coast citadel of self-realization. Here is the charismatic founder of Gestalt therapy displaying his ingenuity and inventiveness, his bravado, zeal for promotion, and tendency to fall back on hip slogans, as well as his unusual clinical acumen. We get to sit in as he improvises lectures, listen to his pronouncements on human nature and contemporary culture delivered with an informal air of final authority, and above all, witness his theatrical style of having people replay their dreams or stage their characters in the form of dialogues and skits. The book is best described as spoken rather than written, since it is made up almost entirely of transcribed tapes from Perls's late workshops and seminars. Nowadays a host of well-known therapists can be found parading their wares in transcribed books or on tape and film. But the genre was relatively new when Perls did it, and rarely does one get so rounded and intimate a portrait as *Verbatim* supplies. Perls did not hide his personality behind his techniques.

There is so much good will and hopeful energy coming from the groups recorded in this book, that you might think its pages are soaked in California sunlight, thawing one's resistance. But *Gestalt Therapy Verbatim* is set firmly in the mood of the sixties, and from this distance, nearly twenty years later, its colors are a bit faded and garish, like an old postcard from an exotic place. It makes no pretense toward setting forth theory or practice in any comprehensive way. Lively, ad hoc, inspirational, it inevitably became Perls's most popular book, a fact which has had an unfortunate consequence. It was received by many people as though it contained all one needed to learn Gestalt therapy, a notion that is patently untrue.

Many of us who read *Gestalt Therapy Verbatim* when it first appeared considered it a manifesto for a therapeutic revolution in an era rampant with manifestos. We felt both delight and unease when Perls cursed the scholasticism of psychoanalytic theory and showed us by example how to free ourselves from the narrow, ritualistic behavior of its practitioners. Perhaps his objections seemed all the more telling by virtue of his own analytic beginnings under several major early Freudians, followers and dissidents alike. His analysts and supervisors included Wilhelm Reich, Karen Horney, Otto Fenichel, and Helene Deutsch among others. Now he was turning the austerity of psychoanalysis inside out as if his mission were to bring showmanship to psychotherapy. He made therapy, of all things, entertaining! Perls's version of Gestalt therapy in Verbatim comes across as a daring apostasy staged like a magic show. One could imagine him as a heretic sawing a woman in half.

Given the iconoclasm of the sixties, this was a highly appealing stance. It explains why *Gestalt Therapy Verbatim* reached well beyond (and may have largely bypassed) professional circles to gain something of a cult status among personal growth faddists, unruly marginal therapists, and college audiences in Berkeley and Cambridge. The spirited doings in *Verbatim* can lead one to forget that Perls at this point was demonstrating Gestalt therapy not practicing it. As a result, the book encouraged some fairly widespread misconceptions: that Gestalt therapy was a batch of techniques, based on using two chairs for the patient instead of one; that it was a quick and easy means to blast through neurotic defenses; and, in general, that Perls's personal style was identical with Gestalt therapy itself.

Such ideas mistake one idiosyncratic phase in the development of Gestalt therapy for the whole of it and overlook what was genuinely radical and innovative, namely its lucid, novel, and commonsensical assumptions about human functioning. Worked out by Perls long before his Esalen years in collaboration with others, these assumptions and their implications represent a lasting contribution to the elusive art of psychotherapy. They are there in *Gestalt Therapy Verbatim*, but you have to pry them loose from the scaffolding Perls erected for demonstration purposes.

The book is best read in the company of his two earlier volumes, *Ego, Hunger and Aggression* and Volume II of *Gestalt Therapy: Excitement and Growth in the Human Personality*. Both of the earlier works were joint ventures — the first with his wife Laura, who remained an invisible coauthor; the second with Paul Goodman, who elaborated a manuscript by Perls into something close to a full-blown theoretical account of Gestalt therapy.

The misunderstandings are not altogether Perls's fault, but neither does he fully escape responsibility. Many notable clinicians and innovators in psychotherapy, from Freud forward — Reich, Jung, Milton Erickson, R. D. Laing, to name a few striking examples — cast ambiguous shadows across the ranks of their followers. They loom before us in a blur of roles: Are they scientists penetrating the secrets of human nature or religious healers? Mesmerists, sleight-of-hand experts? Charlatans? Misunderstood geniuses, cranks, or even madmen? Does their ancestry date back to primitive traditions — shamanism and wizardry — or do they hail from the post-Newtonian world of deductive logic applied to the natural environment? Maybe they have to present themselves as unimpeachable or mystical authorities to coax patients out of their defenses and persuade students to become advocates. It is often said that poets and artists have to create their audiences. Perhaps founders of therapeutic schools have to create both patients and disciples. But to become a highly influential, charismatic figure bears the risk of producing slavish followers and insufficiently judicious critics. Hurrying to spread the word and increasingly indifferent to systematic thought, Perls in his late years left a legacy of mixed blessings to aspiring Gestalt therapists.

Despite the limitations its form imposes — and they reflected Perls's limitations for the most part — *Verbatim* still has much to offer beyond its historical interest. Perls treats neurosis as though it were a kind of trance-state, a secret preoccupation with anxious loose ends of childhood that removes people from vital contact with their present circumstances. The central task of therapy, he declares, is not to convince patients to accept arcane interpretations of their ancient history, but to help them come alive to their immediate experience in the present moment. This aim is achieved neither through flashes of intellectual insight nor rewiring behavioral circuits; but neither does it come about through the mere release of emotion (as Perls sometimes seems to be suggesting). It is more like the awakening to the immediacy and simplicity of the actual described in these lines from a brief poem by Wallace Stevens:

> In my room the world is beyond my understanding;
> But when I walk I see that it consists of three or four
>   hills and a cloud.

From Perls's standpoint, sarcasm, humor, drama, shock could all be used to rouse patients into the open air from the stale rooms of their neuroses, where they have remained behind closed doors in states of befuddled fixation. In principle, his theatrical tactics resemble a Zen teacher's tricks, such as hitting meditating disciples with a wooden sword to remind them of the tangibility of the present.

The wooden sword does not obviate the need for long, disciplined hours spent sitting in meditation. Nor is there any method or technique that eliminates the slow, step-by-step progress made in therapy through exploring and dismantling one's self-defeating, habitual ways of organizing reality. The rapid montages that characterize Perls's demonstrations in *Gestalt Therapy Verbatim* do not translate directly into the rhythms of ongoing psychotherapy. But the underlying principle — his emphasis on awareness and contact in the present moment, which he calls the "here and now" — can be extremely useful. It modifies radically what the therapist and the patient attend to by making it possible to begin at any point, with anything that the patient makes available — a symptom, a dream, a sigh, a facial expression, a way of sitting or a tone of voice, a thought, urge, or sensation, the curling or uncurling of a fist, staring or looking away, a physical tightening, a stutter, a lapse into silence, a sudden flood of speech, or a drift into vague, abstract language and cliches. In Gestalt therapy, these are not treated as murmurs and ripples accompanying a stream of associations, but as the heart of the matter. Medium and message, form and content, have almost the opposite relationship that they have traditionally had in psychoanalysis, where the patient's reports and the therapist's interpretations of mental contents are primary, while the patient's way of presenting himself remains peripheral.

Although this reversal may stand analysis on its head, it does not throw everything out the window along with the couch. The revolutionary import of the present tense for psychotherapy has to be understood in terms of what it borrowed from the Freudians as well as what it abandoned. For instance, to focus on what is occurring at the moment in therapy is the broadest elaboration of the "transference," a phenomenon which analysts have always treated as a present event. In his essay "Remembering, Repeating, and Working-Through," Freud connected transference to the repetition compulsion. He claimed that material from the past which has slipped through cracks in the patient's consciousness shows up "not in his memory but in his behavior; he repeats it, without of course knowing that he is repeating it." In particular, and most importantly for therapy, he repeats it in how he responds to the therapist.

Both the analyst and the Gestalt therapist might view this unaware repetition as evidence of a lingering faulty solution to a past problem. But where the analyst would tend to use the transference primarily as a clue to its sources in the past, and explicate it as such to the patient, the Gestalt therapist would concentrate on helping the patient invent a new solution on the spot by experimenting with the contact between them. For example, an overly submissive (and probably obsessive) patient who inhibits his criticism out of the desire to please, might need to discover how to support and express being critical when it is necessary to cope with something distasteful in his current life, beginning with his criticism of the therapist. This difference represents a momentous shift in the structure of psychotherapy. The search for a workable

solution in the present gives Gestalt therapy its impetus to improvise and experiment rather than to explain. Most of Perls's lively
interventions in *Verbatim* take their cue from this principle.

In modern life we suffer from too many explanations. This
may be an offshoot of the past, like the Age of Reason hanging on
during the Age of Information. We need to move on to something
else, so why cling to explanations in therapy? Perls's Gestalt therapy gave up on explanations; it became impatient for something to
happen. In this respect, it bears some resemblance to modern art,
which also quit explaining and began to concern itself with the
sheer dynamism of the event. Early in this century, the poet Ezra
Pound characterized the change in art: "The age," he wrote, "demanded an image/Of its accelerated grimace." The older modes,
"the obscure reveries/Of the inward gaze" no longer fit the times.
His words could just as well apply to the controversies about psychotherapy in our day. As culture and society change, so do the
forms of mental suffering. The remedies for alleviating psychological distress in one era prove to be inadequate in another. Freud's
"talking cure," for example, worked well with the Victorian neuroses, because their ornate symptoms mirrored the sexual tensions
lurking in the nineteenth century family. Early psychoanalytic
treatment brought people relief from hysterical fainting spells or
tormenting obsessional fantasies by hauling sex, laden with its
burden of guilt and denial, into the light where it could be explained. It was a brilliant stroke, this conversion of family and state
secrets about human impulses into healthy gossip under the guise
of scientific interpretation.

Nowadays most psychotherapists would agree that the
classical neuroses, fixed in languid or rigid poses like marble statues for an entrance hall, have become scarce. One could hardly

depend on them to fill a private practice. People don't go into therapy so much with circumscribed symptoms as with a more general malaise, a remoteness from their own lives. If many of them are still torn about sex, they are often in conflict about everything else as well — intimacy in a broad sense, all contact with others, their work, their very sense of identity and their place in the scheme of things. It has become increasingly doubtful whether, to borrow Pound's phrases, the obscure reveries and inward gaze of psychoanalysis could keep up with the accelerated grimace of the modern neuroses. As a result, the mental health professions have been scrambling to invent new therapies, revise old ones. Analysis itself has moved from the symptomatic to the characterological. By shifting the locus of discovery and change from past to present and from the logic of causes to the drama of effects, Perls was able to go even further: He made it possible for the patient in therapy to illuminate and revise the whole pattern of his existence from the perspective of the moment, like Blake's world in a grain of sand. Thus the patient's construction of his life could become more an option, less a seeming act of fate.

Given his impatience with explanations, Perls's approach to theory tended to be pragmatic and eclectic — some would say opportunistic. In *Verbatim* one finds a patchwork of borrowed concepts stitched from various traditions. From Reich, who had been one of his analysts, Perls took the notion of character armor, which adds the physical tensions in neurotic character to the psychological ones. From Horney, who had both analyzed and supervised him, he took the idea that neurotic behavior is based on manipulation to win love. From Sartrean existentialism, he got his insistence on individual responsibility for shaping one's own life. From experimental Gestalt psychology, he drew on the concepts of figure/ground and the unfinished situation to account for people's differing experience of reality and their tendency to get trapped in their own histories.

What gave all this a kind of coherence was Perls's concentration on the quality of life in the present. He used theoretical concepts like lenses through which to examine people's failures to contact their immediate situations. Ultimately for Perls, the measure of health is the ability to experience what is new as new. This entails a simple, direct, and highly particular relation to one's world. In contrast to psychoanalysis, which assumes that human nature is a deep riddle, Perls liked to call Gestalt therapy the "philosophy of the obvious" and claim that he hadn't invented it but only rediscovered it. Our culture and child-rearing practices, he declared, conspire to block us from grasping the obvious, even though it is our birthright to know it spontaneously. Perls endowed Gestalt therapy with a romantic aura that linked it to the Wordsworthian notion that the child is the best philosopher, to the emphasis in certain Eastern spiritual traditions on emptying the mind in order to know the world without preconceptions, and to the attempts of phenomenology and existentialism to rid our thinking of artificial dualisms such as cause and effect, subject and object, appearance and reality, essence and existence, conscious and unconscious. Gestalt therapy, as Perls conceived it, sought to restore our lost innocence.

III.

Spokesmen for new therapies are frequently tempted into grand flights beyond the clinic or consulting room walls, and Perls was no exception. At times he spoke in dire prophetic tones, as if

Gestalt therapy were the last chance to rescue the world from the clutches of neurotic corruption. In his autobiography, *In and Out the Garbage Pail,* he wrote that he was "the possible creator of a 'new' method of treatment and the exponent of a viable philosophy which could do something for mankind." The first part of that statement is indisputable; but the second opens up a very different set of issues from the ones posed by strict considerations of therapeutic method. Turned into a vision of the good life or of redemption from evil, psychotherapy enters a nebulous zone, where it becomes entangled with moral imperatives and cultural ideologies. (I'm not sure that any important psychotherapy has been so willing to stick to its specialized tasks that it altogether shuns cosmic speculations; neither psychoanalysis nor behaviorism went out of its way to avoid them.)

The idea that health is a kind of return to innocence in Perls's work of the 1960's suggests an answer to an intriguing question: How did a German-Jewish refugee psychiatrist and psychoanalyst, a product of the Weimar Republic and its complex culture, end up as presiding guru at the Esalen Institute? Perls, late in life, framed by virgin redwoods and stark cliffs that plunged without transition into the Pacific Ocean, epitomized a venerable American theme — the Self redefined, made new, responsible only to itself amid the pastoral grandeur of the American wilderness. He even came to look like the Thoreau or Whitman of psychotherapy. The evolution of Gestalt therapy cannot be understood entirely apart from the Americanization of Frederick Perls. Both his life and his changing views could be described as a progression from European history to American innocence.

Born in a Jewish section of Berlin in 1893, Perls had completed medical school by 1921 and undertook training in psychoanalysis during the late twenties and early thirties. He fled Germany in 1933 with his wife Laura and their daughter, the first of their two children, as the Nazis' rise to power began to assume serious proportions. With Ernest Jones's help, Perls found his way to Johannesburg, where he spent the next dozen years. During this period he and Laura wrote *Ego, Hunger, and Aggression*, a book that put forward some of the main ideas, still mostly pinned to a psychoanalytic framework, that later went into the development of Gestalt therapy. He left South Africa for good in 1946 to settle in New York, though after a few years he began the wanderings that eventually landed him in California.

Perls's geographical and cultural migration followed a well-worn path. From the time of America's colonial beginnings, the quest for innocence has been a recurrent national passion. The first families who sailed from Europe to escape religious persecution hoped not only to make a better life, but a brand new life in the New World. When they left Europe, they turned their backs on history, even on the very idea of history. This was a novel attitude, for Europeans have always nestled in the arms of their past, as though it wraps them in security and meaningfulness. History pervades everything in Europe, from landscapes and cities, art and thought, to politics and psychotherapy. But Americans tend to regard the past, especially the recent past, as a source of oppression and corruption, and they periodically reject it or rebel against it in the belief that they can wipe the slate clean and start afresh, like a second chance in Eden. History, from one point of view, does not begin until after the Fall; its task is to carry out the consequences of original sin. In this respect, psychoanalysis is historical to its very core. Freud's view of human nature never really abandoned original sin, which underlies his tolerance for limitation and suffering, as when he remarked that psychoanalysis delivers patients from "hysterical misery into everyday unhappiness." But in America one could presumably have, as Emerson put it, "an original relation with the universe" — a perfectionistic, mystical, and monumentally nostalgic idea that harks back to a timeless paradise before history.

By the time Perls reached California, the streets were filled with the latest outpouring of American innocence, the spectacular, hectic innocence of the sixties. Like a river at flood tide, it carved new tributaries in the culture. Hardly anything was left untouched by the force of its current — love, sex, schools, work, music, dress, modes of play and intoxication, community, government. The nation could no longer sneak so easily into distant civil wars under the guise of anti-communism nor practice racism with impunity. Disenchanted with the liberal welfare state and life in the suburbs, the young launched a wide frontal attack on duplicity and inhibition in American society. Dressed like pioneers, kids who had earned their degrees in urban universities dropped out of the job market and headed for remote rural areas to live off the land. There were a growing number of weekend-workshop therapies dedicated to emotional openness and authenticity. This was a generation that trusted its own impulses above all and preferred early Marx and primitive Christianity. Sometimes its innocence of history thinned into ignorance or denial, causing some political radicals to forget all over again the Stalinist horrors in Russia or to gloss over the Maoist purges in China. In an age of disillusionment, perhaps innocence springs up as the optimistic alternative to its darker sibling, nihilism. Outrageously playful, promiscuous, utopian, rebellious, the mood of the sixties was alternately good-humored and angry, and somehow managed to be at once sophisticated and naive.

In one respect Perls's Gestalt therapy resembled both the militant radicals and the wide-eyed flower children: It favored an aggressive self-expression, bordering on what Sartre characterized as "that diligent and almost sadistic violence I call the full employment of oneself." To live in the here and now, Perls insisted, one had to free oneself from the grip of dependence on others, which he often equated with being controlled by others.

Not that he was a loner. He loved audiences, parties, disciples, and brief sexual encounters. Toward the end of his life he began to form a utopian Gestalt community in Vancouver where therapists mingled with trainees and resident patients, a kind of therapeutic Brook Farm. But he had become increasingly uncomfortable with the commitments that tie marriages and families together. Once established in New York, he left his wife and children there and drifted westward, like one of those cowboy heroes in movies of the forties and fifties, who was at home in a gunfight, saloon, or whorehouse, but who headed for the hills when the local schoolmarm began earnest domestic pursuit. Here was another theme, derived from Perls's character, that blossomed when he reached the United States, infiltrating his therapy and adding to its distinctly American flavor. There is a great deal about fulfillment of individual potential and very little about intimacy in *Gestalt Therapy Verbatim*. Like Emerson, Perls became an apostle of separateness, similar in spirit to Emersonian radical individualism, the gospel of self-reliance. Such was the message in the "Gestalt prayer," with which Perls ends the introduction to *Gestalt Therapy*

Verbatim: "I do my thing, and you do your thing./I am not in this world to live up to your expectations/And you are not in this world to live up to mine . . ." This is a valuable reminder for adolescents struggling to separate from their parents, but it is advice of limited utility for people who are trying to make a successful marriage or live in a family.

The fit between American life in the 1960's and Perls's Gestalt therapy is illustrated by the fact that the "Gestalt prayer" turned up on a popular poster which could be found in those days on the walls of bookstores along Berkeley's Telegraph Avenue sandwiched between portraits, not of Freud and Reich, but of Fidel Castro and the Grateful Dead. Perls got so deeply into the here and now of his times that he left Gestalt therapy with the perplexing task of how to climb back out and move on.

IV.

Sometimes one wonders whether time flies faster in America than anywhere else. Less than twenty-five years have passed since the workshop I described took place and eighteen years since Perls's death. In the meantime, Gestalt therapy has suffered a fate similar to many another radical or avant-garde departure from the dominant strains of American artistic and professional life. It has faded into a partial acceptance, a kind of simultaneous success and failure. Gestalt therapy remains on the margins of the therapeutic establishment where it no longer generates much heat or controversy; most psychotherapists have heard of it, but relatively few know very much about it. Some of its language — contact, awareness, the here and now — has replaced "phallic symbol" and "Oedipus complex" in the stale idiom of cocktail party psychologizing. Now and then the hospitals, clinics, medical schools, departments of psychology and social work, the controlling forces in the world of psychotherapy, open their doors to a lecture or a seminar on Gestalt therapy. College textbooks on methods of psychotherapy usually treat it as a set of techniques and lump it together with psychodrama and the so-called emotive or expressive therapies, a misrepresentation that shows how pervasive the tendency to identify Perls's taste with the whole of Gestalt therapy has become. There are numerous training institutes across the country as well as a host of private practitioners who call themselves Gestalt therapists, there are conferences and a quarterly journal, but it all doesn't seem to be moving anywhere in particular nor clearing much new ground.

Why has Gestalt therapy stagnated or slipped into a middle-aged decline despite its promising revolutionary youth? For one thing, a persistent intellectual thinness continues to plague Gestalt therapy and hamper its further growth. Given Perls's temperament — his intellectual promiscuity, his flair for clever rather than systematic formulations, and his kinship with native American innocence and individualism, which have always emphasized knowing through feeling and action rather than reflective thought — it is not surprising that he transmitted an anti-intellectual bias. "Lose your mind and come to your senses," he used to say. To be sure, the founders of founding Gestalt therapy tried to redress this imbalance long before the era of *Verbatim*. In Paul Goodman's writings on Gestalt therapy, one finds Perls's inspirations reconstructed into far-reaching concepts. For example, there is an intricate definition of the contact boundary as the meeting place between the self and the world where all psychological growth occurs, a careful delineation of the resistances to contact as building blocks of neurotic character, and a phenomenological account of Gestalt (figure/ground) formation as a powerful explanatory principle in understanding human experience. Laura Perls, Isadore From, and others have quietly taught these ideas to multitudes of therapists during the past several decades. Unfortunately, Laura Perls, who, unlike her husband, practiced and taught with patient accuracy, has published only scattered articles, and Isadore From, probably the most reflective, precise, and thoroughgoing trainer of Gestalt therapists, has barely appeared in print.

The Gestalt therapists that have followed on their heels, with few exceptions, have not done much to help expand Gestalt therapy into an important growing body of work. Several interesting books have appeared, but these give too much space to their authors' successful case histories and for the most part take theory and technique for granted. Articles come out with regularity that apply Gestalt therapy to this or that special population of patients or compare, contrast, and combine it with every other brand of psychology and psychotherapy imaginable. But there has been very little of the basic theoretical probing through which psychoanalysis manages to keep on revising and furthering itself. One function of such theorizing is that it creates a public language that clinicians and researchers can draw on to explore, extend, modify, debate, and teach. Gestalt therapy still lacks the underpinning of a full vision of human development and personality (my own belief is that it could make some very important contributions to our understanding of such matters). Nor has it produced anything, though some of Goodman's work comes close, like the grand baroque architecture, tragic hue, and ironical complications that make the best psychoanalytic writing, Freud's own above all, a rich and enduring literature. But then neither have any of the other modern therapies.

For another thing, Gestalt therapy has become prey to the voracious appetite of American culture, capable of swallowing everything in its path, blurring distinctions and pulling the sting from anything that provokes it, whether in art, politics, or psychology. Perhaps this is why our decades seem so clearly demarcated, our social movements so short-lived, as though produced by mood-swings: The radical sixties; the narcissistic seventies; followed by the yuppie eighties, which may have ground to a halt when the stock market crashed on October 19, 1987, as if to prepare us for what? The Spartan nineties, or the Decade of the Deficits? These mood-swings are themselves a dyed-in-the-wool Americanism. Thomas Jefferson thought that the United States ought to have a revolution every generation so that democracy could periodically purge itself of contaminants. He meant political revolutions; we have watered down his advice and created a succession of "lifestyle" revolutions instead. Just at the point when a radical innovation or movement might begin to elicit significant discussion within our social order, it makes the cover of Time and receives testimonials from one or two Hollywood stars. Thus elevated into harmlessness, it is soon discarded, leaving little more than a vague, residual stain on our cultural fashions. If Gestalt therapy never quite reached the cover of a weekly news magazine, it was not due to Perls's reticence. Whereas Freud worried that the American's instant enthusiasm for psychoanalysis would devour it, while robbing it of its complexities, Perls capitalized on enthusiastic receptions.

Is Gestalt therapy already on the way out? Not exactly, but it is threatened with a form of assimilation that will continue to erode its distinctive identity. There are signs that Gestalt therapy is being absorbed, as if by osmosis, into the psychotherapeutic mainstream without recognition or acknowledgment of its contributions. The other day I happened to read a pre-publication manuscript written by Dr. Michael Robbins, a well-known analyst, on the therapy of "primitive personalities," the borderline, narcissistic, and schizoid character types whom many professionals believe have edged out traditional neurotics as the most characteristic troubled people in our day. The author argues in this paper that an orthodox psychoanalytic approach based on inner conflicts, mechanisms of defense, and a therapy intent on bringing unconscious forces to light does not work with such personalities. He wants to revise the traditional analytic so that it will account for the interplay between self and other instead of limiting itself to the inner world of a single individual. He defines introjection and projection as mental constructs that are constantly made and re-made in a person's current relationships, rather than as leftover deposits fixed in the personality from early childhood. He strikes an existentialist note when he suggests that inauthenticity arises from actively distorting oneself to meet others' expectations instead of embracing the truth of one's own being. He conveys respect for the creativity that is lost in symptom-formation; that is, he discerns its roots in children's creative if painful contortions to keep their connection to disturbed family settings that are essential to the children's survival. He gives the patient's experience priority over the therapist's interpretations. And he refuses to reduce the relationship between therapist and patient to a mere instance of transference. This paper sets forth in the language of psychoanalytic object-relations theory virtually all the basic principles of Gestalt therapy, spelled out by Frederick and Laura Perls and Paul

Goodman forty years ago. Maybe Perls was right when he said that he had merely rediscovered them, for now it seems that they are being rediscovered by others.

According to a basic concept in Gestalt therapy, growth and development are dialectical events. They involve an integration of meetings between self and environment across a boundary that preserves the participants' important differences. In such meetings, both are changed. Gestalt therapy can contribute far more to the practice of psychotherapy as a whole through retaining its originality and extending its theoretical reach, compelling the other schools to grapple seriously with its implications. In the process both will be changed. But for this purpose we need to have all the historical writings on Gestalt therapy readily available, so that they can be widely read, argued over, and put to the test. *Gestalt Therapy Verbatim*, in its curious tangle of one man's predilections with a spirit of individualism and improvisation, its theatrical daring combined with accommodation to its era, remains the most dramatic and influential record of Perls's last few years.

— Michael Vincent Miller
Newton, Massachusetts
Summer, 1988

∫ Preface to *S'apparaître À L'occasion*
    D'un Autre by Jean-Marie Robine

The brilliant innovations of Gestalt therapy — its relin-
quishing of the Freudian unconscious for a holistic, field-oriented
conception of human nature and its redirecting the therapy session
from an archeological hunt for causality to creative improvisations
in the present moment of the session itself — first appeared more
than fifty years ago. They have not on the whole been followed by
equally brilliant further elaboration and development. Perhaps the
followers of most intellectual or cultural movements rarely approx-
imate the creativity of its founders. Nevertheless the population of
Gestalt therapists continues to expand, even though the movement
has carried on pretty much from the sidelines. Gestalt therapy
training institutes exist in numerous countries on several continents. Some of them flourish, though most struggle to survive.
There are a growing number of journals and conferences devoted
to Gestalt therapy. Yet no more than a handful of teachers, thinkers, and writers among Gestalt therapists have succeeded in extending very far the lines of inquiry that were first opened when

this beautiful groundbreaking theory and practice originally appeared. Among this small group Jean-Marie Robine, who lives in Bordeaux, France (though he teaches all over the world like a therapeutic nomad with an urgent mission) stands out as one of the most inventive and important figures on the current scene.

Robine's special gift as a theorist is a sensibility that moves with ease from the philosopher's absorption in the task of fine-tuning concepts to the clinician's fascination with the nuances of feeling and behavior. One doesn't find many such sensibilities in the annals of psychological theory. William James (although he wasn't a therapist, he had the eye and intuition of a good clinician), Freud himself, the phenomenological psychiatrists Ludwig Binswanger, Medard Boss, J. Van den Berg, and Erwin Straus, as well as the idiosyncratic Jacques Lacan come to mind. A weave of philosophical acumen with therapeutic finesse seems like an ideal combination of talents for the making of new psychological theory. In this regard one might recall that psychology was considered a branch of philosophy until well into the nineteenth century. But just as psychotherapy was being invented, it became captive to a new social development, the breaking up of professions into specialized secular priesthoods. Both psychotherapy and psychological theory fell under the sway of a medical outlook. Gestalt therapy, however, at least when it was first developed, remained on intimate terms with philosophy. The experience of reading the opening chapters of the volume that Goodman contributed to Perls, Hefferline, and Goodman, *Gestalt Therapy: Excitement and Growth in the Human Personality* is more like coming across a new book by James or Bergson or Merleau-Ponty than it is like reading a conventional psychology textbook or a psychoanalytic monograph (later in the book, the tone and style change somewhat, as the influence of ego psychology gains a heavier grip).

Then a strange thing happened to Gestalt therapy on its way to California in the 1960s. Under the charismatic leadership of Frederick Perls, who left his more literary and philosophically inclined collaborators (including his wife Laura along with Paul Goodman and Isadore From) in New York, Gestalt therapy took on some of the character of an evangelical spiritual movement. In this form it had a moment of rather wide popularity. This version might well be called vulgar Gestalt therapy, because it resembles Perls's and Goodman's original vision about as much as what is called vulgar Marxism resembles the writings of Karl Marx. Live in the Here and Now, Take Responsibility for your Feelings, I am I, and You are You, proclaimed this version of Gestalt therapy. Perfectly sound slogans, to be sure, but impatient, reductive ones, and they offer the practitioner little guidance for the painstakingly intricate and contemplative work of attending to another person's difficulties and untapped possibilities. This was a misfortune not only for Gestalt therapy but for the progress of psychotherapy in general. The message of Perls, Hefferline, and Goodman was lost for the most part in the American enthusiasm for quick fixes (even though Perls himself finally warned against them) and thus disregarded by the majority of clinicians outside Gestalt therapy's immediate circles. The misfortune continues to be transmitted widely in our own day.

Robine has always been deeply committed to Gestalt therapy, but the very nature of his commitment was bound to lead him in a different direction from 1960s Gestalt therapy. He is a radical thinker in the best sense of the word — the kind of radical who opens new frontiers by first going to the root (which is what the word radical actually means). We tend to think of radicals as being so far to the left in breaking with traditional politics or culture as to be off the map. In fact, the best radicals have a conservative streak. They are likely to see present establishments as bureaucratized corruptions of valuable traditions — for example, traditions of freedom or excellence. Going to the root involves a return to origins to recover a spirit or a set of values that has been lost. Robine makes his own radical departure through going back with a fine-tooth comb to the original text of Perls, Hefferline, and Goodman, as well as to the thinkers who influenced Perls and Goodman, such as Otto Rank, Kurt Lewin, and John Dewey. In this pursuit he rather reminds one of Jacques Lacan in his famous return to Freud. Lacan attempted to peel away layers of superficiality and mediocrity that had grown up around Freud's writings in order to investigate their very basis. Robine has done something similar with Goodman. The result is to produce radically new possibilities by bringing to the foreground implications that were overlooked or ignored by generations of followers.

The novelty of Robine's ideas stems partly from the fact that no such going back is merely a return to the past. In his theoretical writings, Robine continually tests the principles of Perls, Hefferline, and Goodman against both his own temperament and the changes that have taken place in western culture since that book first appeared. It is pertinent in this respect that Robine happens to be French. Philosophy as well as the arts took a major turn during the second half of the last century from modernism to what became known as postmodernism. In those branches of thought most relevant to psychology and psychotherapy, this turn moved the center of gravity from Germany and the United States, where the influence of Freud, Husserl, Heidegger, Buber, and Lewin and their American counterparts, such as James and Dewey (to name the ones most relevant to Gestalt therapy) dominated, to France, where Lacan, Merleau-Ponty, Levinas, Derrida, and Deleuze recomposed what they learned from their German ancestors into new paradigms. Robine has filtered Gestalt therapy through the thought of both these groups, going back to those who influenced Perls and Goodman, as well as forward to the more recent group of his countrymen (not including Lacan, in whom Robine exhibits no interest).

Why bring the complications of modern philosophy to bear on psychotherapy? Doesn't this just make the life of the psychotherapist more difficult? No doubt, but the vicissitudes of human existence are themselves subtle and difficult to understand. A common tendency in therapy is to reduce them to determinisms, such as claims that mental disturbance is all biology or childhood trauma or bad conditioning. Such therapy does not begin to address either the complication or the creativity of our psychic lives. This seems a particularly important point to make in our era. In inventing psychoanalysis, Freud drew on an ancient philosophical tradition of Socratic self-knowledge. His idea of relieving mental suffering entailed a discipline of exploring oneself in the presence of a skilled empathic listener and interpreter. This has long been a culturally dominant view of psychotherapy, but it is currently struggling against increasing medicalization and rationalization of health services which are affecting therapeutic practice everywhere. The Socratic may be in danger of fading away, at least in clinical and hospital settings. To preserve the Socratic tradition means bringing philosophy as much as psychological or neurological research to bear on psychotherapy. I think that Robine would agree with me that the best psychotherapy is a kind of applied philosophy.

As I have already suggested, Gestalt therapy lends itself particularly well to a philosophical emphasis. Gestalt therapy subjected what it took from psychoanalysis not only to Gestalt psychology but also to a phenomenological and existentialist outlook with a liberal dose of American pragmatism added to the mix. This gave rise to a mode of practice in which the psychotherapist closely observes, using the therapy session itself as a staging place, how patients confer their own special expressive styles (including symptoms) upon both their experience of themselves and their worlds or, more accurately, their experience of themselves *in* their worlds. Most Gestalt therapists adhere to this principle in practice. But much of Gestalt therapy theory has not kept up. The literature of Gestalt therapy after Perls, Hefferline, and Goodman, especially in English, is strewn with references to "the patients' phenomenology" or "our phenomenological approach," as though it can be taken for granted that everyone knows what these phrases mean. How can you coherently extend an idea into new territory when you take it for granted in a superficial way? If you invoke philosophy at the level of theory, you need to take seriously what the relevant philosophers say. Yet Robine, who has brought to bear on Gestalt therapy theory an encyclopedic knowledge of phenomenological and existential-phenomenological philosophy, has not had a lot of company in this endeavor.

Among other things Robine's borrowings from philosophy support a principle that to some is now an old-fashioned idea — that awareness is the prerequisite of therapeutic change. Self-knowledge is, of course, basic to the Socratic tradition, and it was basic to psychoanalysis' notion that knowing oneself is healing. This has traditionally been taken to imply an introspective search, a journey inward. But here Robine, carrying forward certain implications in Gestalt therapy, makes a fundamental change in point of view. The psychoanalytic enterprise originally concentrated on understanding the individual patient's inner life, with its unconscious conflicts, its blocked instinctual drives, and its mechanisms of defense. More recently psychoanalytic practice and theory has come ever closer to the Gestalt therapy theory of fifty years ago (without acknowledging its predecessor) by focusing on the relational and intersubjective aspects of human conduct. Robine, however, finds themes in Goodman's work that lead him to take Gestalt therapy well beyond, or more precisely, to a stage in the making of experience well before, the relational and inter-subjective perspectives. Although relational and intersubjective psychoanalytic therapies shift attention in varying degrees from the patient's inner life to the relationship between patient and therapist, both assume that such relationship is between selves already individualized into something like finished products.

Robine, however, assumes no such thing. He has never cared much about finished products in psychology. Especially in his recent work both theory and practice begin without preconceptions about individualized selves or established roles. But if it is not the individual self — or even the relational or intersubjective self — that is the subject matter of psychology, what is? And how does this bear on the practice of psychotherapy? The basis for an answer to these questions is already to be found in Goodman's opening remarks in Perls, Hefferline, and Goodman. Goodman writes, "We speak of the organism contacting the environment, but it is the contact that is the simplest and first reality" (1994 [1951], p. 3). In other words, "contact," defined as the continuous, active, fluctuating meetings between organism and environment, is itself the proper and primary subject of psychology. The implication here is that psychological experience is located neither inside the person as a combination of drives and mental representations of an external world, nor in interactions between a subjective self and an objective world, but in active meetings between the person and a world in which he or she is already embedded — that is, in meetings in which each is shaping the other and from which nei-

ther can be separated from the other without profound impover-
ishment of experience and loss of meaning.

Robine began to examine and elaborate these ideas in
"Contact — the First Experience," one of the early essays (1990)
not included in this collection. He made it clear that, for Gestalt
therapy, contact — the very act of meeting — precedes anything
that might be understood as a relationship, whether defined in
terms of object relations or from an existential dialogical standpoint (intersubjectivity). If contacting, then, is the primary phenomenon in human mental life, it is to this activity itself that psychological theory and the practice of psychotherapy must direct its
attention. In bringing this out, Robine throws into relief the single
most radical break that Gestalt therapy made a half a century ago
with western psychological thinking to that point.

Given the elemental place of contact in its theory, what
part does the idea of a "self" play in Gestalt therapy? It is essential
to distinguish, especially to English speaking readers, what Robine
means by the "self" from conventional ways of thinking about it
and why he calls it an "unfolding self." The self has long been a
centerpiece of Anglo-American psychological theory, where it has
been described as though it shared characteristics with material
objects in space (but what kind of space, one might ask, does the
self exist in?). The self has thus taken on a questionable definite-
ness in western psychological thinking, an illusory firmness, as
though it were something that could be enclosed in an outline, and
then studied, diagnosed, and treated by the therapist, or esteemed,
realized, or made authentic by the patient.

Such reified conceptions of the self derive from the Cartesian division of existence into encapsulated individual conscious-
nesses busy trying to govern an objective material world. In western cultures this split had already been put to use by protestant

theologies, especially Calvinist and Puritan ones, which emphasized looking inward (self-scrutiny) and castigating the body. From the secular side, it was subsequently carried forward by nineteenth century positivism. In British and American psychoanalytic schools after Freud, authentic selves, false selves, and core selves sprang up. Even the humanistic psychologies of the mid-twentieth century made the fulfillment of self (self-realization or self-actualization) their goal.

In his nineteen-sixties version of Gestalt therapy, Perls mostly adhered to this individualistic and spatial conception of self. It underpins his vision of layers of false self wrapped around a repressed authentic one waiting to explode into being, and his top dog and underdog, which come across as like pop art versions of the internalizations and identifications of object relations theory. But in Goodman's writings something quite different occurs. In the first part of the theoretical volume of Perls, Hefferline, and Goodman, the self is defined neither from the inside out (as in psychodynamic theories), nor from the outside in (as in behaviorism) but as an aesthetic activity: the activity of shaping experience at that very site where meetings between the person and his or her surrounding environment occur. This is a fascinating suggestion, which defines the self as a temporal process rather than a quasi-spatial entity, and it represents another radical break (although one that Goodman himself by no means maintains consistently) with the prevailing western tradition. It is from this sense of temporal process that Robine takes his cue.

It's not that Robine rejects intrapsychic or other structural views of the psyche out of hand. He knows well enough that they have added considerably to our understanding of human functioning. However he doesn't want the self left there, hanging out to dry, as though suspended in some kind of inner mental space. He is interested in what happens if the theorist follows out Good-man's description of the self as a maker of forms, itself changing form, situated where the organism and the environment engage in constantly changing transactions with one another. Thus put in motion at this edge, the self and its surroundings tend to arise from and dissolve into each other. What is left is a kind of flowing river of momentary, passing forms in which distinctions between self and other, inner and outer, ultimately disappear except as a way of speaking. Robine's conception of self can only be fleetingly and partially grasped as a kind of verb, not by anything so static as a noun. For him, the self is constituted by the passing of time much more than by anything resembling space.

A temporal emphasis does not mean that experience is without structure, but it consists of fluctuating structure in motion. "Gestalt therapy," as Robine puts it, "stems much more from a culture of verbs, or of adverbs, than it does from a culture of nouns. It is not the fixed forms that interest us . . . [here he cites Laura Perls], but the forms in movement, the formation of forms" (p. 10). Robine's vision of the self is rather like a subatomic particle, which can never be pinned down, because it has either already changed or vanished by the time you perceive it and try to name it. Even verbs and adverbs don't quite catch it. With subatomic particles, you only have the sense that they may have been there by the trail they leave behind or because your equations predict that such must be the case. With a temporal self, what is left behind are the forms of experience. These can be frozen in space. A painter paints — and leaves behind his works for us to view. But he has moved on, still painting.

One notices the prevalence of the word "form" in this discussion. Indeed the word appears throughout Robine's work. As in all Gestalt therapy, properly understood, Robine's investigation of experience has always entailed particular attention to how experience is made and thus to the forms one gives to experience in the very act of experiencing ("form" is one of the meanings of the word "Gestalt"). Since the making of form is also a major concern of artists, it is not so surprising as it may seem at first glance that the earliest essay in his previous collection — "An Aesthetic of Psychotherapy" (1984) — looked at Gestalt therapy through the lens of criteria usually reserved for works of art, in contrast to the traditional preoccupation of psychological theory with science. (See also Robine, Ed. *"La psychotherapie comme esthétique,"* Ed. L'exprimerie? Bordeaux (2006) partly translated in *International Gestalt Journal*, vol. XXX, #1, 2007)

For the therapist, you could say that the aesthetic task is to explore what happens (and what else is possible) when people, in regulating the anxieties of living with uncertainty, staunch the flow of experience and thus design their lives around limited, sometimes severely limited, possibilities. In the language of Gestalt therapy, these are called "fixed Gestalts"; in aesthetic terms, they become stereotypes imposed on experience that cramp it into ill-fitting, inappropriate configurations. This is how Gestalt therapy enters the realm of psychopathology. Robine sees a parallel dangerous tendency in psychological theory itself — to substitute the name or concept itself for what that name or concept momentarily and inadequately points toward. Against this tendency he directs much of his own theorizing. To Robine, the worst sin is to build a theory around names and then claim that such a theory predicts "truths" or give a description of "reality." Such theories, rather than suggestively guiding and supporting the therapist's capacity to improvise, lead to the application of reductive therapeutic formulas to the mysteries of the patient's existence.

The essays in this book illuminate one facet of Gestalt therapy after another from fresh points of view. Despite Robine's taste for the philosophical, there are passages of personal reflection alongside samples drawn from individual and group sessions, so that one comes away from the book with a sense of intimate connection between his development as a theorist and his experience as a therapist. One aspect of this connection in particular merits further discussion here because Robine has drawn upon it for a formulation that may well constitute his most important contribution to the relationship between theory and practice.

Robine's approach to a therapy session is to wait with as few preconceptions as possible and to try to remain open to everything that happens. As figures, shapes, forms, patterns, and roles emerge, the therapist and the patient can scrutinize how these configurations are actually in a process of being put together in the session itself. In the language of postmodernism, one might think of this as a method of experiential deconstruction. Robine treats the therapy session itself as a particular kind of construction, an improvised arrangement in a field of potentials from which an indefinite number of constructions could be made. The aim is to heighten awareness of possibilities (besides the usually fixed, symptomatic one that the patient brings in) in the ongoing stream of experience as it forms. From this vantage point the theorist can investigate, and the therapist can experiment with, how patient and therapist together actively and collaboratively go about giving structure and meaning to the present *situation*, a word that he borrows from Goodman, and which Goodman took over from John Dewey. In the case of a therapy session, the situation might be described as this room in which these two people — this patient and this therapist — sit down together and begin to speak (no doubt innumerable other descriptions are possible). The situation, understood in this way, is a wide-open arena, with nothing taken for granted, ripe for collaborative creative exploration and experimentation. For Robine, phenomenological innocence, the bracketing of assumptions, is the point of departure, one that has its roots planted firmly in the classical theory of Gestalt therapy.

Taking the situation, an everyday word, as a fundamental theoretical concept for psychotherapy may seem, at first glance, too simple an idea for a discipline traditionally given to arcane terminology. As Robine uses it, in fact, it is a concept of considerable power and complexity, arrived at in his recent writing through a developmental trajectory that runs throughout these essays. To understand its full import, one needs to see how it is related to the traditional place of field theory in Gestalt therapy.

Since Gestalt therapy conceives of human experience as a sequence of transitory constructions, the question naturally arises, from what raw material is experience made, if one is not to end up with a claim that it is made *ex nihilo*? (To make such a claim would confuse the phenomenological basis of Gestalt therapy with an extreme relativism that says nothing exists except our fabrications. Neither Goodman's text nor Robine's postmodern reworking of it would settle for this sort of solipsistic or nihilistic position.) Perls and Goodman assumed that what exists before experience was the "organism/environment field," an undifferentiated landscape of potentialities that precedes every human encounter, every appearance of the self, every separation into categories or entities (such as self and other). The idea that a primitive condition of unity is the prerequisite for division into organism and environment filtered into Gestalt therapy from a number of sources — among them, the holistic theories of J. C. Smuts and Kurt Goldstein (both of whom deeply influenced Perls), the interactionist social psychology of Dewey, and the social science field theory of the Gestalt psychologist Kurt Lewin. To the extent that field theory has provided a framework for much of the thinking about Gestalt therapy during the past dozen years or so, it has helped in turning recent theory away from Perls's later individualistic bias toward a more relational and ecological emphasis.

However, the organism/environment field, perhaps too much ploughed over, has begun to show signs of fatigue. It seems headed for a fate like that which befell the "self" — of becoming abstract and reified. In part this is due to Kurt Lewin's influence. Lewin was a physicist before he turned to social science and psychology. He derived his ideas from the electromagnetic and quantum field theories, which attempted to account for the impact of the whole on the part and the part on the whole, even across such distances that it can be far from obvious how parts and wholes are related to each other. Field theory has revolutionized physics, but it represents a high order of abstraction, especially when applied to human behavior. Thus much of recent Gestalt therapy field theory has tended to replace the drama of particulars that make up human experience with grand abstractions that seem remote from what psychotherapists actually do.

In his own writings, Robine has often tackled the question of the organism/environment conception of field theory. Several of the essays here address it, although with increasing dissatisfaction about its Lewinian leaning toward abstraction, as well as its tendency, despite its holistic premises, toward giving too much credibility once again to the individual organism, which can drift back into what Robine calls a "one-person psychology." (It seems incredibly difficult to keep psychological theory from slipping into this single-minded focus on the encapsulated individual — a difficulty that probably stems not from human nature but from the conditioning of the western mind.) So in characteristic fashion he returned recently to Perls's and Goodman's text and found there a series of hints about the "situation," which he elaborated into alternative, more concrete way of describing the psychotherapy session as a special kind of two-person field.

Robine gives a lovely example of how the Gestalt therapist pays attention to the way in which one contacts one's world as the elemental psychological fact that underlies all one's shaping of experience, including that of relationships. He tells of "the patient who complained to me of being invaded and overwhelmed by her relational environment, which intruded on her life and demanded ever more of her. As she was speaking to me, she seemed unaware of a brilliant ray of sunshine which was striking her face and blinding her: she would only have needed to shift her chair a few centimeters to regain some minimal degree of comfort" (p. 7). The example also illustrates perfectly how a therapist might make use of what is available in the present situation.

This transformation of the "field" into a specifically therapeutic "situation" is an impressive accomplishment, because it re-grounds field theory phenomenologically in the actual practice of psychotherapy. It is also a difference in theoretical focal length, like the difference between a geological map and a photograph of a local neighborhood. Both are useful, depending on what you are looking for. But it seems to me that the photograph is far more useful to the psychotherapist and to the student of human nature as well. Without sailing off into cosmic abstraction or sinking back into an individualistic model, Robine manages to build a theory that restores the therapy session as a stage for the idiosyncratic, unpredictable drama of human existence.

$\int$ Elegy for Laura

I first met Laura Perls in the early 1970's, when Richard Borofsky and I were directing training programs at the Boston Gestalt Institute. We began bringing her to Boston to lead weekend workshops for our training groups, like a local symphony orchestra bringing in a distinguished guest conductor. Laura, already nearing seventy, made a striking impression. She had the slim, graceful shape of a woman decades younger, and an alert, restless self-assurance, as though circumstances would never find her at a loss. There was a suggestion of aristocracy in her bearing, not uncommon among educated upper-middle class German Jews who grew up in the early years of the century. Laura's personality was a union of elegance and vitality. She radiated animal energy tamed by cultural refinement.

---

*From *The Gestalt Journal* Vol. XIII, (Fall, 1990) No. 2). Reprinted with permission.

The sense of culture that Laura brought with her was not merely a veneer; it was the product of her deep immersion from childhood in European humanistic values. A wide-ranging background of knowledge and accomplishments informed her work. She had trained seriously in music and modern dance; she knew literature and languages; she had learned psychology from some of the important innovative researchers and clinicians of her youth; she was a swimmer in the currents of contemporary European thought.

I think that Laura always delighted in her accomplishments. When she was off stage professionally, she would allow herself a touch of exhibitionism (though no one was more shy at a lectern in front of a large audience). In the cozy paneled library of the private school where we held our training sessions, she discovered a piano during a lunch break and sat down at once to play, I don't remember exactly what, Brahms or Schubert. She was out of practice, but her playing nevertheless had an old stamp of authority, the air of someone used to commanding an audience's attention. Approaching seventy, she was still a perennial wunderkind, a prodigy.

But when she took over a training group, she gave her undivided attention to the person working or to the unfolding group event. As a therapist and teacher, she could let her presence subside into the background, like a lamp turned down low, giving off just the right amount of illumination. She didn't need to loom large in her work. She surrendered herself to the patient's need and to the task of explicating the principles involved in the therapeutic situation.

I never studied with Laura in any formal sense. But I imbibed a good deal of therapeutic wisdom from simply observing her at work in Boston as well as through conversations over lunch or dinner when I visited her in New York. Laura taught me that psychotherapy could be conceived in terms of aesthetic values, not merely technical ones. It was clear, however, that she was less concerned with the artistic creativity of the therapist than that of the patient. She treated the patient as a failing artist, one in need of careful and discriminating coaching to help convert symptoms into more graceful modes of self-expression. Her conception of the therapist's role was closer to that of the literary or art critic than that of the artist.

There were also any number of specific therapeutic ideas I learned from watching her teach in a group setting. Let me describe a few instances that remain vivid in my memory.

When someone asked her at the end of a demonstration whether an especially obstinate and spiteful volunteer "patient" had made her angry, Laura replied, "I no longer get angry when I work. But I am willing to be firm."

She showed in a simple, clear way how to make use of the continuum of mind and body. A man in a training group announced at one point that he felt a little nauseous, and Laura asked him "what is it about me that you can't stomach?" In another demonstration, as a volunteer's forceful feeling extinguished itself in an inconclusive defeat, Laura stopped him to point out how his torso had caved in at just that moment. "You don't back yourself up," she told him. Then she proceeded to oversee a detailed investigation of the tensions and sensations from his shoulder blades to his tail bone. "Many people live as though they have no back," she pointed out to the group. Without awareness of some self behind them, she explained, they experience themselves as if they were all front, which leads them to feel chronically overexposed. Thus they are easily shamed or defeated. Turning again to the "patient," she asked him to retain his new consciousness of his back and try once more to express his feelings. Here was a perfect illustration of therapeutic experiment with support and contact, Laura Perls's two central principles.

Someone complained that her therapeutic episodes lacked final resolution or closure. Laura replied that she had lost interest in closing things in therapy. She preferred to plant a seed that might open up something new, leaving it to the patient to carry it forward in accord with his or her own needs and rhythms. "Growth occurs in small steps," she added, for small steps are all that an individual can assimilate at one time.

When a woman told her, "I want to have more contact with you," Laura answered that contact is an activity, not a state one is in or out of. Contact is more a verb than a noun.

Frederick Perls, who first lured me to Gestalt therapy by showing how clinical work could be dramatic and exciting and immediate, is dead. So is Paul Goodman, who convinced me that the ideals of health in psychotherapy could be extended to a radical and utopian criticism of sickness in the social order. So is Bill Warner, another of my teachers, from whom I learned a different kind of drama — the drama of waiting patiently, not with the silence of the psychoanalyst, encouraging projection or regression in the patient, but with the silence of a cat stalking its prey, waiting till the conditions are ripe for a true meeting.

And now, after a brief but terrible illness, Laura Perls, who contributed greatly to the formulation of Gestalt therapy, who broadened its context to include culture, art, and philosophy, and who taught and practiced it with simplicity and precision, is gone. I guess I have reached an age where the illnesses and the dying of those who have most influenced my direction in life, those whom I care most about, is a more and more frequent event. Sometimes it seems to me that my world is unraveling. With Laura's death, another shadow, another hint of the coming dusk, has fallen across my life, dimming the contours of a landscape of meanings and relationships that I had come to take for granted.

∫ To the Memory of Miriam Polster

> Then Miriam, the prophetess, the sister of Aaron,
> took a timbrel in her hand; and all the women went
> out after her with timbrels and dancing. And Mir-
> iam sang to them ...
>
> Exodus 15, verses 20-21

The death of Miriam Polster from a recurrence of cancer on December 19, 2001 deprived Gestalt therapy of its loveliest and warmest diva, if one dare apply this term to someone who had as much generous nobility of soul as Miriam. Even noble souls live their lives in human bodies, and Miriam throughout her life was too down-to-earth and colorful a personality to be a mere angel, although I have no doubt that she is residing among the angelic orders now. She was a genuine diva among teachers of psychother-apy, a natural aristocrat in a profession that, alas, too often seems to breed teachers who claim for themselves unearned powers and

---

* From *The Gestalt Journal*, Vol. XXIV, No. 2. (Fall, 2001). Used with permission.

accomplishments. It is true that the word "diva" may suggest a prima donna, and Miriam had a touch of the prima donna, although I have never seen anyone wear it more gracefully, easily, and, if one can accept the oxymoron, humbly. But the word also suggests a quality that partakes of the divine, and there was indeed something divine about Miriam. Her death took from me, along with countless others throughout much of the western world, our wonderful teacher and friend.

That life is over for Miriam also diminishes the world's store of pleasure. Pleasure is not just internal gratification, nor does it reside wholly in that which yields pleasure. It's a relationship that includes the experience of radiating warmth, well-being, and excitement in response to what one receives from the world's abundance. People who make evident their pleasure at receiving something good give something good back to the world. Miriam went further; she made pleasure contagious. To have dinner with Miriam in a gourmet restaurant or to listen with her to great music was like going sightseeing in a new city with a wise and enthusiastic guide.

This quality was evident in her teaching and in her manner of doing therapy. In her work as in her life Miriam loved to play in all senses of the word. She loved the play of words, the interplay of dialogue, the staging of a play or performance, and the moments in a melody line that resemble the soaring playfulness of a bird's flight. It's worth emphasizing that play does not necessarily suggest something that is light, happy, or frivolous. The Dutch historian Huizinga considered "serious play," as he called it, the most innovative force in culture. In a sense, Miriam used "serious play" to create innovative openings for her patients. In one of her best essays, "The Language of Experience," originally delivered as a keynote speech at *The Gestalt Journal's* 1980 Annual International

Conference in Boston, she tells how an instance of her playing with the concrete liveliness and metaphoric resonances of a phrase made a difference in the life of one patient. The patient was filled with profound sorrow over all the leave-takings throughout his life. He was just now retiring from a meaningful career and ending a long marriage. "In describing his sadness," writes Miriam, "he said a phrase that to me was magical. He said, 'I guess I'll have to pick up my baggage and leave.' I said to him, 'It sounds to me as if you are not leaving empty-handed.' This was something that had not occurred to him but it had a great deal of significance for him."

Like many of the most important teachers of Gestalt therapy, her commitment to psychology and psychotherapy came after an earlier devotion to an artistic discipline. In her youth she had trained as a serious classical vocalist, a performer of lieder and operatic music. Her first college degree was a B.A. in music. An artistic sensibility remained the foundation of her professional as well as her personal life. The idea that one can draw on the aesthetic element in human experience to liberate the personality from neurotic fixations is close to the heart of what makes Gestalt therapy distinctive. Miriam was among the leading figures who made an aesthetic perspective a practice as well as a theory. Her very style exemplified it as did her thinking about Gestalt therapy. During a symposium that I moderated at the same conference I just mentioned, she made a beautifully articulated case in musical terms for dialogue over identity as the pulse-beat of psychotherapy. She pointed out that "anybody who worries about having an identity, doesn't have an identity, and is compelled instead to take positions, to deal in pat phrases and set attitudes . . . I talk about music as much as I can. And it came to me that what you find in a good performance in music, or in a composition beautifully written, or in artistry in general, is the spirit of dialogue."

"When you listen to a fine performance of a concerto, for example," she continued, "what you hear is dialogue between the solo instrument and the orchestra. The solo instrument proposes an idea. The orchestra considers it and responds and the solo instrument is then affected by this, and it goes back and forth. So what I want to consider then, is how will we as Gestalt therapists carry on our dialogue with the environment, with otherness in its myriad forms, without allowing a struggle for our identity to intrude and become obsessively figural?"

The artistic dimension of Miriam's Gestalt therapy is among the reasons I consider her one of my most valued teachers. After my initial training experiences with Frederick Perls in 1966 and 1970, I decided that I wanted to join my professional life to Gestalt therapy, and I planned to follow him to Vancouver for further training. However, Perls died within days of my making that decision. Then, in the early 1970s, I discovered Erving and Miriam while they were both still teaching at the Gestalt Institute of Cleveland, and I spent two years in a training program that they directed in Boston. Both of them influenced me a great deal; indeed, they probably made it possible for me to become a Gestalt therapist. As fascinated as I was with the slashing insights and powerful theatrical methods that characterized Perls's experiential teaching, I didn't know what to make of his highly directive, often confrontational manner and his tendency toward anti-intellectualism. The gentle, good-humored compassion with which both Erving and Miriam approached their work was a revelation to me. At the time I was still teaching at M.I.T. and deeply involved in the student and faculty protests against the war in Vietnam. Erv helped me discover the inventiveness of intuition and feeling. At the same time he made clear the importance of intellectual and political awareness. But it was Miriam in particular who opened up for me the aesthetic possibilities of psychotherapy.

When Miriam worked with a group of trainees, her presence was dramatic. She had a kind of imperious grace, quite different from the sly, mischievous hair-trigger gracefulness of her husband. They exhibited quite distinct ways of being alert to the potential for something new inherent in each moment. Whether standing or sitting, Erving seemed already moving in response to the forming action, like a restless shortstop ready to go for the ball no matter where the it came from. Miriam was more like an actress or concert artist waiting eagerly for the curtain to rise, so that she could play her part in making a yet unknown, improvised script come to life. Erving's eyes gleamed with warm curiosity and a hint of mischief. Miriam's sparkled with excitement at the performance that was about to unfold.

She could be as gentle as anyone I have ever known, but there was a tougher side to her as well. As with all those who care about artistic integrity, she had little tolerance for duplicity or the cliches of inauthentic expression. You might say that she insisted that the singing be in tune. Support for expressive truth, I believe, was her guiding ideal. She was extremely patient, but she also knew how and when to draw the line. She drew it, however, not with aggressive confrontation but through humor and irony. In the many training workshops and demonstrations that I participated in with her during the 1970s, I never once saw her shame a trainee. She could provoke her students into bringing out their best by telling jokes, playing pranks, and involving them in inventive skits of a kind that were never at the expense of a student's dignity.

Although I have to delve back nearly thirty years for my own personal memories of Miriam as a teacher, there was one incident during my training with her that I have never forgotten. I think it captures something of her essence as a teacher. I was a hopeful novice therapist making a transition from ten years of having been a professor of literature to becoming a psychologist. I was in the early stages of the two-year program directed by the Polsters. It was a hot summer day, and our training group was working outdoors, broken up into triads, each little threesome busily trying practicum sessions with one another. Suddenly Miriam appeared, wearing a peasant blouse, a long skirt, and sandals. She sat down in the grass to observe my triad. I was playing the role of therapist, and I instantly became tongue-tied in the face of having to make therapeutic "interventions" (whatever those were!) under the judgmental gaze (as I imagined it) of this commanding woman with her reddish-gold hair tied back like a ballet dancer. I was mostly silent while my "patient" chattered on. At the end, I expected the worst. But Miriam, looking amused, only said, "Michael, you sure have a noisy face!"

How liberating I found her words! They have stayed with me to this day. I realized that I had been responding the entire time, whether I thought I was or not, whether I wanted to cover my tracks or not. I felt teased, but not all shamed — teased, if anything, into being more fully present. And I came away with an important insight: That therapy was not a matter of coming up with the right thing to say or a clever intervention, but sprang from the way one was there with the patient. Like a painter who can change the mood of a canvas with one brush stroke, Miriam needed only a few words to help me transform my embarrassed silence from a symptom into a creative possibility.

∫ Elegiac Reflections on Isadore From

Isadore From's death on June 27, 1994 represents the end of an era for Gestalt therapy, the closing of a chapter that now spans nearly a half-century. His own contributions to Gestalt therapy are woven throughout its entire history. During the early 1950's, he joined the small circle that gathered for discussions in Frederick and Laura Perls' Manhattan apartment. Since his previous studies had been mainly in philosophy, not psychology, he was able to give clear and definite shape to an important perception that several other members of this founding group had also begun to recognize: that the far-reaching implications of Gestalt therapy's radical split with psychoanalysis amounted to nothing less than a shift in the fundamental paradigm for understanding human conduct — a shift away from causal natural science to the phenomenology of Husserl and his successors.

---

[*] From the *British Gestalt Journal,* 1994, 3. Reprinted with permission.

From that time forward, Isadore's devotion to Gestalt therapy was unwavering. (If my use of his first name here seems an overly familiar touch, I have to add that I find it uncommonly stiff and formal to write about him using only his last name. To everyone who studied with him or cared about him for more than five minutes, he immediately became Isadore. I can't recollect having heard anyone, perhaps with the exception of a plumber or the mailman arriving at his townhouse on the upper West side, call him "Mr. From.") He continued to practice and teach Gestalt therapy in New York for more then three decades. He also traveled regularly, both throughout the United States and in Europe, especially in Germany and Italy, to conduct training and supervision groups. It would not be misleading to say that Isadore From, along with Frederick Perls, Laura Perls, and Paul Goodman, did the most to set the direction for Gestalt therapy. And Isadore's voice was at least as important as any in sustaining it. But now all those voices have been silenced.

*   *   *

Among the attributes for which Isadore was revered by those who studied with him were his integrity and precision. Whether he was teaching, supervising, or doing psychotherapy, his work always had an impeccable quality: It was meticulous and lucid, although he was perfectly capable of sailing out on a wild intuitive expedition if the situation so moved him. An important part of his unusual ability to range freely yet still remain in tune with a patient's or student's intimate concerns was that he was not one of those people who have to be right at all costs. Like a good experimental researcher, he regarded his hunches as provisional hypotheses, equally open to being confirmed or disconfirmed.

But if I were forced to try to capture the essence of Isadore's sensibility in a word, the one I would choose would be passion. Of course, to pick so loaded a term in our times requires careful definition. And what's more, Isadore, in his customary fashion, would have demanded that I define it carefully. Passion, after all, is in some disrepute in the modern world. In our post-romantic frame of mind, torn and ambivalent because in various ways we are still driven by the romantic ideal even when many of us seem to reject it intellectually, we tend to link passion to irrational impulses that might lead to fanaticism, obsession, or even abuse. Passion strikes the cool postmodern temperament as at once too passive and egotistical, too self-serving a surrender to internal cravings or overwhelmingly tempting external forces.

Passion, though, can also mean something much more active and concentrated, as when we speak of a passionate absorption, a passionately committed attention to and involvement with the matter at hand. Isadore From was passionate in the sense that Kierkegaard must have had in mind when he titled a book *Purity of Heart is to Will One Thing.* Few people seem to have that capacity. Isadore is one of those who did, both personally and intellectually. Such passion involves a fundamental seriousness, though not the kind of seriousness that sits heavily on the soul like puritan theology. It is more like the serious playfulness that the Dutch historian J. Huizinge describes, in his wonderful book *Homo Luclens*, as a civilizing virtue. Huizinge thought that this form of profound play was the heart of culture, art, and religion. In Isadore From's practice, it was also the heart of psychotherapy.

Passion in this sense, Isadore would have explained to us, is not passive; it has considerable aggression in it. Here, too, a precise definition is required. When he spoke of aggression, he intended it to be understood in the affirmative sense that Gestalt therapy interprets aggression: as a beneficial, self-expressive, and creative human power to make something or to make something happen, to be willing to give oneself back to the world as well as to receive from the world. This is anything but the hostile warlike exercise of power over others that we generally think of as aggression nowadays. That kind of response, Isadore would point out, does not originate in freely spontaneous aggression. It is rather the symptom of bottled-up aggression, a state that causes people to crave control and certitude in their relationships. Such hostile aggression stems from fear of impotence or from greed arising out of frustrated needs.

To illustrate the positive meaning of aggression in Gestalt therapy, Isadore distinguished between listening to a piece of music, which he regarded as aggressive because one brought oneself, one's personality and history, to the experience, and hearing the music, which he thought of as a more generalized, aimless, and therefore vague taking in. The same kind of distinction holds, From maintained, between looking and seeing. Not that there is anything wrong with hearing or seeing, but people who characteristically say "I see what you mean" or "I hear you" are probably introjecting or otherwise absenting themselves from the conversation. Characteristic remarks like that are clues that alert the therapist to the need for further exploration.

* * *

Indeed, such clues were typically the observable evidence, for Isadore, that indicates disturbances of contact. In the eager-to-please patient's lack of disagreement or unqualified praise, Isadore would suspect a characterological habit of introjecting, so he would be apt to follow up by doing what he could to elicit the patient's criticism of him, though he would probe gently at the same time to see how anxious his suggestions might make the patient. If someone used global, abstract language to describe their experience in very general terms, Isadore explained to his students, one ought to suspect projection because such vagueness creates at the moment of contact between people a blank space that serves as a projection screen.

He also liked to dissect those little linguistic intensifiers that people use automatically so that he could show how projection works in protesting too much. Which would you rather be told, he would ask a training group, "I love you" or "I really love you?" The second phrase ought to put one at least a little on guard, he would then propose, because the speaker may be projecting that he won't be believed, which suggests that he doubts it himself.

Similarly, Isadore would single out the sort of ritualized idiom that we tend to take for granted, like the common use of "you know" after every few sentences, to show how it reflects a hidden assumption of confluence. The "you know" takes the listener into the speaker's confidence, as though the speaker were saying, in effect, "We are so close that you can read my mind." When a person used "you know" in this manner, Isadore might reply, "No, I don't know. You are telling me," thus sharpening the difference between the two selves attempting to contact each other through talking and listening. Working to preserve differences is an important aspect of psychotherapy, according to Isadore's scheme of things. Without differences, relationships dissolve into a soup.

*   *   *

Such insistence on careful, even minute distinctions was essential in Isadore From's approach to therapy. He felt that change and growth proceeded in small steps rather than dramatic breakthroughs. In this respect, he differed strongly with Frederick Perls. Patients could more readily assimilate small steps, Isadore thought, than overwhelming dramas. Moreover, small changes can make significant differences: When you make even a slight change in an established gestalt configuration, the outcome is a new configuration.

Thus Isadore paid close attention in his work to virtually every idiosyncratic gesture or word through which one presented oneself to others; to how one sat, walked, said hello or goodbye, breathed fully or failed to; and (following what he had learned from the early writings of Reich) to all the ways in which anxiety and character deposit themselves as bodily tensions or (his own special contribution) show up as vague or evasive language. The point is that all these phenomena are observable in what is going on between the therapist and the patient. Therefore the therapist can hand over his observations immediately for testing by the patient's experience.

This direct interplay of observation and experience was the primary meaning, in Isadore's view, of the present moment in Gestalt therapy. Drawing on fragments of tangible evidence, his interpretations or interventions — his "experiments," as he called them — frequently came across as inspired poetic leaps and syntheses. The ultimate source of his inspirations, however, was for the most part that which is immediately given and therefore easily overlooked — the obvious, so to speak. The method inherent in a psychotherapy like this could be described as practical phenomenology. In teaching it, Isadore tried to show students how to do it for themselves. When he gave demonstrations, he would patiently take apart his observations and conclusions step by step. He had no interest in obscurity or mystification.

Despite his concern with physical presence, dream imagery, and every other kind of available cue that might be useful to the therapist, Isadore still regarded language as the consummately human act of self-expression and communication. Clear speech, in his view, was an indication of health. He was as careful with diction as a poet and with semantics as a logician. Language for Isadore meant the direct spoken idiom of the tribe, that which an influential school of twentieth-century philosophers has called "ordinary language," not the jargon, the abstract, overly elaborate terminology of social science and psychology. It is true, of course, that he taught Gestalt therapy using the terms, such as "contact boundary," "retroflection," "confluence," and so on, through which it had differentiated itself from the ruling Freudian approaches. But then he would explain these concepts, even while he demonstrated their use, in language sufficiently simple and precise as to make their implications unmistakable.

It would not be too wild a comparison to say that Isadore From was the Wittgenstein of psychotherapy.

* * *

The principles of Gestalt therapy, unlike certain dominant trends in Western thought, refuse to break human nature down into a series of dualisms, such as consciousness and biology, inner and outer, gleaming ideal and tarnished appearance. For this reason among others, Gestalt therapy has often been compared to Zen Buddhism and other Eastern philosophies, a comparison that is not without some merit. But the East was not the vantage point for Isadore From's vision of Gestalt therapy. He was every inch a Western humanistic thinker, and, like his friend Paul Goodman, he preferred to find the possibilities for a unified psychology within the classical Western tradition. He believed with Kant, who was perhaps first to put forward the idea forward in modern times, with the nineteenth-century English and German romantic poets, and with organicist thinkers like Bergson, William James, and John Dewey, that you half-create what you perceive.

This radical line of epistemology (which like so many radicalisms is also a return to something very ancient) includes the subjectivity of the knower in what is known. It surfaced toward the end of the eighteenth century in opposition to the Enlightenment emphasis that objective knowledge was the only worthwhile knowledge. What the Enlightenment had succeeded in bringing about, along with its other accomplishments, was a definitive split between the subject and the object, the mind and the body, the I and the Thou of human experience. Having thus lost its intimate connection with otherness, the self had to try to repossess it through conquest. This effort was expressed in the famous Baconian formula that knowledge, implying objective knowledge of nature, is power. Science became applied science, ushering in our technological age.

In our own century, the new epistemology was inherited by Gestalt psychologists, like Wertheimer and Koffka, who became convinced that the act of perception itself completed what was perceived; and that this was how humans made the unified wholes, characterized by form and pattern, that constituted their actual experience. A similar insistence on the subjective element in knowledge also appeared in the thought of the early phenomenological philosophers, such as Brentano and Husserl. The common denominator of these revolutions in thought, from Kant and the romantics to the phenomenologists, was the attempt to heal the split between the subject and object, thus restoring the continuity between mind and nature that had largely been a basic premise in Western civilization from the ancient Greeks through the Middle Ages.

All these ideas formed the intellectual backdrop against which Isadore From joined forces with Frederick and Laura Perls and Paul Goodman. What distinguished their thinking was their combined realization that dualism produced not only cultural disrepair but individual neurosis. So they took a unique step: They condensed the search for unity into something immediately applicable to individual suffering — a new psychotherapy.

Frederick Perls soon went on to California to preside over the development and transmission of his own brand of Gestalt therapy, still focused on present experience but increasingly supplemented by psychodrama-like techniques to bring about cathartic emotional release. After a brief spell of working as a therapist and teaching the theory about which he had written so powerfully, Paul Goodman went on to other concerns altogether (though his social and political thought were always strongly colored by the principles of Gestalt therapy). It was left largely to Laura Perls and Isadore From to carry out the original spirit of Gestalt therapy, particularly through their teaching.

* * *

Isadore From remained a purist about Gestalt therapy and, in this respect, a conservative (in the sense of conserving, not in the political sense) voice among its leading teachers end practitioners. In recent years, he had continually warned against the pollution of

Gestalt therapy by crosscurrent and tides bearing the flotsam and jetsam from numerous other approaches to psychotherapy that were springing up everywhere in the twentieth century. But he was no ideologue, though there were those who accused him of being one. His painstaking care in defining what was consistent with Gestalt therapy and what was not made no claims for its superiority to everything else; it was motivated by his persistent worry that if the distinctive features of Gestalt therapy were not rigorously differentiated from other prevalent methods and theories, Gestalt therapy would get lost in the shuffle. And indeed, the historical record has proven him to be not completely unjustified in this concern.

Perhaps he became somewhat too unyielding about accepting the benefits Gestalt therapy might gain from assimilating fresh ideas from other new therapies growing up around it. After all, he knew perfectly well, if anyone did, how eclectic the origins of Gestalt therapy had been in its mingling of psychoanalysis, Gestalt psychology, phenomenology, and existentialism with techniques drawn from body-oriented therapies and the performance arts. His growing alarm, however, came from tendencies within Gestalt therapy itself: He was perturbed that Frederick Perls's last teachings seemed aimed at producing conversion experiences — and therefore emphasized rather florid techniques but made relatively little provision for theory; that people with a smattering of training in Gestalt therapy, partly as a result of Perls's efforts, partly as a result of our therapeutic culture, were prematurely packaging it with other approaches and selling this mixture as though it were a coherent integration: that the key theoretical text — Goodman's expansive transformation of Perls's original formulations in Volume Two of the book they collaborated on with Ralph Hefferline — went out of print for several years.

Among the gifts that Isadore From has left behind for Gestalt therapy are the richest sense of its roots as well as evidence that its theory and practice form an abundant and consistent whole. He never implied that this was the end of the story; he always said that there was a great deal more work to be done. Neither did he, in fact, shut out the possibility of drawing nourishment from neighboring disciplines. It's simply that he felt, quite rightly, I think, that first Gestalt therapy has to be securely anchored in what is most insistently itself. He regarded his life work as the furthering of that aim.

As it goes on to evolve and perhaps branch out, Gestalt therapy needs, perhaps now more than ever, to take firm hold of Isadore's legacy. This is a matter of self-preservation, like someone who slips on a stairway but grabs hold of the handrail. And not only self-preservation, for it is the best way for Gestalt therapy to stretch its horizons. After all, sound practice in Gestalt therapy, Isadore might have added, if only he were here to say it one last time, requires us to keep in mind that the most fruitful integrations come from meetings, whether of persons or of schools of thought, that have their own separate existences clearly defined.

Lightning Source UK Ltd.
Milton Keynes UK
UKHW020635240122
397612UK00005B/230

9 780939 266708